W9-BWK-388

ON LIBERTY

A NORTON CRITICAL EDITION

W. W. NORTON & COMPANY, INC.
also publishes

THE NORTON ANTHOLOGY OF AMERICAN LITERATURE
edited by Nina Baym et al.

THE NORTON ANTHOLOGY OF CONTEMPORARY FICTION
edited by R. V. Cassill

THE NORTON ANTHOLOGY OF ENGLISH LITERATURE
edited by M. H. Abrams et al.

THE NORTON ANTHOLOGY OF LITERATURE BY WOMEN
edited by Sandra M. Gilbert and Susan Gubar

THE NORTON ANTHOLOGY OF MODERN POETRY
edited by Richard Ellmann and Robert O'Clair

THE NORTON ANTHOLOGY OF POETRY
edited by Alexander W. Allison et al.

THE NORTON ANTHOLOGY OF SHORT FICTION
edited by R. V. Cassill

THE NORTON ANTHOLOGY OF WORLD MASTERPIECES
edited by Maynard Mack et al.

THE NORTON FACSIMILE OF
THE FIRST FOLIO OF SHAKESPEARE
prepared by Charlton Hinman

THE NORTON INTRODUCTION TO LITERATURE
edited by Carl E. Bain, Jerome Beaty, and J. Paul Hunter

THE NORTON INTRODUCTION TO THE SHORT NOVEL
edited by Jerome Beaty

THE NORTON READER
edited by Arthur M. Eastman et al.

THE NORTON SAMPLER
edited by Thomas Cooley

A NORTON CRITICAL EDITION

JOHN STUART MILL
ON LIBERTY

ANNOTATED TEXT
SOURCES AND BACKGROUND
CRITICISM

Edited by

DAVID SPITZ

CITY UNIVERSITY OF NEW YORK

W · W · NORTON & COMPANY

New York · London

["The Writing of 'On Liberty,' "] from *The Autobiography of John Stuart Mill* (New York: Columbia University Press, 1924). Excerpts reprinted by permission of the publisher.

["An Early Essay on Toleration,"] from *John Stuart Mill and Harriet Taylor*, by F. A. Hayek (Chicago, 1951). Excerpts reprinted by permission of Augustus M. Kelley Publishers, New Jersey.

"Mill on Liberty," anonymous essay from *The National Review*, 8 (1859), 393-424.

["Mill's Fallacies,"] from *Liberty, Equality, Fraternity*, by James Fitzjames Stephen (London, 1873). Excerpts reprinted by permission of Cambridge University Press.

"The 'Open Society' and Its Fallacies," by Willmoore Kendall, from *The American Political Science Review*, 54 (1960). Reprinted by permission of the publisher.

["The Illiberalism of John Stuart Mill,"] from *Mill and Liberalism*, by Maurice Cowling (Cambridge, 1963). Excerpts reprinted by permission of the publisher.

Adapted from "Morals and the Criminal Law," from *The Enforcement of Morals*, by Patrick Devlin. © Oxford University Press, 1965. Reprinted by permission of the publisher.

"The Value of Freedom," by Albert William Levi, from *Ethics, 70* (1959). Reprinted by permission of the publisher.

"Freedom and Individuality," by David Spitz, from *Liberty*, edited by Carl J. Friedrich (New York, 1962). Reprinted by permission of the publishers, Lieber-Atherton, Inc. Copyright © 1962. All rights reserved.

"Mill on Self-Regarding Actions," by C. L. Ten, taken from *Philosophy*, 43 (1968). Reprinted by permission of the author and the Royal Institute of Philosophy, London.

"Immorality and Treason," by II. L. A. Hart, taken from *The Listener*, 62 (July 30, 1959). Excerpts reprinted by permission of the author and the BBC Publications, London.

COPYRIGHT © 1975 BY W. W. NORTON & COMPANY, INC.

W. W. Norton & Company, Inc., 500 Fifth Avenue, New York, N.Y. 10110

W. W. Norton & Company Ltd., 10 Coptic Street, London, WC1A 1PU

Library of Congress Cataloging in Publication Data

Mill, John Stuart, 1806–1873.
  On liberty.

  (A Norton critical edition)
  Bibliography: p.
  Includes index.
  1. Liberty.   I. Spitz, David, 1916–   ed.

II. Title.
JC585.M6 1975   323.44   74–32203

All Rights Reserved

PRINTED IN THE UNITED STATES OF AMERICA

9 0

ISBN 0-393-04400-9 CL
ISBN 0-393-09252-6 PBK

Contents

HERBERT J. MULLER is the general editor of Norton Critical Editions in the history of ideas.

Preface

The *Communist Manifesto* apart, it is doubtful that any single work in nineteenth- or twentieth-century political theory has excited as much attention, given rise to as vast and controversial a body of literature, and had as profound an impact as has John Stuart Mill's essay *On Liberty* (1859). Certainly, no tract has been more significant as a statement of the liberal position on the importance of freedom for the discovery of truth and for the full development of individuality. Far more than the restrictive defenses of liberty set forth in Milton's *Areopagitica* (1644) and Locke's *Letters on Toleration* (1689–92), it is the classic argument for freedom of thought and expression and the right of privacy.

Yet *On Liberty* is not without problems, or without detractors. Many of Mill's contemporaries found it deficient in argument, wrong in its factual assertions, and morally offensive[1]—"an infidel book," as Mill himself anticipated it would be termed.[2] In a book-length assault, James Fitzjames Stephen castigated Mill for departing from what he took to be the proper principles of utilitarianism (see pp. 142–53 below). A writer in the *National Review* sought to demonstrate that Mill's premises led to contrary conclusions than those Mill himself posited (see pp. 123–42 below). Thomas Carlyle reacted to Mill's volume with a torrent of invective, "as if," he said, "it were a sin to control, or coerce into better methods, human swine in any way; . . . Ach Gott im Himmel!"[3] Later critics like Bernard Bosanquet[4] and the Italian philosopher Benedetto Croce condemned the book in harsh terms, the latter being especially contemptuous of what he called its "cheap" and "ignoble arguments," its "wretched and fallacious reasonings."[5] Present-day critics like Willmoore Kendall and Maurice Cowling (see pp. 154–67 and 167–77 below) go so far as to contend that it is an evil and illiberal work. Henry M. Magid thinks it is so confused that "On the basis of his assumptions, it is not possible to justify absolute and unlimited freedom of thought; nor is it possible, in Mill's terms, to justify limitations on freedom of thought."[6] And Gertrude Himmelfarb,

1. See J. C. Rees, *Mill and His Early Critics* (Leicester, England, 1956).
2. Letter to George Jacob Holyoake, February 1859, in *The Later Letters of John Stuart Mill, 1849–1873, Collected Works*, Mineka and Lindley, eds. (University of Toronto Press, 1972), 15:593.
3. Quoted in Michael St. John Packe, *The Life of John Stuart Mill* (New York, 1954), p. 405.

4. *The Philosophical Theory of the State*, 4th ed. (London, 1923), pp. 56–65.
5. "The Roots of Liberty," in Ruth N. Anshen, ed., *Freedom: Its Meaning* (New York, 1940), p. 34.
6. "Mill and the Problem of Freedom of Thought," *Social Research*, 21 (1954), 43.

though not denying that *On Liberty* is a liberal statement, finds it not only internally chaotic but also at odds with the bulk of Mill's other writings, with what she calls the "other" or "earlier" Mill.[7]

Many commentators believe that *On Liberty* reflects less Mill's ideas than those of Harriet Taylor, later Mrs. Mill.[8] Whether her influence was indeed controlling, or essentially peripheral, as others contend,[9] or whether, as Mill himself insisted in his *Autobiography*, the essay was their joint product, is a still unresolved and much disputed question.[1] So too is the extent to which Mill departed from the teachings of his father, James, and of Jeremy Bentham, in whose utilitarian philosophy he had been raised. Yet both influences were sufficiently marked to lead Bertrand Russell, certainly not one to disclaim a general kinship with the libertarian spirit of Mill's political philosophy, to write:

> Morals and intellect were perpetually at war in his [Mill's] thought, morals being incarnate in Mrs. Taylor and intellect in his father. . . . The amalgam which resulted was practically beneficent, but theoretically somewhat incoherent.[2]

All this, however, is very far from the universal reaction to Mill and his essay *On Liberty*. A contemporary like John Morley, for example, spoke of Mill as "my chief master" and confessed his "young disciple's reverence."[3] Gladstone, in what has since become a household phrase, termed him "the Saint of Rationalism";[4] while the noted historian Henry T. Buckle said of Mill that he was "beyond dispute the deepest of our living thinkers" and described his essay as "this noble treatise, so full of wisdom and of thought."[5] Charles Kingsley, finding *On Liberty* in Parker's bookshop, sat down and read it through then and there, remarking that it made him "a clearer-headed, braver-minded man on the spot."[6] Even so captious a critic as Matthew Arnold could say of Mill that he was a lover "of free and clear thought, . . . a writer deserving all attention and respect," and that *On Liberty* was "one of the few books that inculcate tolerance in an unalarming and inoffensive way."[7] Later critics like Halévy, Harrison, and MacIver, despite certain reserva-

---

7. *On Liberty and Liberalism: The Case of John Stuart Mill* (New York, 1974).

8. See F. A. Hayek, *John Stuart Mill and Harriet Taylor: Their Friendship and Subsequent Marriage* (Chicago, 1951); also Himmelfarb, *op. cit.*, and Packe, *op. cit.*

9. E.g., J. C. Rees, "A Phase in the Development of Mill's Ideas on Liberty," *Political Studies*, 6 (1958), 35–44, and C. L. Ten, "Mill and Liberty," *Journal of the History of Ideas*, 30 (1969), 47–68.

1. See the editors' introduction to Mill's *Later Letters, Collected Works*, 14: xxiii–xxxiv.

2. *Portraits from Memory* (London, 1956), pp. 114–15.

3. *Recollections* (New York, 1917), 2:363; 1:53.

4. W. L. Courtney, *Life of John Stuart Mill* (London, 1889), p. 142.

5. "Mill on Liberty," in his *Essays* (New York, 1864), pp. 74, 115.

6. Charles Kingsley, *His Letters and Memories of His Life*, Mrs. Kingsley, ed. (London, 1877), 2:88.

7. Quoted in Edward Alexander, *Matthew Arnold and John Stuart Mill* (New York, 1965), p. 32.

tions, nonetheless found it a major and impressive defense of freedom of thought and of individuality,[8] while in a more recent article
(see pp. 191–203 below), A. W. Levi pronounced it "a statement of
liberal principle so radical and at the same time so fundamental
that it surely ranks with *The Social Contract* and *The Communist
Manifesto* as a source for the political and social theory of the
Western world." Clearly, *On Liberty* has not lacked a considerable
outpouring of genuine agreement and admiration.

What are the issues that have given rise to so disparate a set of
judgments? As the critical readings will show, these range from specific disagreements over Mill's language—what is meant by a
"mature" people, by "harm"?—to conflicts over his central propositions.

What, for example, is the validity of Mill's distinction between
self-regarding and other-regarding conduct? Granted the importance
of privacy, to what extent, and on the basis of what principle, may
society properly interfere with an individual, either to protect him
or itself from "harm" or to further its notion of the common good?
Has a community no right to restrict practices that violate ordinary
standards of decency, such as the public exhibition of nudity or
solicitation in the streets by prostitutes? Are homosexuality and
abortion and drunkenness purely or primarily private matters or are
they legitimate concerns of a society committed to a certain conception of morality?

What, to take a second realm of controversy, can be said in
defense of Mill's notion that freedom of expression, like freedom of
thought, ought to be unrestrained? Mill himself admitted that freedom of expression is in certain respects distinct from freedom of
thought, for the former, unlike the latter, clearly affects persons
other than the individual uttering an idea; hence it is permissible,
even in Mill's view, to interfere with that utterance when the circumstances are such as to constitute that utterance "a positive instigation to some mischievous act." If this is so, why not censor por-
nographic films and books? Why not prohibit speech that mocks
revered beliefs, say in the deity or monogamy, or that reviles an
individual or a minority group, say the blacks or the Jews? If a professor teaches erroneous, perhaps loathsome, ideas, should not students have a right to silence him or to protect other students from
being contaminated by his views by preventing them from entering
his classroom? Has a community no right to defend its truth from
error?

Why, to move to another area of disagreement, should freedom

8. Elie Halévy, *The Growth of Philosophic Radicalism* (New York, 1949), p.
285; Frederic Harrison, *Tennyson, Rus-*
kin, Mill (New York, 1900), p. 276; R.
M. MacIver, *The Modern State* (London, 1926), pp. 456–60.

be construed as narrowly as Mill construes it? Mill adopts what may be termed a "negative" view of freedom, one that views freedom simply as the absence of restraints, and that consequently allows him to condemn law and social hindrances, including customs, as interferences with liberty. Is it not the case, however, that human action—to the extent that it is volitional rather than determined—is always directed toward the attainment of some particular goal, which (at least to rational men) is deemed good? Men do not, it is often argued, seek freedom simply to be left alone; they seek freedom to do the right things. If, however, they do not know what is right, or do not know what means are appropriate to achieve that right, is it not the business of society and the state to direct them in doing what they really want to do? Is not "positive" freedom—doing what is right—the real purpose of human life? If this is so, or to the extent that it may be so—and surely compulsory vaccination laws, to cite but one example, testify to this truth—then (the critics contend) Mill's "negative" freedom is an insufficient principle on which to build a communal life.

All this, of course, leads to still another dispute, one turning on Mill's understanding (or lack of understanding) of community, of the nature and importance of the ties that bind a people into a single nation. Individuals do not live in isolation; they are not a conglomerate of Robinson Crusoes; they are born into, exist within, and find identity and meaning only among the society of their fellow men. Do we not therefore require a theory of liberty that takes full account of the individual's need for community, rather than, as Mill would have it, a theory that looks only (or primarily) to individuality? Do we not need to inculcate in our citizens a respect for common values, a desire to protect and promote the community's way of life, rather than a concern only for the pursuit of their personal values?

Now, what makes Mill important and timeless is not that he gave final and easy answers to these and similar questions but that he recognized and articulated them as problems of the first magnitude; that he not only posed these crucial issues but offered reasoned arguments to aid in their resolution; and that he set forth what he took to be abiding principles to guide us in our practical conduct with respect to these matters. What is more, in *On Liberty*, as in its companion volume *Representative Government* (1861), Mill pushed to the forefront the question that most concerns those who value liberty and are committed to the principle of democracy: namely, how in democratic states can individuals and minorities be protected against the possible tyranny of majorities? This is why, for more than a century, every serious debate on these questions has turned on the name and work of John Stuart Mill. But it is also why the criticism of Mill has been so persistent and intensive.

Most of these and other "open questions" are treated in the critical readings below. Because of limitations of space, they cannot, of course, do full justice to the complete range of issues deriving from *On Liberty*; nor can they always deal as fully as the subject requires with some of the major specific areas of disagreement, as, for example, the controversy over "negative" and "positive" freedom.[9] It is hoped, however, that they touch on enough of these questions, and suggest enough of the character of the debate, to give the undergraduate student a meaningful introduction to the problems. For further exploration, the Bibliography should prove useful.

I wish to thank the Research Foundation of the City University of New York for financial assistance that made possible the valuable secretarial help of Ellen Sheinfeld. I am grateful to James L. Mairs of W. W. Norton & Company for his patience, encouragement, and advice. I am most indebted to my former research assistant Elaine Mates, who worked with me through all the annotations to the text and the selection of the critical essays; without her devoted support this volume would not yet have come into being.

DAVID SPITZ

New York City
July, 1974

9. Cf. Isaiah Berlin, "Two Concepts of Liberty," in his *Four Essays on Liberty* (Oxford, 1969), chap. 3, and *contra* C. B. Macpherson, "Berlin's Division of Liberty," in his *Democratic Theory* (Oxford, 1973), chap. 5.

Annotated Text of
On Liberty

The grand, leading principle, towards which every argument unfolded in these pages directly converges, is the absolute and essential importance of human development in its richest diversity.—Wilhelm von Humboldt: *Sphere and Duties of Government.*[1]

To the beloved and deplored memory of her[2] *who was the inspirer, and in part the author, of all that is best in my writings— the friend and wife whose exalted sense of truth and right was my strongest incitement, and whose approbation was my chief reward— I dedicate this volume. Like all that I have written for many years, it belongs as much to her as to me; but the work as it stands has had, in a very insufficient degree, the inestimable advantage of her revision; some of the most important portions having been reserved for a more careful re-examination, which they are now never destined to receive. Were I but capable of interpreting to the world one half the great thoughts and noble feelings which are buried in her grave, I should be the medium of a greater benefit to it, than is ever likely to arise from anything that I can write, unprompted and unassisted by her all but unrivalled wisdom.*

1. **Baron Karl Wilhelm von Humboldt** (1767–1835), German philologist, active in Prussian political and educational reform movements. An English translation of his book appeared in 1854; the quotation is from p. 65.

2. Harriet Taylor Mill. For their relationship, see F. A. Hayek, *John Stuart Mill and Harriet Taylor* (Chicago, 1951), and Michael St. John Packe, *The Life of John Stuart Mill* (New York, 1954).

Chapter I

The subject of this Essay is not the so-called Liberty of the Will so unfortunately opposed to the misnamed doctrine of Philosophical Necessity;[1] but Civil, or Social Liberty: the nature and limits of the power which can be legitimately exercised by society over the individual. A question seldom stated, and hardly ever discussed, in general terms, but which profoundly influences the practical controversies of the age by its latent presence, and is likely soon to make itself recognised as the vital question of the future. It is so far from being new, that, in a certain sense, it has divided mankind, almost from the remotest ages; but in the stage of progress into which the more civilised portions of the species have now entered, it presents itself under new conditions, and requires a different and more fundamental treatment.

The struggle between Liberty and Authority is the most conspicuous feature in the portions of history with which we are earliest familiar, particularly in that of Greece, Rome, and England. But in old times this contest was between subjects, or some classes of subjects, and the Government. By liberty, was meant protection against the tyranny of the political rulers. The rulers were conceived (except in some of the popular governments of Greece) as in a necessarily antagonistic position to the people whom they ruled. They consisted of a governing One, or a governing tribe or caste, who derived their authority from inheritance or conquest, who, at all events, did not hold it at the pleasure of the governed, and whose supremacy men did not venture, perhaps did not desire, to contest, whatever precautions might be taken against its oppressive exercise. Their power was regarded as necessary, but also as highly dangerous; as a weapon which they would attempt to use against their subjects, no less than against external enemies. To prevent the weaker members of the community from being preyed upon by innumerable vultures, it was needful that there should be an animal of prey stronger than the rest, commissioned to keep them down. But as the king of the vultures would be no less bent upon preying on the flock than any of the minor harpies, it was indispensable to be in a perpetual attitude of defence against his beak and claws. The aim, therefore, of patriots was to set limits to the power which the ruler should be

---

1. The doctrine of Philosophical Necessity, of man as a determined creature rather than one whose will, by influencing some of his circumstances, can exercise real power over the formation of his own character, is discussed by Mill in his earlier work, *A System of Logic*, Book 6, chap. 2; see also his *Autobiography*, Columbia University Press ed. (New York, 1924), pp. 118–20.

suffered to exercise over the community; and this limitation was what they meant by liberty. It was attempted in two ways. First, by obtaining a recognition of certain immunities, called political liberties or rights, which it was to be regarded as a breach of duty in the ruler to infringe, and which if he did infringe, specific resistance, or general rebellion, was held to be justifiable. A second, and generally a later expedient, was the establishment of constitutional checks, by which the consent of the community, or of a body of some sort, supposed to represent its interests, was made a necessary condition to some of the more important acts of the governing power. To the first of these modes of limitation, the ruling power, in most European countries, was compelled, more or less, to submit. It was not so with the second; and, to attain this, or when already in some degree possessed, to attain it more completely, became everywhere the principal object of the lovers of liberty. And so long as mankind were content to combat one enemy by another, and to be ruled by a master, on condition of being guaranteed more or less efficaciously against his tyranny, they did not carry their aspirations beyond this point.

A time, however, came, in the progress of human affairs, when men ceased to think it a necessity of nature that their governors should be an independent power, opposed in interest to themselves. It appeared to them much better that the various magistrates of the State should be their tenants or delegates, revocable at their pleasure. In that way alone, it seemed, could they have complete security that the powers of government would never be abused to their disadvantage. By degrees this new demand for elective and temporary rulers became the prominent object of the exertions of the popular party, wherever any such party existed; and superseded, to a considerable extent, the previous efforts to limit the power of rulers. As the struggle proceeded for making the ruling power emanate from the periodical choice of the ruled, some persons began to think that too much importance had been attached to the limitation of the power itself. *That* (it might seem) was a resource against rulers whose interests were habitually opposed to those of the people. What was now wanted was, that the rulers should be identified with the people; that their interest and will should be the interest and will of the nation. The nation did not need to be protected against its own will. There was no fear of its tyrannising over itself. Let the rulers be effectually responsible to it, promptly removable by it, and it could afford to trust them with power of which it could itself dictate the use to be made. Their power was but the nation's own power, concentrated, and in a form convenient for exercise. This mode of thought, or rather perhaps of feeling, was common among the last generation of European liberalism,[2] in the Continental section of which it still apparently predominates. Those who admit any limit to what a government may do, except in the case of such governments as they think ought not to exist, stand out as brilliant exceptions among the political thinkers of the Continent.[3] A similar tone of sentiment might by this time have been prevalent in our own country, if the circumstances which for a time encouraged it, had continued unaltered.

But, in political and philosophical theories, as well as in persons, success discloses faults and infirmities which failure might have concealed from observation. The notion, that the people have no need to limit their power over themselves, might seem axiomatic, when popular government was a thing only dreamed about, or read of as having existed at some distant period of the past. Neither was that notion necessarily disturbed by such temporary aberrations as those of the French Revolution, the worst of which were the work of a usurping few, and which, in any case, belonged, not to the permanent working of popular institutions, but to a sudden and convulsive outbreak against monarchical and aristocratic depotism. In time, however, a democratic republic came to occupy a large portion of the earth's surface,[4] and made itself felt as one of the most powerful members of the community of nations; and elective and responsible government became subject to the observations and criticisms which wait upon a great existing fact. It was now perceived that such phrases as "self-government," and "the power of the people over themselves," do not express the true state of the case. The "people" who exercise the power are not always the same people with those over whom it is exercised; and the "self-government" spoken of is not the government of each by himself, but of each by all the rest. The will of the people, moreover, practically means the will of the most numerous or the most active *part* of the people; the majority, or those who succeed in making themselves accepted as the majority; the people, consequently, *may* desire to oppress a part of their number; and precautions are as much needed against this as against any other abuse of power. The limitation, therefore, of the power of government over individuals loses none of its importance when the holders of power are regularly accountable to the community, that is, to the strongest party therein. This view

2. European liberals embracing this view included such British philosophers as Jeremy Bentham (1748–1832) and James Mill (1773–1836), and such Continental writers as Benjamin Constant (1767–1830) and Wilhelm von Humboldt. These writers formed part of a school of social thought (prominent in the late eighteenth and early nineteenth centuries) characterized by a belief in man's goodness, rationality, and perfectibility; an insistence on liberty and equal opportunities for each individual; and an energetic opposition to all remnants of feudal privileges.
3. Mill might have had in mind here Charles Louis de Secondat, Baron de Montesquieu (1689–1755).
4. The United States of America.

of things, recommending itself equally to the intelligence of thinkers and to the inclination of those important classes in European
society to whose real or supposed interests democracy is adverse, has
had no difficulty in establishing itself; and in political speculations
"the tyranny of the majority" is now generally included among the
evils against which society requires to be on its guard.

Like other tyrannies, the tyranny of the majority was at first, and
is still vulgarly, held in dread, chiefly as operating through the acts
of the public authorities.[5] But reflecting persons[6] perceived that
when society is itself the tyrant—society collectively over the separate individuals who compose it—its means of tyrannising are not
restricted to the acts which it may do by the hands of its political
functionaries. Society can and does execute its own mandates; and
if it issues wrong mandates instead of right, or any mandates at all
in things with which it ought not to meddle, it practises a social tyranny more formidable than many kinds of political oppression,
since, though not usually upheld by such extreme penalties, it
leaves fewer means of escape, penetrating much more deeply into
the details of life, and enslaving the soul itself. Protection, therefore, against the tyranny of the magistrate is not enough: there
needs protection also against the tyranny of the prevailing opinion
and feeling; against the tendency of society to impose, by other
means than civil penalties, its own ideas and practices as rules of
conduct on those who dissent from them; to fetter the development, and, if possible, prevent the formation, of any individuality
not in harmony with its ways, and compels all characters to fashion themselves upon the model of its own. There is a limit to the
legitimate interference of collective opinion with individual independence: and to find that limit, and maintain it against encroachment, is as indispensable to a good condition of human affairs, as
protection against political despotism.[7]

But though this proposition is not likely to be contested in general terms, the practical question, where to place the limit—how to
make the fitting adjustment between individual independence and
social control—is a subject on which nearly everything remains to
be done. All that makes existence valuable to any one, depends on
the enforcement of restraints upon the actions of other people.
Some rules of conduct, therefore, must be imposed, by law in the

5. So James Madison, for example, argued in *The Federalist* (1787–88), no. 10.
6. Mill probably refers here to Alexis de Tocqueville, *Democracy in America* (1835, 1840), especially vol. 1, chap. 15.
7. This way of putting the central prob-lem of the essay—that society, through both government and social pressure, can legitimately interfere with individuals, but that in a good society there must be some principled limits to such interfer-ence—has, despite Mill's anticipation to the contrary (as stated in the following sentence of the text), given rise to great contestation. Cf. the discussion and liter-ature cited in the critical essays below.

first place, and by opinion on many things which are not fit subjects for the operation of law.[8] What these rules should be is the principal question in human affairs; but if we except a few of the most obvious cases, it is one of those which least progress has been made in resolving. No two ages, and scarcely any two countries, have decided it alike; and the decision of one age or country is a wonder to another. Yet the people of any given age and country no more suspect any difficulty in it, than if it were a subject on which mankind had always been agreed. The rules which obtain among themselves appear to them self-evident and self-justifying. This all but universal illusion is one of the examples of the magical influence of custom, which is not only, as the proverb says, a second nature, but is continually mistaken for the first. The effect of custom, in preventing any misgiving respecting the rules of conduct which mankind impose on one another, is all the more complete because the subject is one on which it is not generally considered necessary that reasons should be given, either by one person to others or by each to himself. People are accustomed to believe, and have been encouraged in the belief by some who aspire to the character of philosophers, that their feelings, on subjects of this nature, are better than reasons, and render reasons unnecessary. The practical principle which guides them to their opinions on the regulation of human conduct, is the feeling in each person's mind that everybody should be required to act as he, and those with whom he sympathises, would like them to act. No one, indeed, acknowledges to himself that his standard of judgment is his own liking; but an opinion on a point of conduct, not supported by reasons, can only count as one person's preference;[9] and if the reasons, when given, are a mere appeal to a similar preference felt by other people, it is still only many people's liking instead of one. To an ordinary man, however, his own preference, thus supported, is not only a perfectly satisfactory reason, but the only one he generally has for any of his notions of morality, taste, or propriety, which are not expressly written in his religious creed; and his chief guide in the interpretation even of that. Men's opinions, accordingly, on what is laudable or blamable, are affected by all the multifarious causes which influence their wishes in regard to the conduct of others, and which are as numerous as those which determine their wishes on any other subject. Sometimes their reason—at other times their prejudices or supersti-

8. Despite these sentences, some of Mill's critics have contended that his essay is a plea for the complete absence of social and legal restraints over the individual, even for anarchy or nihilism.
9. Mill here rejects a number of commonly held positions: that nonrational preferences represent God's will, or the inherited accumulated wisdom of the ages, or attitudes and principles natural to man and in conformity with his highest destiny. He discusses these elsewhere, e.g., in his essays on Bentham and Coleridge, in *Essays on Ethics, Religion and Society, Collected Works* (Toronto, 1969), 10:75–163.

tions: often their social affections, not seldom their antisocial ones, their envy or jealousy, their arrogance or contemptuousness: but most commonly their desires or fears for themselves—their legitimate or illegitimate self-interest. Wherever there is an ascendant class, a large portion of the morality of the country emanates from its class interests, and its feelings of class superiority. The morality between Spartans and Helots,[1] between planters and negroes, between princes and subjects, between nobles and roturiers,[2] between men and women, has been for the most part the creation of these class interests and feelings: and the sentiments thus generated react in turn upon the moral feelings of the members of the ascendant class, in their relations among themselves. Where, on the other hand, a class, formerly ascendant, has lost its ascendancy, or where its ascendancy is unpopular, the prevailing moral sentiments frequently bear the impress of an impatient dislike of superiority.[3] Another grand determining principle of the rules of conduct, both in act and forbearance, which have been enforced by law or opinion, has been the servility of mankind towards the supposed preferences or aversions of their temporal masters or of their gods. This servility, though essentially selfish, is not hypocrisy; it gives rise to perfectly genuine sentiments of abhorrence; it made men burn magicians and heretics. Among so many baser influences, the general and obvious interests of society have of course had a share, and a large one, in the direction of the moral sentiments: less, however, as a matter of reason, and on their own account, than as a consequence of the sympathies and antipathies which grew out of them: and sympathies and antipathies which had little or nothing to do with the interests of society, have made themselves felt in the establishment of moralities with quite as great force.

The likings and dislikings of society, or of some powerful portion of it, are thus the main thing which has practically determined the rules laid down for general observance, under the penalties of law or opinion. And in general, those who have been in advance of society in thought and feeling, have left this condition of things unassailed in principle, however they may have come into conflict with it in some of its details. They have occupied themselves rather in inquiring what things society ought to like or dislike, than in questioning whether its likings or dislikings should be a law to individuals. They preferred endeavouring to alter the feelings of mankind on the particular points on which they were themselves heretical, rather than make common cause in defence of freedom, with heretics generally.

1. The Helots in the Greek city-state of Sparta were state slaves under allotment to landowners.
2. Persons of low rank; commoners; plebeians.
3. As in the slogan "Liberté, Egalité, Fraternité," at the time of the French Revolution.

The only case in which the higher ground has been taken on principle and maintained with consistency, by any but an individual here and there, is that of religious belief: a case instructive in many ways, and not least so as forming a most striking instance of the fallibility of what is called the moral sense: for the *odium theologicum,*[4] in a sincere bigot, is one of the most unequivocal cases of moral feeling. Those who first broke the yoke of what called itself the Universal Church,[5] were in general as little willing to permit differences of religious opinion as that church itself. But when the heat of the conflict was over, without giving a complete victory to any party, and each church or sect was reduced to limit its hopes to retaining possession of the ground it already occupied; minorities, seeing that they had no chance of becoming majorities, were under the necessity of pleading to those whom they could not convert, for permission to differ. It is accordingly on this battlefield, almost solely, that the rights of the individual against society have been asserted on broad grounds of principle, and the claim of society to exercise authority over dissentients openly controverted. The great writers to whom the world owes what religious liberty it possesses,[6] have mostly asserted freedom of conscience as an indefeasible right, and denied absolutely that a human being is accountable to others for his religious belief. Yet so natural to mankind is intolerance in whatever they really care about, that religious freedom has hardly anywhere been practically realised, except where religious indifference, which dislikes to have its peace disturbed by theological quarrels, has added its weight to the scale. In the minds of almost all religious persons, even in the most tolerant countries, the duty of toleration is admitted with tacit reserves. One person will bear with dissent in matters of church government, but not of dogma; another can tolerate anybody, short of a Papist[7] or a Unitarian;[8] another every one who believes in revealed religion; a few extend their charity a little further, but stop at the belief in a God and in a future state. Wherever the sentiment of the majority is still genuine and intense, it is found to have abated little of its claim to be obeyed.

In England, from the peculiar circumstances of our political history, though the yoke of opinion is perhaps heavier, that of law is lighter, than in most other countries of Europe; and there is considerable jealousy of direct interference, by the legislative or the executive power, with private conduct; not so much from any just regard for the independence of the individual, as from the still sub-

4. The hatred occasioned by bitter, emotionally charged religious controversy.
5. The Roman Catholic Church.
6. For example, the British philosopher John Locke (1632–1704).
7. An adherent of the Pope; a member

of the Roman Catholic Church.
8. A member of a religious sect that rejects the doctrine of the Trinity and looks to reason and conscience as guides to conduct.

sisting habit of looking on the government as representing an opposite interest to the public. The majority have not yet learnt to feel the power of the government their power, or its opinions their opinions. When they do so, individual liberty will probably be as much exposed to invasion from the government, as it already is from public opinion. But, as yet, there is a considerable amount of feeling ready to be called forth against any attempt of the law to control individuals in things in which they have not hitherto been accustomed to be controlled by it; and this with very little discrimination as to whether the matter is, or is not, within the legitimate sphere of legal control; insomuch that the feeling, highly salutary on the whole, is perhaps quite as often misplaced as well grounded in the particular instances of its application. There is, in fact, no recognised principle by which the propriety or impropriety of government interference is customarily tested. People decide according to their personal preferences. Some, whenever they see any good to be done, or evil to be remedied, would willingly instigate the government to undertake the business; while others prefer to bear almost any amount of social evil, rather than add one to the departments of human interest amenable to governmental control. And men range themselves on one or the other side in any particular case, according to this general direction of their sentiments; or according to the degree of interest which they feel in the particular thing which it is proposed that the government should do, or according to the belief they entertain that the government would, or would not, do it in the manner they prefer; but very rarely on account of any opinion to which they consistently adhere, as to what things are fit to be done by a government. And it seems to me that in consequence of this absence of rule or principle, one side is at present as often wrong as the other; the interference of government is, with about equal frequency, improperly invoked and improperly condemned.

The object of this Essay is to assert one very simple principle, as entitled to govern absolutely the dealings of society with the individual in the way of compulsion and control, whether the means used be physical force in the form of legal penalties, or the moral coercion of public opinion. That principle is, that the sole end for which mankind are warranted, individually or collectively, in interfering with the liberty of action of any of their number, is self-protection.[9] That the only purpose for which power can be rightfully exercised over any member of a civilised community, against

9. This principle has been much commented upon. Critics have argued, for example, that it neglects the need for interference to promote the well-being of others or the common good. Defenders have pointed, among other things, to Mill's own awareness of such considerations in the second paragraph following this passage, as well as in other portions of the essay, e.g., chap. 4.

his will, is to prevent harm[1] to others. His own good, either physical or moral, is not a sufficient warrant. He cannot rightfully be compelled to do or forbear because it will be better for him to do so, because it will make him happier, because, in the opinions of others, to do so would be wise, or even right. These are good reasons for remonstrating with him, or reasoning with him, or persuading him, or entreating him, but not for compelling him, or visiting him with any evil in case he do otherwise. To justify that, the conduct from which it is desired to deter him must be calculated to produce evil to some one else. The only part of the conduct of any one, for which he is amenable to society, is that which concerns others. In the part which merely concerns himself, his independence is, of right, absolute. Over himself, over his own body and mind, the individual is sovereign.

It is, perhaps hardly necessary to say that this doctrine is meant to apply only to human beings in the maturity of their faculties. We are not speaking of children, or of young persons below the age which the law may fix as that of manhood or womanhood. Those who are still in a state to require being taken care of by others, must be protected against their own actions as well as against external injury. For the same reason, we may leave out of consideration those backward states of society in which the race itself may be considered as in its nonage. The early difficulties in the way of spontaneous progress are so great, that there is seldom any choice of means for overcoming them; and a ruler full of the spirit of improvement is warranted in the use of any expedients that will attain an end, perhaps otherwise unattainable. Despotism is a legitimate mode of government in dealing with barbarians, provided the end be their improvement, and the means justified by actually effecting that end.[2] Liberty, as a principle, has no application to any state of things anterior to the time when mankind have become capable of being improved by free and equal discussion. Until then, there is nothing for them but implicit obedience to an Akbar or a Charlemagne,[3] if they are so fortunate as to find one. But as soon as mankind have attained the capacity of being guided to their own improvement by conviction or persuasion (a period long since reached in all nations with whom we need here concern ourselves),

1. So, too, there is controversy over the notion of "harm." Does it, for example, refer to moral or merely physical harm, or to acts injurious to the interests of others? Does it apply only to individuals, or does it include harm to society? Cf. the controversy between Patrick Devlin, *The Enforcement of Morals* (London, 1965), especially chap. 6, and H. L. A. Hart, *Law, Liberty and Morality* (London, 1963) and *The Morality of the Criminal Law* (Jerusalem, 1965), Lecture 2.

2. For Mill's further development of this theme, see his *Representative Government*, chap. 18.

3. Akbar (1542–1605), a Mogul emperor of India, and Charlemagne (742–814), King of the Franks and the first Holy Roman Emperor, were both noted for benevolent and skillful rule and for their promotion of culture and learning.

compulsion, either in the direct form or in that of pains and penalties for non-compliance, is no longer admissible as a means to their own good, and justifiable only for the security of others.

It is proper to state that I forego any advantage which could be derived to my argument from the idea of abstract right, as a thing independent of utility.[4] I regard utility as the ultimate appeal on all ethical questions; but it must be utility in the largest sense, grounded on the permanent interests of man[5] as a progressive being. Those interests, I contend, authorise the subjection of individual spontaneity to external control, only in respect to those actions of each, which concern the interest[6] of other people. If any one does an act hurtful to others, there is a *prima facie*[7] case for punishing him, by law, or, where legal penalties are not safely applicable, by general disapprobation. There are also many positive acts for the benefit of others, which he may rightfully be compelled to perform; such as to give evidence in a court of justice; to bear his fair share in the common defence, or in any other joint work necessary to the interest of the society of which he enjoys the protection; and to perform certain acts of individual beneficence, such as saving a fellow-creature's life, or interposing to protect the defenceless against ill-usage, things which whenever it is obviously a man's duty to do, he may rightfully be made responsible to society for not doing. A person may cause evil to others not only by his actions but by his inaction, and in either case he is justly accountable to them for the injury. The latter case, it is true, requires a much more cautious exercise of compulsion than the former. To make any one answerable for doing evil to others is the rule; to make him answerable for not preventing evil is, comparatively speaking, the exception. Yet there are many cases clear enough and grave enough to

4. Despite this explicit statement, some critics have alleged that Mill's argument does in fact appeal to natural or abstract right. For the controversy, see David Spitz, "Freedom and Individuality: Mill's *Liberty* in Retrospect," in C. J. Friedrich, ed., *Liberty* (New York, 1962), pp. 190–94.

5. Some editions, because of a printer's error, have inserted the word "a" before the word "man," thereby giving a more individualistic slant to the sentence than is warranted by the correct text. To be sure, the original manuscript of *On Liberty* has never been located, but all the early editions of the essay, both in England and in the United States, omit the "a"; and Mill explicitly stated in his *Autobiography* that because of the death of his wife and collaborator he would never revise the text. What seems to have happened is that the printer of the People's (a low-priced) edition inadvertently inserted the word "a" and this was incorporated in later reprints, e.g., the widely used Everyman's edition. Regrettably, this mistake has led to some serious misunderstandings of Mill's teaching; see, for example, John Rawls, *A Theory of Justice* (Cambridge, Mass., 1971), p. 209.

6. The concept of what concerns others seems to be qualified here by the introduction of the word "interest." For the importance of this term, see J. C. Rees, "A Re-Reading of Mill on Liberty," *Political Studies*, 8 (1960), 113–29; but see *contra* C. L. Ten, "Mill on Self-Regarding Actions," *Philosophy* 43 (1968), 29–37, and Richard Wollheim, "John Stuart Mill and the Limits of State Action," *Social Research*, 40 (1973), 1–30.

7. At first sight; on the face of it.

justify that exception. In all things which regard the external relations of the individual, he is *de jure*[8] amenable to those whose interests are concerned, and, if need be, to society as their protector. There are often good reasons for not holding him to the responsibility; but these reasons must arise from the special expediencies of the case: either because it is a kind of case in which he is on the whole likely to act better, when left to his own discretion, than when controlled in any way in which society have it in their power to control him; or because the attempt to exercise control would produce other evils, greater than those which it would prevent. When such reasons as these preclude the enforcement of responsibility, the conscience of the agent himself should step into the vacant judgment seat, and protect those interests of others which have no external protection; judging himself all the more rigidly, because the case does not admit of his being made accountable to the judgment of his fellow-creatures.

But there is a sphere of action in which society, as distinguished from the individual, has, if any, only an indirect interest; comprehending all that portion of a person's life and conduct which affects only himself, or if it also affects others, only with their free, voluntary, and undeceived consent and participation. When I say only himself, I mean directly, and in the first instance; for whatever affects himself, may affect others *through* himself; and the objection which may be grounded on this contingency, will receive consideration in the sequel. This, then, is the appropriate region of human liberty. It comprises, first, the inward domain of consciousness; demanding liberty of conscience in the most comprehensive sense; liberty of thought and feeling; absolute freedom of opinion and sentiment on all subjects, practical or speculative, scientific, moral, or theological. The liberty of expressing and publishing opinions may seem to fall under a different principle, since it belongs to that part of the conduct of an individual which concerns other people; but, being almost of as much importance as the liberty of thought itself, and resting in great part on the same reasons, is practically inseparable from it. Secondly, the principle requires liberty of tastes and pursuits; of framing the plan of our life to suit our own character; of doing as we like, subject to such consequences as may follow: without impediment from our fellow-creatures, so long as what we do does not harm them, even though they should think our conduct foolish, perverse, or wrong. Thirdly, from this liberty of each individual, follows the liberty, within the same limits, of combination among individuals; freedom to unite, for any purpose not involving

8. According to law, or by right.

harm to others: the persons combining being supposed to be of full age, and not forced or deceived.[9]

No society in which these liberties are not, on the whole, respected, is free, whatever may be its form of government; and none is completely free in which they do not exist absolute and unqualified. The only freedom which deserves the name, is that of pursuing our own good in our own way, so long as we do not attempt to deprive others of theirs, or impede their efforts to obtain it. Each is the proper guardian of his own health, whether bodily, or mental and spiritual. Mankind are greater gainers by suffering each other to live as seems good to themselves, than by compelling each to live as seems good to the rest.

Though this doctrine is anything but new, and, to some persons, may have the air of a truism, there is no doctrine which stands more directly opposed to the general tendency of existing opinion and practice. Society has expended fully as much effort in the attempt (according to its lights) to compel people to conform to its notions of personal as of social excellence. The ancient commonwealths thought themselves entitled to practise, and the ancient philosophers countenanced, the regulation of every part of private conduct by public authority, on the ground that the State had a deep interest in the whole bodily and mental discipline of every one of its citizens;[1] a mode of thinking which may have been admissible in small republics surrounded by powerful enemies, in constant peril of being subverted by foreign attack or internal commotion, and to which even a short interval of relaxed energy and self-command might so easily be fatal that they could not afford to wait for the salutary permanent effects of freedom. In the modern world, the greater size of political communities, and, above all, the separation between spiritual and temporal authority (which placed the direction of men's consciences in other hands than those which controlled their worldly affairs), prevented so great an interference by law in the details of private life; but the engines of moral repression have been wielded more strenuously

9. This paragraph, delineating the self-regarding sphere of human action and setting forth the primary liberties, in particular the liberties of thought and of expression, is perhaps the focal point of the many assaults on Mill's essay. Typical of criticisms are James Fitzjames Stephen, *Liberty, Equality, Fraternity* (London, 1873), and Willmoore Kendall, "The 'Open Society' and Its Fallacies," *American Political Science Review*, 54 (1960), 972–79. In defense of Mill, see J. M. Robson, *The Improvement of Mankind: The Social and Political Thought of John Stuart Mill* (Toronto, 1968), especially Part 2; A. W. Levi,

"The Value of Freedom: Mill's Liberty (1859–1959)," *Ethics*, 70 (1959), 37–46; and Spitz, *op. cit.*, pp. 176–226.
1. Whether Mill correctly read the practices of the ancient commonwealths (say, Athens rather than Sparta), or the teachings of the ancient philosophers (e.g., Plato), may be contested. For contrasting views, see Karl Popper, *The Open Society and Its Enemies*, 3rd ed. (London, 1957), vol. 1, whose account would support Mill's description, and Werner Jaeger, *Paideia*, 3 vols., trans. Highet (New York, 1939, 1943, 1944), who offers a different view.

against divergence from the reigning opinion in self-regarding, than even in social matters; religion, the most powerful of the elements which have entered into the formation of moral feeling, having almost always been governed either by the ambition of a hierarchy, seeking control over every department of human conduct, or by the spirit of Puritanism.[2] And some of those modern reformers who have placed themselves in strongest opposition to the religions of the past, have been noway behind either churches or sects in their assertion of the right of spiritual domination: M. Comte, in particular, whose social systems, as unfolded in his *Système de Politique Positive*, aims at establishing (though by moral more than by legal appliances) a despotism of society over the individual, surpassing anything contemplated in the political ideal of the most rigid disciplinarian among the ancient philosophers.[3]

Apart from the peculiar tenets of individual thinkers, there is also in the world at large an increasing inclination to stretch unduly the powers of society over the individual, both by the force of opinion and even by that of legislation; and as the tendency of all the changes taking place in the world is to strengthen society, and diminish the power of the individual, this encroachment is not one of the evils which tend spontaneously to disappear, but, on the contrary, to grow more and more formidable. The disposition of mankind, whether as rulers or as fellow-citizens, to impose their own opinions and inclinations as a rule of conduct on others, is so energetically supported by some of the best and by some of the worst feelings incident to human nature, that it is hardly ever kept under restraint by anything but want of power; and as the power is not declining, but growing,[4] unless a strong barrier of moral conviction can be raised against the mischief, we must expect, in the present circumstances of the world, to see it increase.

It will be convenient for the argument, if, instead of at once entering upon the general thesis, we confine ourselves in the first instance to a single branch of it, on which the principle here stated is, if not fully, yet to a certain point, recognised by the current

2. The beliefs of dissenters in sixteenth-century England who wished further to remove the Church of England from Roman Catholic influences by simplifying worship and affecting greater strictness in personal morality and religious principles. The term is used pejoratively by Mill (and often in our own time) to indicate excessively rigid control of personal conduct.

3. Auguste Comte (1798–1857), French sociologist and founder of positivism. His central doctrine postulates the evolution of human society from the theological to the metaphysical to the scientific or positive stage of history. In his *Système de politique positive* (1851–54), he expounded in minute detail his plan for the practical reorganization of society under a "religion of humanity." In Mill's view, this plan entailed a despotism even more rigid than that he conceived to reside in Plato's *Republic*. See Mill's "Auguste Comte and Positivism," in his *Essays on Ethics, Religion and Society, Collected Works*, 10:261–368.

4. Mill seems to refer here to the spread of democracy and the progressive enfranchisement of the masses.

opinions. This one branch is the Liberty of Thought: from which it is impossible to separate the cognate liberty of speaking and of writing. Although these liberties, to some considerable amount, form part of the political morality of all countries which profess religious toleration and free institutions, the grounds, both philosophical and practical, on which they rest, are perhaps not so familiar to the general mind, nor so thoroughly appreciated by many even of the leaders of opinion, as might have been expected. Those grounds, when rightly understood, are of much wider application than to only one division of the subject, and a thorough consideration of this part of the question will be found the best introduction to the remainder. Those to whom nothing which I am about to say will be new, may therefore, I hope, excuse me, if on a subject which for now three centuries has been so often discussed, I venture on one discussion more.

Chapter II

OF THE LIBERTY OF THOUGHT AND DISCUSSION

The time, it is to be hoped, is gone by, when any defence would be necessary of the "liberty of the press" as one of the securities against corrupt or tyrannical government. No argument, we may suppose, can now be needed, against permitting a legislature or an executive, not identified in interest with the people, to prescribe opinions to them, and determine what doctrines or what arguments they shall be allowed to hear. This aspect of the question, besides, has been so often and so triumphantly enforced by preceding writers, that it needs not be specially insisted on in this place. Though the law of England, on the subject of the press, is as servile to this day as it was in the time of the Tudors,[1] there is little danger of its being actually put in force against political discussion, except during some temporary panic, when fear of insurrection drives ministers and judges from their propriety;[2] and, speaking generally, it is not, in constitutional countries, to be apprehended, that the government, whether completely responsible to the people or not, will often attempt to control the expression of opinion, except when in doing so it makes itself the organ of the general intolerance of the public. Let us suppose, therefore, that the government is entirely at one

1. The ruling royal family in England from 1485 (Henry VII) to 1603 (Elizabeth I).
2. [Mill's note] These words had scarcely been written, when, as if to give them an emphatic contradiction, occurred the Government Press Prosecutions of 1858. [Editor: For the publication in Britain of views in defense of those who would assassinate Napoleon III.] That ill-judged interference with the liberty of public discussion has not, however, induced me to alter a single word in the text, nor has it at all weakened my conviction that, moments of panic excepted, the era of pains and penalties for political discussion has, in our own country, passed away. For, in the first place, the prosecutions were not persisted in; and, in the second, they were never, properly speaking, political prosecutions. The offence charged was not that of criticising institutions, or the acts or persons of rulers, but of circulating what was deemed an immoral doctrine, the lawfulness of Tyrannicide.

If the arguments of the present chapter are of any validity, there ought to exist the fullest liberty of professing and discussing, as a matter of ethical conviction, any doctrine, however immoral it may be considered. [Editor: This statement seems to have given especial affront to conservatives, some of whom (e.g., Kendall, op. cit.) have interpreted it to imply a kind of liberal absolutism.] It would, therefore, be irrelevant and out of place to examine here, whether the doctrine of Tyrannicide deserves that title. I shall content myself with saying that the subject has been at all times one of the open questions of morals; that the act of a private citizen in striking down a criminal, who, by raising himself above the law, has placed himself beyond the reach of legal punishment or control, has been accounted by whole nations, and by some of the best and wisest of men, not a crime, but an act of exalted virtue; and that, right or wrong, it is not of the nature of assassination, but of civil war. As such, I hold that the instigation to it, in a specific case, may be a proper subject of punishment, but only if an overt act has followed, and at least a probable connection can be established between the act and the instigation. Even then, it is not a foreign government, but the very government assailed, which alone, in the exercise of self-defence, can legitimately punish attacks directed against its own existence.

with the people, and never thinks of exerting any power of coercion unless in agreement with what it conceives to be their voice. But I deny the right of the people to exercise such coercion, either by themselves or by their government. The power itself is illegitimate. The best government has no more title to it than the worst. It is as noxious, or more noxious, when exerted in accordance with public opinion, than when in opposition to it. If all mankind minus one were of one opinion, and only one person were of the contrary opinion, mankind would be no more justified in silencing that one person, than he, if he had the power, would be justified in silencing mankind.[3] Were an opinion a personal possession of no value except to the owner; if to be obstructed in the enjoyment of it were simply a private injury, it would make some difference whether the injury was inflicted only on a few persons or on many. But the peculiar evil of silencing the expression of an opinion is, that it is robbing the human race; posterity as well as the existing generation; those who dissent from the opinion, still more than those who hold it. If the opinion is right, they are deprived of the opportunity of exchanging error for truth: if wrong, they lose, what is almost as great a benefit, the clearer perception and livelier impression of truth, produced by its collision with error.

It is necessary to consider separately these two hypotheses, each of which has a distinct branch of the argument corresponding to it. We can never be sure that the opinion we are endeavouring to stifle is a false opinion; and if we were sure, stifling it would be an evil still.[4]

First: the opinion which it is attempted to suppress by authority may possibly be true. Those who desire to suppress it, of course deny its truth; but they are not infallible. They have no authority to decide the question for all mankind, and exclude every other person from the means of judging. To refuse a hearing to an opinion, because they are sure that it is false, is to assume that *their* certainty is the same thing as *absolute* certainty. All silencing of discussion is an assumption of infallibility.[5] Its condemnation may be allowed to rest on this common argument, not the worse for being common.

Unfortunately for the good sense of mankind, the fact of their fallibility is far from carrying the weight in their practical judgment which is always allowed to it in theory; for while every one well knows himself to be fallible, few think it necessary to take any pre-

---

3. This has become one of the most quoted sentences of the essay.
4. It may be noted, *en passant*, that this is clearly a utilitarian argument, not an appeal to abstract right.
5. This need not, as some critics (e.g.,

Kendall) have alleged, entail the enthronement of skepticism about ultimate values. See Richard Wollheim, "Without Doubt or Dogma: The Logic of Liberalism," *The Nation*, 183 (July 28, 1956), 74–76.

cautions against their own fallibility, or admit the supposition that any opinion, of which they feel very certain, may be one of the examples of the error to which they acknowledge themselves to be liable. Absolute princes, or others who are accustomed to unlimited deference, usually feel this complete confidence in their own opinions on nearly all subjects. People more happily situated, who sometimes hear their opinions disputed, and are not wholly unused to be set right when they are wrong, place the same unbounded reliance only on such of their opinions as are shared by all who surround them, or to whom they habitually defer; for in proportion to a man's want of confidence in his own solitary judgment, does he usually repose, with implicit trust, on the infallibility of "the world" in general. And the world, to each individual, means the part of it with which he comes in contact; his party, his sect, his church, his class of society; the man may be called, by comparison, almost liberal and large-minded to whom it means anything so comprehensive as his own country or his own age. Nor is his faith in this collective authority at all shaken by his being aware that other ages, countries, sects, churches, classes, and parties have thought, and even now think, the exact reverse. He devolves upon his own world the responsibility of being in the right against the dissentient worlds of other people; and it never troubles him that mere accident has decided which of these numerous worlds is the object of his reliance, and that the same causes which make him a Churchman[6] in London, would have made him a Buddhist[7] or a Confucian[8] in Pekin.[9] Yet it is as evident in itself, as any amount of argument can make it, that ages are no more infallible than individuals; every age having held many opinions which subsequent ages have deemed not only false but absurd; and it is as certain that many opinions now general will be rejected by future ages, as it is that many, once general, are rejected by the present.

The objection likely to be made to this argument would probably take some such form as the following. There is no greater assumption of infallibility in forbidding the propagation of error, than in any other thing which is done by public authority on its own judgment and responsibility. Judgment is given to men that they may use it. Because it may be used erroneously, are men to be told that they ought not to use it at all? To prohibit what they think pernicious, is not claiming exemption from error, but fulfilling the duty incumbent on them, although fallible, of acting on their conscien-

---

6. An adherent of the Church of England.
7. A follower of Buddhism, a religious system founded by Prince Siddhartha, or Gautama Buddha, a great religious teacher who lived in northern India about the fifth or sixth century B.C.
8. A follower of the Chinese philosopher Kung Fû-tse, or Confucius (551–478 B.C.).
9. Peking, the capital of China.

tious conviction. If we were never to act on our opinions, because
those opinions may be wrong, we should leave all our interests
uncared for, and all our duties unperformed. An objection which
applies to all conduct can be no valid objection to any conduct in
particular. It is the duty of governments, and of individuals, to form
the truest opinions they can; to form carefully, and never impose
them upon others unless they are quite sure of being right. But
when they are sure (such reasoners may say), it is not conscientiousness but cowardice to shrink from acting on their opinions, and
allow doctrines which they honestly think dangerous to the welfare
of mankind, either in this life or in another, to be scattered abroad
without restraint, because other people, in less enlightened times,
have persecuted opinions now believed to be true. Let us take care,
it may be said, not to make the same mistake: but governments and
nations have made mistakes in other things, which are not denied
to be fit subjects for the exercise of authority: they have laid on bad
taxes, made unjust wars. Ought we therefore to lay on no taxes,
and, under whatever provocation, make no wars? Men and governments, must act to the best of their ability. There is no such thing
as absolute certainty, but there is assurance sufficient for the purposes of human life. We may, and must, assume our opinion to be
true for the guidance of our own conduct: and it is assuming no
more when we forbid bad men to pervert society by the propagation
of opinions which we regard as false and pernicious.

I answer, that it is assuming very much more. There is the greatest difference between presuming an opinion to be true, because,
with every opportunity for contesting it, it has not been refuted,
and assuming its truth for the purpose of not permitting its refuta-
tion. Complete liberty of contradicting and disproving our opinion
is the very condition which justifies us in assuming its truth for purposes of action; and on no other terms can a being with human faculties have any rational assurance of being right.

When we consider either the history of opinion, or the ordinary
conduct of human life, to what is it to be ascribed that the one and
the other are no worse than they are? Not certainly to the inherent
force of the human understanding; for, on any matter not self-evident, there are ninety-nine persons totally incapable of judging of it
for one who is capable; and the capacity of the hundredth person is
only comparative; for the majority of the eminent men of every past
generation held many opinions now known to be erroneous, and did
or approved numerous things which no one will now justify. Why is
it, then, that there is on the whole a preponderance among mankind of rational opinions and rational conduct? If there really is this
preponderance—which there must be unless human affairs are, and

have always been, in an almost desperate state—it is owing to a quality of the human mind, the source of everything respectable in man either as an intellectual or as a moral being, namely, that his errors are corrigible. He is capable of rectifying his mistakes, by discussion and experience.[1] Not by experience alone. There must be discussion, to show how experience is to be interpreted. Wrong opinions and practices gradually yield to fact and argument; but facts and arguments, to produce any effect on the mind, must be brought before it. Very few facts are able to tell their own story, without comments to bring out their meaning. The whole strength and value, then, of human judgment, depending on the one property, that it can be set right when it is wrong, reliance can be placed on it only when the means of setting it right are kept constantly at hand. In the case of any person whose judgment is really deserving of confidence, how has it become so? Because he has kept his mind open to criticism on his opinions and conduct. Because it has been his practice to listen to all that could be said against him; to profit by as much of it as was just, and expound to himself, and upon occasion to others, the fallacy of what was fallacious. Because he has felt, that the only way in which a human being can make some approach to knowing the whole of a subject, is by hearing what can be said about it by persons of every variety of opinion, and studying all modes in which it can be looked at by every character of mind. No wise man ever acquired his wisdom in any mode but this; nor is it in the nature of human intellect to become wise in any other manner. The steady habit of correcting and completing his own opinion by collating it with those of others, so far from causing doubt and hesitation in carrying it into practice, is the only stable foundation for a just reliance on it: for, being cognisant of all that can, at least obviously, be said against him, and having taken up his position against all gainsayers—knowing that he has sought for objections and difficulties, instead of avoiding them, and has shut out no light which can be thrown upon the subject from any quarter—he has a right to think his judgment better than that of any person, or any multitude, who have not gone through a similar process.

It is not too much to require that what the wisest of mankind, those who are best entitled to trust their own judgment, find necessary to warrant their relying on it, should be submitted to by that miscellaneous collection of a few wise and many foolish individuals, called the public. The most intolerant of churches, the Roman Catholic Church, even at the canonisation of a saint, admits, and

1. Mill's fuller exposition of the role of reason and experience may be found in his *System of Logic* and the essay on Coleridge.

listens patiently to, a "devil's advocate."[2] The holiest of men, it appears, cannot be admitted to posthumous honours, until all that the devil could say against him is known and weighed. If even the Newtonian philosophy[3] were not permitted to be questioned, mankind could not feel as complete assurance of its truth as they now do. The beliefs which we have most warrant for have no safeguard to rest on, but a standing invitation to the whole world to prove them unfounded. If the challenge is not accepted, or is accepted and the attempt fails, we are far enough from certainty still; but we have done the best that the existing state of human reason admits of; we have neglected nothing that could give the truth a chance of reaching us: if the lists are kept open, we may hope that if there be a better truth, it will be found when the human mind is capable of receiving it; and in the meantime we may rely on having attained such approach to truth as is possible in our own day. This is the amount of certainty attainable by a fallible being, and this the sole way of attaining it.

Strange it is, that men should admit the validity of the arguments for free discussion, but object to their being "pushed to an extreme"; not seeing that unless the reasons are good for an extreme case, they are not good for any case. Strange that they should imagine that they are not assuming infallibility, when they acknowledge that there should be free discussion on all subjects which can possibly be *doubtful*, but think that some particular principle or doctrine should be forbidden to be questioned because it is so *certain*, that is, because *they are certain* that it is certain. To call any proposition certain, while there is any one who would deny its certainty if permitted, but who is not permitted, is to assume that we ourselves, and those who agree with us, are the judges of certainty, and judges without hearing the other side.

In the present age—which has been described as "destitute of faith, but terrified at scepticism"[4]—in which people feel sure, not so much that their opinions are true, as that they should not know what to do without them—the claims of an opinion to be protected from public attack are rested not so much on its truth, as on its importance to society. There are, it is alleged, certain beliefs so useful, not to say indispensable, to well-being that it is as much the duty of governments to uphold those beliefs, as to protect any

2. The *advocatus diaboli* is a person formally assigned by the Church to prepare arguments in opposition to the proposed beatification and canonization of a saint. Currently a technique employed in many situations to assure representation of diverse views.
3. Explanatory principles about the natural world derived from the science of

mechanics developed by Isaac Newton (1642–1727).
4. From Carlyle's "Memoirs of the Life of Scott," first published in Mill's periodical, *London and Westminster Review* (1838), reprinted in Thomas Carlyle, *Critical and Miscellaneous Essays* (New York, 1880), p. 520.

other of the interests of society. In a case of such necessity, and so directly in the line of their duty, something less than infallibility may, it is maintained, warrant, and even bind, governments to act on their own opinion, confirmed by the general opinion of mankind. It is also often argued, and still oftener thought, that none but bad men would desire to weaken these salutary beliefs; and there can be nothing wrong, it is thought, in restraining bad men, and prohibiting what only such men would wish to practise. This mode of thinking makes the justification of restraints on discussion not a question of the truth of doctrines, but of their usefulness; and flatters itself by that means to escape the responsibility of claiming to be an infallible judge of opinions. But those who thus satisfy themselves, do not perceive that the assumption of infallibility is merely shifted from one point to another. The usefulness of an opinion is itself matter of opinion: as disputable, as open to discussion, and requiring discussion as much as the opinion itself. There is the same need of an infallible judge of opinions to decide an opinion to be noxious, as to decide it to be false, unless the opinion condemned has full opportunity of defending itself. And it will not do to say that the heretic may be allowed to maintain the utility or harmlessness of his opinion, though forbidden to maintain its truth. The truth of an opinion is part of its utility. If we would know whether or not it is desirable that a proposition should be believed, is it possible to exclude the consideration of whether or not it is true? In the opinion, not of bad men, but of the best men, no belief which is contrary to truth can be really useful: and can you prevent such men from urging that plea, when they are charged with culpability for denying some doctrine which they are told is useful, but which they believe to be false? Those who are on the side of received opinions never fail to take all possible advantage of this plea: you do not find *them* handling the question of utility as if it could be completely abstracted from that of truth: on the contrary, it is, above all, because their doctrine is "the truth," that the knowledge or the belief of it is held to be so indispensable. There can be no fair discussion of the question of usefulness when an argument so vital may be employed on one side, but not on the other. And in point of fact, when law or public feeling do not permit the truth of an opinion to be disputed, they are just as little tolerant of a denial of its usefulness. The utmost they allow is an extenuation of its absolute necessity, or of the positive guilt of rejecting it.

In order more fully to illustrate the mischief of denying a hearing to opinions because we, in our own judgment, have condemned them, it will be desirable to fix down the discussion to a concrete case; and I choose, by preference, the cases which are least favourable to me—in which the argument against freedom of opinion, both on the score of truth and on that of utility, is considered the strongest. Let the opinions impugned be the belief in a God and in a future state, or any of the commonly received doctrines of morality. To fight the battle on such ground gives a great advantage to an unfair antagonist; since he will be sure to say (and many who have no desire to be unfair will say it internally), Are these the doctrines which you do not deem sufficiently certain to be taken under the protection of law? Is the belief in a God one of the opinions to feel sure of which you hold to be assuming infallibility? But I must be permitted to observe, that it is not the feeling sure of a doctrine (be it what it may) which I call an assumption of infallibility. It is the undertaking to decide that question *for others*, without allowing them to hear what can be said on the contrary side. And I denounce and reprobate this pretension not the less, if put forth on the side of my most solemn convictions. However positive any one's persuasion may be, not only of the falsity but of the pernicious consequences—not only of the pernicious consequences, but (to adopt expressions which I altogether condemn) the immorality and impiety of an opinion; yet if, in pursuance of that private judgment, though backed by the public judgment of his country or his cotemporaries, he prevents the opinion from being heard in its defence, he assumes infallibility. And so far from the assumption being less objectionable or less dangerous because the opinion is called immoral or impious, this is the case of all others in which it is most fatal. These are exactly the occasions on which the men of one generation commit those dreadful mistakes which excite the astonishment and horror of posterity. It is among such that we find the instances memorable in history, when the arm of the law has been employed to root out the best men and the noblest doctrines; with deplorable success as to the men, though some of the doctrines have survived to be (as if in mockery) invoked in defence of similar conduct towards those who dissent from *them*, or from their received interpretation.

Mankind can hardly be too often reminded, that there was once a man named Socrates,[5] between whom and the legal authorities and public opinion of his time there took place a memorable collision. Born in an age and country abounding in individual greatness, this man has been handed down to us by those who best knew both him and the age, as the most virtuous man in it; while *we* know him as the head and prototype of all subsequent teachers of virtue,

---

5. Athenian philosopher (469?–399 B.C.), condemned to death, according to the allegation, for teaching disrespect of the gods and corrupting the youth. For his trial and death, see Plato's dialogues *Euthyphro, Apology, Crito*, and *Phaedo*.

the source equally of the lofty inspiration of Plato[6] and the judicious utilitarianism of Aristotle,[7] "*i maëstri di color che sanno*," the two headsprings of ethical as of all other philosophy. This acknowledged master of all the eminent thinkers who have since lived—whose fame, still growing after more than two thousand years, all but outweighs the whole remainder of the names which make his native city illustrious—was put to death by his countrymen, after a judicial conviction, for impiety and immorality. Impiety, in denying the gods recognised by the State; indeed his accuser asserted (see the "Apologia"[8]) that he believed in no gods at all. Immorality, in being, by his doctrines and instructions, a "corruptor of youth." Of these charges the tribunal, there is every ground for believing, honestly found him guilty, and condemned the man who probably of all then born had deserved best of mankind to be put to death as a criminal.

To pass from this to the only other instance of judicial iniquity, the mention of which, after the condemnation of Socrates, would not be an anti-climax: the event which took place on Calvary[9] rather more than eighteen hundred years ago. The man who left on the memory of those who witnessed his life and conversation such an impression of his moral grandeur that eighteen subsequent centuries have done homage to him as the Almighty in person, was ignominiously put to death, as what? As a blasphemer. Men did not merely mistake their benefactor; they mistook him for the exact contrary of what he was, and treated him as that prodigy of impiety which they themselves are now held to be for their treatment of him. The feelings with which mankind now regard these lamentable transactions, especially the later of the two, render them extremely unjust in their judgment of the unhappy actors. These were, to all appearance, not bad men—not worse than men commonly are, but rather the contrary; men who possessed in a full, or somewhat more than a full measure, the religious, moral and patriotic feelings of their time and people: the very kind of men who, in all times, our own included, have every chance of passing through life blameless and respected. The high-priest[1] who rent his garments when the words were pronounced, which, according to all the ideas of his country, constituted the blackest guilt, was in all probability quite as sincere in his horror and indignation as the generality of respecta-

6. Greek philosopher (427?–347 B.C.) and pupil of Socrates.
7. Greek philosopher (384–322 B.C.) and pupil of Plato. The quotation, "the masters of those who know," was adapted by Mill from Dante's description of Aristotle, in the *Divine Comedy* (*Inferno*, Canto 4, line 131). Aristotle propounded an ethics based on an equation of happiness and goodness, but differing in crucial respects from the utilitarianism of Bentham and James Mill.
8. Plato's *Apology*, which gives an account of Socrates' trial.
9. Site of Jesus' crucifixion.
1. Caiaphas (Matthew 26:65).

ble and pious men now are in the religious and moral sentiments they profess; and most of those who now shudder at his conduct, if they had lived in his time, and been born Jews, would have acted precisely as he did. Orthodox Christians who are tempted to think that those who stoned to death the first martyrs must have been worse men than they themselves are, ought to remember that one of those persecutors was Saint Paul.[2]

Let us add one more example, the most striking of all, if the impressiveness of an error is measured by the wisdom and virtue of him who falls into it. If ever any one, possessed of power, had grounds for thinking himself the best and most enlightened among his contemporaries, it was the Emperor Marcus Aurelius.[3] Absolute monarch of the whole civilised world, he preserved through life not only the most unblemished justice, but what was less to be expected from his Stoical[4] breeding, the tenderest heart. The few failings which are attributed to him were all on the side of indulgence: while his writings, the highest ethical product of the ancient mind, differ scarcely perceptibly, if they differ at all, from the most characteristic teachings of Christ. This man, a better Christian in all but the dogmatic sense of the word than almost any of the ostensibly Christian sovereigns who have since reigned, persecuted Christianity. Placed at the summit of all the previous attainments of humanity, with an open, unfettered intellect, and a character which led him of himself to embody in his moral writings the Christian ideal, he yet failed to see that Christianity was to be a good and not an evil to the world,[5] with his duties to which he was so deeply penetrated. Existing society he knew to be in a deplorable state. But such as it was, he saw, or thought he saw, that it was held together, and prevented from being worse, by belief and reverence of the received divinities. As a ruler of mankind, he deemed it his duty not to suffer society to fall in pieces; and saw not how, if its existing ties were removed, any others could be formed which could again knit it together. The new religion openly aimed at dissolving these ties:

2. Jewish-born Saul, later St. Paul, "Apostle to the Gentiles" and great Christian missionary (died A.D. ca. 67), who, prior to his conversion, persecuted the followers of Jesus.
3. Marcus Aurelius Antoninus (121–80), Roman emperor, author of *Meditations* (a book of Stoic philosophy), and a ruler celebrated for his virtue and humanitarianism.
4. The Stoics were members of a Greek school of philosophy founded by Zeno of Citium (336?–264? B.C.), who preached the virtues of self-control, personal austerity and fortitude, and indifference to pleasure or pain, all of which became dominant values in Roman civilization.
5. Despite these (and later) statements, some critics have charged Mill with attacking Christianity. See, for example, Maurice Cowling, *Mill and Liberalism* (Cambridge, 1963), pp. xiii, 12–15, 140–42, and chap. 4. But cf. further Mill's *Utilitarianism*, chap. 2, where he says: "In the golden rule of Jesus of Nazareth, we read the complete spirit of the ethics of utility. To do as you would be done by, and to love your neighbor as yourself, constitute the ideal perfection of utilitarian morality."

unless, therefore, it was his duty to adopt that religion, it seemed to be his duty to put it down. Inasmuch then as the theology of Christianity did not appear to him true or of divine origin; inasmuch as this strange history of a crucified God was not credible to him, and a system which purported to rest entirely upon a foundation to him so wholly unbelievable, could not be foreseen by him to be that renovating agency which, after all abatements, it has in fact proved to be; the gentlest and most amiable of philosophers and rulers, under a solemn sense of duty, authorised the persecution of Christianity. To my mind this is one of the most tragical facts in all history. It is a bitter thought, how different a thing the Christianity of the world might have been, if the Christian faith had been adopted as the religion of the empire under the auspices of Marcus Aurelius instead of those of Constantine.[6] But it would be equally unjust to him and false to truth to deny, that no one plea which can be urged for punishing anti-Christian teaching was wanting to Marcus Aurelius for punishing, as he did, the propagation of Christianity. No Christian more firmly believes that Atheism is false, and tends to the dissolution of society, than Marcus Aurelius believed the same things of Christianity; he who, of all men then living, might have been thought the most capable of appreciating it. Unless any one who approves of punishment for the promulgation of opinions, flatters himself that he is a wiser and better man than Marcus Aurelius —more deeply versed in the wisdom of his time, more elevated in his intellect above it—more earnest in his search for truth, or more single-minded in his devotion to it when found; let him abstain from that assumption of the joint infallibility of himself and the multitude, which the great Antoninus made with so unfortunate a result.

Aware of the impossibility of defending the use of punishment for restraining irreligious opinions by any argument which will not justify Marcus Antoninus, the enemies of religious freedom, when hard pressed, occasionally accept this consequence, and say, with Dr. Johnson,[7] that the persecutors of Christianity were in the right; that persecution is an ordeal through which truth ought to pass, and always passes successfully, legal penalties being, in the end, powerless against truth, though sometimes beneficially effective against mischievous errors. This is a form of the argument for religious intolerance sufficiently remarkable not to be passed without notice.

6. Constantine the Great (288?–337), Roman emperor who in 313 made Christianity a lawful religion and then persecuted dissenters.

7. Samuel Johnson (1709–84), British lexicographer, critic, poet, and conversationalist.

A theory which maintains that truth may justifiably be perse-cuted because persecution cannot possibly do it any harm, cannot be charged with being intentionally hostile to the reception of new truths; but we cannot commend the generosity of its dealing with the persons to whom mankind are indebted for them. To discover to the world something which deeply concerns it, and of which it was previously ignorant; to prove to it that it had been mistaken on some vital point of temporal or spiritual interest, is as important a service as a human being can render to his fellow-creatures, and in certain cases, as in those of the early Christians and of the Reform-ers, those who think with Dr. Johnson believe it to have been the most precious gift which could be bestowed on mankind. That the authors of such splendid benefits should be requited by martyrdom; that their reward should be to be dealt with as the vilest of crimi-nals, is not, upon this theory, a deplorable error and misfortune, for which humanity should mourn in sackcloth and ashes, but the normal and justifiable state of things. The propounder of a new truth, according to this doctrine, should stand, as stood, in the legis-lation of the Locrians,[8] the proposer of a new law, with a halter round his neck, to be instantly tightened if the public assembly did not, on hearing his reasons, then and there adopt his proposition. People who defend this mode of treating benefactors cannot be sup-posed to set much value on the benefit; and I believe this view of the subject is mostly confined to the sort of persons who think that new truths may have been desirable once, but that we have had enough of them now.

But, indeed, the dictum that truth always triumphs over persecu-tion is one of those pleasant falsehoods which men repeat after one another till they pass into commonplaces, but which all experience refutes. History teems with instances of truth put down by persecu-tion. If not suppressed for ever, it may be thrown back for cen-turies. To speak only of religious opinions: the Reformation[9] broke out at least twenty times before Luther,[1] and was put down. Arnold of Brescia[2] was put down. Fra Dolcino[3] was put down. Savonarola[4]

---

8. The inhabitants of Locri, a Greek col-ony in southern Italy, who had perhaps the first written code of laws in Europe, drawn up by the lawgiver Zaleucus, a slave, in the seventh century B.C.
9. The great religious movement in the sixteenth century, having for its object the reform of the doctrines and practices of Roman Catholicism, and ending in the establishment of the Protestant churches.
1. Martin Luther (1483–1546), German priest and theologian who led the Protes-tant Reformation and profoundly influ-enced both German politics and thought.

2. Arnold of Brescia (1090?–1155), Ital-ian priest who fought the Church's tem-poral power, became a leader of the Roman republic, and was eventually exe-cuted as a political rebel by the Roman Curia.
3. Dolcino of Novario (died 1307), he-retical preacher who was tortured to death.
4. Girolamo Savonarola (1452–98), pop-ular and briefly powerful Florentine preacher, renowned both for his eloquent attacks on church laxity and for his ex-treme severity; he was eventually hanged and burned at the stake for heresy.

was put down. The Albigeois[5] were put down. The Vaudois[6] were put down. The Lollards[7] were put down. The Hussites[8] were put down. Even after the era of Luther,. wherever persecution was persisted in, it was successful. In Spain, Italy, Flanders, the Austrian empire, Protestantism was rooted out;[9] and, most likely, would have been so in England, had Queen Mary[1] lived, or Queen Elizabeth[2] died. Persecution has always succeeded, save where the heretics were too strong a party to be effectually persecuted. No reasonable person can doubt that Christianity might have been extirpated in the Roman Empire. It spread, and became predominant, because the persecutions were only occasional, lasting but a short time, and separated by long intervals of almost undisturbed propagandism. It is a piece of idle sentimentality that truth, merely as truth, has any inherent power denied to error of prevailing against the dungeon and the stake. Men are not more zealous for truth than they often are for error, and a sufficient application of legal or even of social penalties will generally succeed in stopping the propagation of either. The real advantage which truth has consists in this, that when an opinion is true, it may be extinguished once, twice, or many times, but in the course of ages there will generally be found persons to rediscover it, until some one of its reappearances falls on a time when from favourable circumstances it escapes persecution until it has made such head as to withstand all subsequent attempts to suppress it.

It will be said, that we do not now put to death the introducers of new opinions: we are not like our fathers who slew the prophets, we even build sepulchres to them. It is true we no longer put heretics to death; and the amount of penal infliction which modern feel-

---

5. Also known as Albigenses, or Albigensians, a heretical southern French religious sect that flourished in the twelfth and thirteenth centuries but disappeared under the combined assault of the Inquisition, missionary preaching, and Pope Innocent III's crusade against them in 1209.
6. Also known as Waldenses, or Waldensians, after their leader Pierre Waldo, a wealthy merchant of Lyons, France, who in the twelfth century gave away his wealth and organized an ascetic and heretical religious sect which was strongly persecuted but survived to merge with the German Protestants in the sixteenth century.
7. Members of an ascetic and anti-sacerdotal English and Scottish movement for ecclesiastical reform led by John Wyclif, or Wycliffe (1324–84), and popular among both middle and lower classes until driven underground by suppressive measures.
8. Followers of John Huss (1369?–1415),
who led a popular movement in Bohemia and Moravia that was strongly influenced by the religious teachings of Wycliffe but also involved a national struggle between Czechs and Germans, and a social struggle against feudalism; its influence was dissipated by internal schism, military defeat, and widespread defection, but remnants of the group survived to unite with the sixteenth-century Reformers.
9. By the Counter-Reformation following the Protestant Reformation of the sixteenth century.
1. Mary I, also Mary Tudor or "Bloody Mary" (1516–58), who as Queen of England (1553–58) tried to re-establish the supremacy of the Roman Catholic Church.
2. Born in 1533, daughter of Henry VIII and Anne Boleyn, and Queen of England from 1558 to 1603, she succeeded Mary and ensured the continuation of the Church of England as the official national church.

ing would probably tolerate, even against the most obnoxious opinions, is not sufficient to extirpate them. But let us not flatter ourselves that we are yet free from the stain even of legal persecution. Penalties for opinion, or at least for its expression, still exist by law; and their enforcement is not, even in these times, so unexampled as to make it all incredible that they may some day be revived in full force. In the year 1857, at the summer assizes[3] of the county of Cornwall, an unfortunate man,[4] said to be of unexceptionable conduct in all relations of life, was sentenced to twenty-one months' imprisonment, for uttering, and writing on a gate, some offensive words concerning Christianity. Witin a month of the same time, at the Old Bailey,[5] two persons, on two separate occasions,[6] were rejected as jurymen, and one of them grossly insulted by the judge and by one of the counsel, because they honestly declared that they had no theological belief; and a third, a foreigner,[7] for the same reason, was denied justice against a thief. This refusal of redress took place in virtue of the legal doctrine, that no person can be allowed to give evidence in a court of justice who does not profess belief in a God (any god is sufficient) and in a future state;[8] which is equivalent to declaring such persons to be outlaws, excluded from the protection of the tribunals; who may not only be robbed or assaulted with impunity, if no one but themselves, or persons of similar opinions, be present, but any one else may be robbed or assaulted with impunity, if the proof of the fact depends on their evidence. The assumption on which this is grounded is that the oath is worthless of a person who does not believe in a future state; a proposition which betokens much ignorance of history in those who assent to it (since it is historically true that a large proportion of infidels in all ages have been persons of distinguished integrity and honour); and would be maintained by no one who had the smallest conception how many of the persons in greatest repute with the world, both for virtues and attainments, are well known, at least to their intimates, to be unbelievers. The rule, besides, is suicidal, and cuts away its own foundation. Under pretence that atheists must be liars, it admits the testimony of all atheists who are willing to lie, and rejects only those who brave the obloquy of publicly confessing a detested creed rather than affirm a falsehood. A rule thus self-convicted of absurdity so far as regards its professed purpose, can be kept in force only as a badge of hatred, a relic of persecution; a persecution, too, having the peculiarity that the qual-

---

3. Courts that meet periodically in the counties of England to hear both civil and criminal cases.

4. [Mill's note] Thomas Pooley, Bodmin Assizes, July 31, 1857. In December following, he received a free pardon from the Crown.

5. London's central criminal court.

6. [Mill's note] George Jacob Holyoake, August 17, 1857; Edward Truelove, July 1857.

7. [Mill's note] Baron de Gleichen, Marlborough Street Police Court, August 4, 1857.

8. Since 1888 this is no longer the law of England.

ification for undergoing it is the being clearly proved not to deserve it. The rule, and the theory it implies, are hardly less insulting to believers than to infidels. For if he who does not believe in a future state necessarily lies, it follows that they who do believe are only prevented from lying, if prevented they are, by the fear of hell. We will not do the authors and abettors of the rule the injury of supposing that the conception which they have formed of Christian virtue is drawn from their own consciousness.

These, indeed, are but rags and remnants of persecution, and may be thought to be not so much an indication of the wish to persecute, as an example of that very frequent infirmity of English minds, which makes them take a preposterous pleasure in the assertion of a bad principle, when they are no longer bad enough to desire to carry it really into practice. But unhappily there is no security in the state of the public mind that the suspension of worse forms of legal persecution, which has lasted for about the space of a generation, will continue. In this age the quiet surface of routine is as often ruffled by attempts to resuscitate past evils, as to introduce new benefits. What is boasted of at the present time as the revival of religion, is always, in narrow and uncultivated minds, at least as much the revival of bigotry; and where there is the strong permanent leaven of intolerance in the feelings of a people, which at all times abides in the middle classes of this country, it needs but little to provoke them into actively persecuting those whom they have never ceased to think proper objects of persecution.[9] For it is this

9. [Mill's note] Ample warning may be drawn from the large infusion of the passions of a persecutor, which mingled with the general display of the worst parts of our national character on the occasion of the Sepoy insurrection. [Editor: The mutiny in 1857–59 of the native soldiers (sepoys) in the Bengal Army of the East India Company, who were offended by military policies repugnant to their religion. Though the rebellion was put down, it resulted in the transfer of the administration of India from the East India Company to the Crown.] The ravings of fanatics or charlatans from the pulpit may be unworthy of notice; but the heads of the Evangelical party [Editor: One of three major organized parties within the Church of England; the Low Church party as distinct from the Broad and High Church parties.] have announced as their principle for the government of Hindoos and Mahomedans, that no schools be supported by public money in which the Bible is not taught, and by necessary consequence that no public employment be given to any but real or pretended Christians. An Under-Secretary of State [Editor: *The* (London) *Times* (November 14, 1857) attributes the following words to W. N. Massey, then in Lord Palmerston's ministry, in an address to his constituents in Salford.], in a speech delivered to his constituents on the 12th of November, 1857, is reported to have said: "Toleration of their faith" (the faith of a hundred millions of British subjects), "the superstition which they called religion, by the British Government, had had the effect of retarding the ascendancy of the British name, and preventing the salutary growth of Christianity. . . . Toleration was the great corner-stone of the religious liberties of this country; but do not let them abuse that precious word toleration. As he understood it, it meant the complete liberty to all, freedom of worship, *among Christians, who worshipped upon the same foundation.* It meant toleration of all sects and denominations of *Christians who believed in the one mediation.*" I desire to call attention to the fact, that a man who has been deemed fit to fill a high office in the government of this country under a liberal ministry, maintains the doctrine that all who do not believe in the divinity of Christ are beyond the pale of toleration. Who, after this imbecile display, can indulge the illusion that religious persecution has passed away, never to return?

—it is the opinions men entertain, and the feelings they cherish, respecting those who disown the beliefs they deem important, which makes this country not a place of mental freedom. For a long time past, the chief mischief of the legal penalties is that they strengthen the social stigma. It is that stigma which is really effective, and so effective is it, that the profession of opinions which are under the ban of society is much less common in England than is, in many other countries, the avowal of those which incur risk of judicial punishment.[1] In respect to all persons but those whose pecuniary circumstances make them independent of the good will of other people, opinion, on this subject, is as efficacious as law; men might as well be imprisoned, as excluded from the means of earning their bread. Those whose bread is already secured, and who desire no favours from men in power, or from bodies of men, or from the public, have nothing to fear from the open avowal of any opinions, but to be ill-thought of and ill-spoken of, and this it ought not to require a very heroic mould to enable them to bear. There is no room for any appeal *ad misericordiam*[2] in behalf of such persons. But though we do not now inflict so much evil on those who think differently from us as it was formerly our custom to do, it may be that we do ourselves as much evil as ever by our treatment of them. Socrates was put to death, but the Socratic philosophy rose like the sun in heaven, and spread its illumination over the whole intellectual firmament. Christians were cast to the lions, but the Christian church grew up a stately and spreading tree, overtopping the older and less vigorous growths, and stifling them by its shade. Our merely social intolerance kills no one, roots out no opinions, but induces men to disguise them, or to abstain from any active effort for their diffusion. With us, heretical opinions do not perceptibly gain, or even lose, ground in each decade or generation; they never blaze out far and wide, but continue to smoulder in the narrow circles of thinking and studious persons among whom they originate, without ever lighting up the general affairs of mankind with either a true or a deceptive light. And thus is kept up a state of things very satisfactory to some minds, because, without the unpleasant process of fining or imprisoning anybody, it maintains all prevailing opinions outwardly undisturbed, while it does not absolutely interdict the exercise of reason by dissentients afflicted with the malady of thought. A convenient plan for having peace in the intellectual world, and keeping all things going on therein very much as they do already. But the price paid for this sort of intellectual pacification is

1. Here and in the passages that follow, Mill reflects the influence on him of Tocqueville's belief that the major threat to liberty in modern society may stem from social rather than from legal forces.

2. An argument appealing for clemency on merciful and compassionate grounds.

the sacrifice of the entire moral courage of the human mind. A state of things in which a large portion of the most active and inquiring intellects find it advisable to keep the general principles and grounds of their convictions within their own breasts, and attempt, in what they address to the public, to fit as much as they can of their own conclusions to premises which they have internally re-nounced, cannot send forth the open, fearless characters, and logical, consistent intellects who once adorned the thinking world. The sort of men who can be looked for under it, are either mere conformers to commonplace, or time-servers for truth, whose arguments on all great subjects are meant for their hearers, and are not those which have convinced themselves. Those who avoid this alternative, do so by narrowing their thoughts and interest to things which can be spoken of without venturing within the region of principles, that is, to small practical matters, which would come right of themselves, if but the minds of mankind were strengthened and enlarged, and which will never be made effectually right until then: while that which would strengthen and enlarge men's minds, free and daring speculation on the highest subjects, is abandoned.

Those in whose eyes this reticence on the part of heretics is no evil should consider, in the first place, that in consequence of it there is never any fair and thorough discussion of heretical opinions; and that such of them as could not stand such a discussion, though they may be prevented from spreading, do not disappear. But it is not the minds of heretics that are deteriorated most by the ban placed on all inquiry which does not end in the orthodox conclu-sions. The greatest harm done is to those who are not heretics, and whose whole mental development is cramped, and their reason cowed, by the fear of heresy. Who can compute what the world loses in the multitude of promising intellects combined with timid characters, who dare not follow out any bold, vigorous, independent train of thought, lest it should land them in something which would admit of being considered irreligious or immoral? Among them we may occasionally see some man of deep conscientiousness, and subtle and refined understanding, who spends a life in sophisti-cating with an intellect which he cannot silence, and exhausts the resources of ingenuity in attempting to reconcile the promptings of his conscience and reason with orthodoxy, which yet he does not, perhaps, to the end succeed in doing. No one can be a great thinker who does not recognise, that as a thinker it is his first duty to follow his intellect to whatever conclusions it may lead. Truth gains more even by the errors of one who, with due study and preparation, thinks for himself, than by the true opinions of those who only hold them because they do not suffer themselves to think. Not that it is solely, or chiefly, to form great thinkers, that freedom of thinking is required. On the contrary, it is as much and even more indispensable to enable average human beings to attain the mental stature which they are capable of. There have been, and may again be, great individual thinkers in a general atmosphere of mental slavery. But there never has been, nor ever will be, in that atmosphere an intellectually active people. Where any people has made a temporary approach to such a character, it has been because the dread of heterodox speculation was for a time suspended. Where there is a tacit convention that principles are not to be disputed; where the discussion of the greatest questions which can occupy humanity is considered to be closed, we cannot hope to find that generally high scale of mental activity which has made some periods of history so remarkable. Never when controversy avoided the subjects which are large and important enough to kindle enthusiasm, was the mind of a people stirred up from its foundations, and the impulse given which raised even persons of the most ordinary intellect to something of the dignity of thinking beings. Of such we have had an example in the condition of Europe during the times immediately following the Reformation; another, though limited to the Continent and to a more cultivated class, in the speculative movement of the latter half of the eighteenth century;[3] and a third, of still briefer duration, in the intellectual fermentation of Germany during the Goethian[4] and Fichtean[5] period. These periods differed widely in the particular opinions which they developed; but were alike in this, that during all three the yoke of authority was broken. In each, an old mental despotism had been thrown off, and no new one had yet taken its place. The impulse given at these three periods has made Europe what it now is. Every single improvement which has taken place either in the human mind or in institutions, may be traced distinctly to one or other of them. Appearances have for some time indicated that all three impulses are well nigh spent; and we can expect no fresh start until we again assert our mental freedom.

Let us now pass to the second division of the argument, and dismissing the supposition that any of the received opinions may be false, let us assume them to be true, and examine into the worth of the manner in which they are likely to be held, when their truth is not freely and openly canvassed. However unwillingly a person who has a strong opinion may admit the possibility that his opinion may be false, he ought to be moved by the consideration that, however

3. Mill is apparently referring here to French and German thinkers of the Enlightenment, e.g., Voltaire (1694–1788) and Rousseau (1712–78), Montesquieu and Diderot (1713–84), Kant (1724–1804) and Lessing (1729–81). See Peter Gay, *The Enlightenment*, 2 vols. (New York, 1966, 1969).
4. Johann Wolfgang von Goethe (1749–1832), German poet, dramatist, novelist, and statesman.
5. Johann Gottlieb Fichte (1762–1814), German philosopher.

true it may be, if it is not fully, frequently, and fearlessly discussed, it will be held as a dead dogma, not a living truth.

There is a class of persons (happily not quite so numerous as formerly) who think it enough if a person assents undoubtingly to what they think true, though he has no knowledge whatever of the grounds of the opinion, and could not make a tenable defence of it against the most superficial objections. Such persons, if they can once get their creed taught from authority, naturally think that no good, and some harm, comes of its being allowed to be questioned. Where their influence prevails, they make it nearly impossible for the received opinion to be rejected wisely and considerately, though it may still be rejected rashly and ignorantly; for to shut out discussion entirely is seldom possible, and when it once gets in, beliefs not grounded on conviction are apt to give way before the slightest semblance of an argument. Waiving, however, this possibility—assuming that the true opinion abides in the mind, but abides as a prejudice, a belief independent of, and proof against, argument—this is not the way in which truth ought to be held by a rational being. This is not knowing the truth. Truth, thus held, is but one superstition the more, accidentally clinging to the words which enunciate a truth.

If the intellect and judgment of mankind ought to be cultivated, a thing which Protestants at least do not deny,[6] on what can these faculties be more appropriately exercised by any one, than on the things which concern him so much that it is considered necessary for him to hold opinions on them? If the cultivation of the understanding consists in one thing more than in another, it is surely in learning the grounds of one's own opinions. Whatever people believe, on subjects on which it is of the first importance to believe rightly, they ought to be able to defend against at least the common objections. But, some one may say, "Let them be *taught* the grounds of their opinions. It does not follow that opinions must be merely parroted because they are never heard controverted. Persons who learn geometry do not simply commit the theorems to memory, but understand and learn likewise the demonstrations; and it would be absurd to say that they remain ignorant of the grounds of geometrical truths, because they never hear any one deny, and attempt to disprove them." Undoubtedly: and such teaching suffices on a subject like mathematics, where there is nothing at all to be said on the wrong side of the question.

6. Mill seems to separate Protestant from Catholic teaching on this subject, although the issue is not a doctrinal matter for either persuasion. Traditions that favor intellectual cultivation or downgrade its importance can be found prominently in the history of both groups. Compare, for example, Thomas à Kempis' *The Imitation of Christ* with John Henry Newman's stress on the development of the mind in *The Idea of a University*, published but seven years before Mill's essay.

The peculiarity of the evidence of mathematical truths is that all the argument is on one side. There are no objections, and no answers to objections. But on every subject on which difference of opinion is possible, the truth depends on a balance to be struck between two sets of conflicting reasons. Even in natural philosophy, there is always some other explanation possible of the same facts; some geocentric theory instead of heliocentric,[7] some phlogiston instead of oxygen;[8] and it has to be shown why that other theory cannot be the true one: and until this is shown, and until we know how it is shown, we do not understand the grounds of our opinion. But when we turn to subjects infinitely more complicated, to morals, religion, politics, social relations, and the business of life, three-fourths of the arguments for every disputed opinion consist in dispelling the appearances which favour some opinion different from it. The greatest orator, save one, of antiquity,[9] has left it on record that he always studied his adversary's case with as great, if not still greater, intensity than even his own. What Cicero practised as the means of forensic success requires to be imitated by all who study any subject in order to arrive at the truth. He who knows only his own side of the case, knows little of that. His reasons may be good, and no one may have been able to refute them. But if he is equally unable to refute the reasons on the opposite side; if he does not so much as know what they are, he has no ground for preferring either opinion. The rational position for him would be suspension of judgment, and unless he contents himself with that, he is either led by authority, or adopts, like the generality of the world, the side to which he feels most inclination. Nor is it enough that he should hear the arguments of adversaries from his own teachers, presented as they state them, and accompanied by what they offer as refutations. That is not the way to do justice to the arguments, or bring them into real contact with his own mind. He must be able to hear them from persons who actually believe them; who defend them in earnest, and do their very utmost for them. He must know them in their most plausible and persuasive form; he must feel the whole force of the difficulty which the true view of the subject has to encounter and dispose of; else he will never really possess himself of the portion of truth which meets and removes that difficulty. Ninety-nine in a hundred of what are called educated men are in

7. Conflicting theories about the nature of the planetary system: the geocentric theory holds that the earth is at the center of the system; the heliocentric theory asserts that the sun is at the center.
8. Phlogiston: a nonexistent substance which, prior to the discovery of oxygen, was believed to reside in all inflammable matter and to be released during combustion.
9. Marcus Tullius Cicero (106–43 B.C.), Roman statesman and orator, reputedly exceeded in forensic ability only by the Athenian orator Demosthenes (384?–322 B.C.). Cicero's major political treatise has been translated as *On the Commonwealth*, trans. Sabine and Smith (Columbus, Ohio, 1929).

this condition; even of those who can argue fluently for their opinions. Their conclusion may be true, but it might be false for anything they know: they have never thrown themselves into the
mental position of those who think differently from them, and considered what such persons may have to say; and consequently they
do not, in any proper sense of the word, know the doctrine which
they themselves profess. They do not know those parts of it which
explain and justify the remainder; the considerations which show
that a fact which seemingly conflicts with another is reconcilable
with it, or that, of two apparently strong reasons, one and not the
other ought to be preferred. All that part of the truth which turns
the scale, and decides the judgment of a completely informed mind,
they are strangers to; nor is it ever really known, but to those who
have attended equally and impartially to both sides, and endeavoured to see the reasons of both in the strongest light. So essential
is this discipline to a real understanding of moral and human subjects, that if opponents of all important truths do not exist, it is
indispensable to imagine them, and supply them with the strongest
arguments which the most skilful devil's advocate can conjure up.[1]

To abate the force of these considerations, an enemy of free discussion may be supposed to say, that there is no necessity for mankind in general to know and understand all that can be said against
or for their opinions by philosophers and theologians. That it is not
needful for common men to be able to expose all the misstatements
or fallacies of an ingenious opponent. That it is enough if there is
always somebody capable of answering them, so that nothing likely
to mislead uninstructed persons remains unrefuted. That simple
minds, having been taught the obvious grounds of the truths inculcated on them, may trust to authority for the rest, and being aware
that they have neither knowledge nor talent to resolve every
difficulty which can be raised, may repose in the assurance that all
those which have been raised have been or can be answered, by
those who are specially trained to the task.

Conceding to this view of the subject the utmost that can be
claimed for it by those most easily satisfied with the amount of
understanding of truth which ought to accompany the belief of it;
even so, the argument for free discussion is no way weakened. For
even this doctrine acknowledges that mankind ought to have a
rational assurance that all objections have been satisfactorily
answered; and how are they to be answered if that which requires to
be answered is not spoken? or how can the answers be known to be

---

1. Some critics of Mill, fearing that
falsehood might then prevail over truth,
have been particularly incensed by this
proposal. See, for example, Gerhart Niemeyer, "A Reappraisal of the Doctrine
of Free Speech," *Thought*, 25 (1950),
251–74.

satisfactory, if the objectors have no opportunity of showing that it is unsatisfactory? If not the public, at least the philosophers and theologians who are to resolve the difficulties, must make themselves familiar with those difficulties in their most puzzling form; and this cannot be accomplished unless they are freely stated, and placed in the most advantageous light which they admit of. The Catholic Church has its own way of dealing with this embarrassing problem. It makes a broad separation between those who can be permitted to receive its doctrines on conviction, and those who must accept them on trust. Neither, indeed, are allowed any choice as to what they will accept; but the clergy, such at least as can be fully confided in, may admissibly and meritoriously make themselves acquainted with the arguments of opponents, in order to answer them, and may, therefore, read heretical books; the laity, not unless by special permission, hard to be obtained.[2] This discipline recognises a knowledge of the enemy's case as beneficial to the teachers, but finds means, consistent with this, of denying it to the rest of the world: thus giving to the *élite* more mental culture, though not more mental freedom, than it allows to the mass. By this device it succeeds in obtaining the kind of mental superiority which its purposes require; for though culture without freedom never made a large and liberal mind, it can make a clever *nisi prius*[3] advocate of a cause. But in countries professing Protestantism, this resource is denied; since Protestants hold, at least in theory, that the responsibility for the choice of a religion must be borne by each for himself, and cannot be thrown off upon teachers. Besides, in the present state of the world, it is practically impossible that writings which are read by the instructed can be kept from the uninstructed. If the teachers of mankind are to be cognisant of all that they ought to know, everything must be free to be written and published without restraint.

If, however, the mischievous operation of the absence of free discussion, when the received opinions are true, were confined to leaving men ignorant of the grounds of those opinions, it might be thought that this, if an intellectual, is no moral evil, and does not affect the worth of the opinions, regarded in their influence on the character. The fact, however, is, that not only the grounds of the opinion are forgotten in the absence of discussion, but too often the meaning of the opinion itself. The words which convey it cease to

2. Since 1564, by authority of Pius IV, the Roman Catholic Church has published a list of books which Catholics are forbidden to read (the *Index librorum prohibitorum*, or Prohibitory Index), or which they may read only in expurgated editions (the *Index expurgatorius*, or Expurgatory Index). Though forbidden to the general reader, these books are available to priests and intellectuals.

3. A term derived from English legal proceedings; used more generally to mean that a law is presumed valid unless shown otherwise.

suggest ideas, or suggest only a small portion of those they were originally employed to communicate. Instead of a vivid conception
and a living belief there remain only a few phrases retained by rote;
or, if any part, the shell and husk only of the meaning is retained,
the finer essence being lost. The great chapter in human history
which this fact occupies and fills, cannot be too earnestly studied
and meditated on.

It is illustrated in the experience of almost all ethical doctrines
and religious creeds. They are all full of meaning and vitality to
those who originate them, and to the direct disciples of the origina-
tors. Their meaning continues to be felt in undiminished strength,
and is perhaps brought out into even fuller consciousness, so long as
the struggle lasts to give the doctrine or creed an ascendancy over
other creeds. At last it either prevails, and becomes the general
opinion, or its progress stops; it keeps possession of the ground it
has gained, but ceases to spread further. When either of these
results has become apparent, controversy on the subject flags, and
gradually dies away. The doctrine has taken its place, if not as a
received opinion, as one of the admitted sects or divisions of opinion: those who hold it have generally inherited, not adopted it; and
conversion from one of these doctrines to another, being now an
exceptional fact, occupies little place in the thoughts of their professors. Instead of being, as at first, constantly on the alert either to
defend themselves against the world, or to bring the world over to
them, they have subsided into acquiescence, and neither listen,
when they can help it, to arguments against their creed, nor trouble
dissentients (if there be such) with arguments in its favour. From
this time may usually be dated the decline in the living power of
the doctrine. We often hear the teachers of all creeds lamenting the
difficulty of keeping up in the minds of believers a lively apprehension of the truth which they nominally recognise, so that it may
penetrate the feelings, and acquire a real mastery over the conduct.
No such difficulty is complained of while the creed is still fighting for
its existence: even the weaker combatants then know and feel what
they are fighting for, and the difference between it and other doctrines; and in that period of every creed's existence, not a few persons may be found, who have realised its fundamental principles in
all the forms of thought, have weighed and considered them in all
their important bearings, and have experienced the full effect on the
character which belief in that creed ought to produce in a mind
thoroughly imbued with it. But when it has come to be an hereditary creed, and to be received passively, not actively—when the mind
is no longer compelled, in the same degree as at first, to exercise its
vital powers on the questions which its belief presents to it, there is
a progressive tendency to forget all of the belief except the formu-

laries, or to give it a dull and torpid assent, as if accepting it on trust dispensed with the necessity of realising it in consciousness, or testing it by personal experience, until it almost ceases to connect itself at all with the inner life of the human being. Then are seen the cases, so frequent in this age of the world as almost to form the majority, in which the creed remains as it were outside the mind, incrusting and petrifying it against all other influences addressed to the higher parts of our nature; manifesting its power by not suffering any fresh and living conviction to get in, but itself doing nothing for the mind or heart, except standing sentinel over them to keep them vacant.

To what an extent doctrines intrinsically fitted to make the deepest impression upon the mind may remain in it as dead beliefs, without being ever realised in the imagination, the feelings, or the understanding, is exemplified by the manner in which the majority of believers hold the doctrines of Christianity. By Christianity I here mean what is accounted such by all churches and sects—the maxims and precepts contained in the New Testament. These are considered sacred, and accepted as laws, by all professing Christians. Yet it is scarcely too much to say that not one Christian in a thousand guides or tests his individual conduct by reference to those laws. The standard to which he does refer it, is the custom of his nation, his class, or his religious profession. He has thus, on the one hand, a collection of ethical maxims, which he believes to have been vouchsafed to him by infallible wisdom as rules for his government; and on the other a set of every-day judgments and practices, which go a certain length with some of those maxims, not so great a length with others, stand in direct opposition to some, and are, on the whole, a compromise between the Christian creed and the interests and suggestions of worldly life. To the first of these standards he gives his homage; to the other his real allegiance. All Christians believe that the blessed are the poor and humble, and those who are ill-used by the world; that it is easier for a camel to pass through the eye of a needle than for a rich man to enter the kingdom of heaven; that they should judge not, lest they be judged; that they should swear not at all; that they should love their neighbour as themselves; that if one take their cloak, they should give him their coat also; that they should take no thought for the morrow; that if they would be perfect they should sell all that they have and give it to the poor.[4] They are not insincere when they say that they believe these things. They do believe them, as people believe what they have always heard lauded and never discussed. But in the sense of that living belief which regulates conduct, they believe these doctrines just up to the point to which it is usual to act upon them.

4. These maxims are drawn from the Gospel according to Matthew, save for the fourth (concerning swearing), which is from the Epistle of James.

The doctrines in their integrity are serviceable to pelt adversaries with; and it is understood that they are to be put forward (when possible) as the reasons for whatever people do that they think laudable. But any one who reminded them that the maxims require an infinity of things which they never even think of doing, would gain nothing but to be classed among those very unpopular characters who affect to be better than other people. The doctrines have no hold on ordinary believers—are not a power in their minds. They have an habitual respect for the sound of them, but no feeling which spreads from the words to the things signified, and forces the mind to take *them* in, and make them conform to the formula. Whenever conduct is concerned, they look round for Mr. A and B to direct them how far to go in obeying Christ.

Now we may be well assured that the case was not thus, but far otherwise, with the early Christians. Had it been thus, Christianity never would have expanded from an obscure sect of the despised Hebrews into the religion of the Roman empire. When their enemies said, "See how these Christians love one another"[5] (a remark not likely to be made by anybody now), they assuredly had a much livelier feeling of the meaning of their creed than they have ever had since. And to this cause, probably, it is chiefly owing that Christianity now makes so little progress in extending its domain, and after eighteen centuries is still nearly confined to Europeans and the descendants of Europeans. Even with the strictly religious, who are much in earnest about their doctrines, and attach a greater amount of meaning to many of them than people in general, it commonly happens that the part which is thus comparatively active in their minds is that which was made by Calvin,[6] or Knox,[7] or some such person much nearer in character to themselves. The sayings of Christ coexist passively in their minds, producing hardly any effect beyond what is caused by mere listening to words so amiable and bland. There are many reasons, doubtless, why doctrines which are the badge of a sect retain more of their vitality than those common to all recognised sects, and why more pains are taken by teachers to keep their meaning alive; but one reason certainly is, that the peculiar doctrines are more questioned, and have to be oftener defended against open gainsayers. Both teachers and learners go to sleep at their post, as soon as there is no enemy in the field.

The same thing holds true, generally speaking, of all traditional

5. From the *Apologeticus* (39.7) of Tertullian (Quintus Septimius Florens Tertullianus), a famous Christian writer of the late second and early third centuries.
6. John Calvin (1509–64), French theologian and leader of the Proetstant Reformation, who as ruler of Geneva attempted to put into practice the austere religious ideas articulated in his *Institutes of the Christian Religion.* His doctrines greatly influenced Puritanism in England and America.
7. John Knox (1505–72), leader of the Protestant Reformation in Scotland and founder of the Presbyterian Church.

doctrines—those of prudence and knowledge of life, as well as of morals or religion. All languages and literatures are full of general observations on life, both as to what it is, and how to conduct oneself in it; observations which everybody knows, which everybody repeats, or hears with acquiescence, which are received as truisms, yet of which most people first truly learn the meaning when experience, generally of a painful kind, has made it a reality to them. How often, when smarting under some unforeseen misfortune or disappointment, does a person call to mind some proverb or common saying, familiar to him all his life, the meaning of which, if he had ever before felt it as he does now, would have saved him from the calamity. There are indeed reasons for this, other than the absence of discussion; there are many truths of which the full meaning *cannot* be realised until personal experience has brought it home. But much more of the meaning even of these would have been understood, and what was understood would have been far more deeply impressed on the mind, if the man had been accustomed to hear it argued *pro* and *con* by people who did understand it. The fatal tendency of mankind to leave off thinking about a thing when it is no longer doubtful, is the cause of half their errors. A cotemporary author has well spoken of "the deep slumber of a decided opinion."[8]

But what! (it may be asked) Is the absence of unanimity an indispensable condition of true knowledge? Is it necessary that some part of mankind should persist in error to enable any to realise the truth? Does a belief cease to be real and vital as soon as it is generally received—and is a proposition never thoroughly understood and felt unless some doubt of it remains? As soon as mankind have unanimously accepted a truth, does the truth perish within them? The highest aim and best result of improved intelligence, it has hitherto been thought, is to unite mankind more and more in the acknowledgement of all important truths; and does the intelligence only last as long as it has not achieved its object? Do the fruits of conquest perish by the very completeness of the victory?

I affirm no such thing. As mankind improve, the number of doctrines which are no longer disputed or doubted will be constantly on the increase: and the well-being of mankind may almost be measured by the number and gravity of the truths which have reached the point of being uncontested.[9] The cessation, on one question after another, of serious controversy, is one of the necessary incidents of the consolidation of opinion; a consolidation of sal-

8. This contemporary author and quotation are unknown to the Editor.
9. Despite this statement, some critics (e.g., Kendall) have contended that Mill did not believe in the possibility or desirability of attaining truth or unanimity of belief.

utary in the case of true opinions, as it is dangerous and noxious when the opinions are erroneous. But though this gradual narrowing of the bounds of diversity of opinion is necessary in both senses of the term, being at once inevitable and indispensable, we are not therefore obliged to conclude that all its consequences must be beneficial. The loss of so important an aid to the intelligent and living apprehension of a truth, as is afforded by the necessity of explaining it to, or defending it against, opponents, though not sufficient to outweigh, is no trifling drawback from, the benefit of its universal recognition. Where this advantage can no longer be had, I confess I should like to see the teachers of mankind endeavouring to provide a substitute for it; some contrivance for making the difficulties of the question as present to the learner's consciousness, as if they were pressed upon him by a dissentient champion, eager for his conversion.

But instead of seeking contrivances for this purpose, they have lost those they formerly had. The Socratic dialectics, so magnificently exemplified in the dialogues of Plato, were a contrivance of this description. They were essentially a negative discussion of the great question of philosophy and life, directed with consummate skill to the purpose of convincing any one who had merely adopted the commonplaces of received opinion that he did not understand the subject—that he as yet attached no definite meaning to the doctrines he professed; in order that, becoming aware of his ignorance, he might be put in the way to obtain a stable belief, resting on a clear apprehension both of the meaning of doctrines and of their evidence. The school disputations[1] of the Middle Ages had a somewhat similar object. They were intended to make sure that the pupil understood his own opinion, and (by necessary correlation) the opinion opposed to it, and could enforce the grounds of the one and confute those of the other. These last-mentioned contests had indeed the incurable defect, that the premises appealed to were taken from authority, not from reason; and, as a discipline to the mind, they were in every respect inferior to the powerful dialectics which formed the intellects of the "Socratici viri";[2] but the modern mind owes far more to both than it is generally willing to admit, and the present modes of education contain nothing which in the smallest degree supplies the place either of the one or of the other. A person who derives all his instruction from teachers or books, even if he escape the besetting temptation of contenting himself with cram, is under no compulsion to hear both sides; accordingly it is far from a frequent accomplishment, even among thinkers, to

---

1. Formal arguments on set subjects conducted as part of the training of students in medieval educational institutions.

2. Disciples (literally, "men") of Socrates.

know both sides; and the weakest part of what everybody says in defence of his opinion is what he intends as a reply to antagonists. It is the fashion of the present time to disparage negative logic— that which points out weaknesses in theory or errors in practice, without establishing positive truths. Such negative criticism would indeed be poor enough as an ultimate result; but as a means to attaining any positive knowledge or conviction worthy the name, it cannot be valued too highly; and until people are again systematically trained to it, there will be few great thinkers, and a low general average of intellect, in any but the mathematical and physical departments of speculation. On any other subject no one's opinions deserve the name of knowledge, except so far as he has either had forced upon him by others, or gone through of himself, the same mental process which would have been required of him in carrying on an active controversy with opponents. That, therefore, which when absent, it is so indispensable, but so difficult, to create, how worse than absurd it is to forego, when spontaneously offering itself! If there are any persons who contest a received opinion, or who will do so if law or opinion will let them, let us thank them for it, open our minds to listen to them, and rejoice that there is some one to do for us what we otherwise ought, if we have any regard for either the certainty or the vitality of our convictions, to do with much greater labour for ourselves.

It still remains to speak of one of the principal causes which make diversity of opinion advantageous, and will continue to do so until mankind shall have entered a stage of intellectual advancement which at present seems at an incalculable distance. We have hitherto considered only two possibilities: that the received opinion may be false, and some other opinion, consequently, true; or that, the received opinion being true, a conflict with the opposite error is essential to a clear apprehension and deep feeling of its truth. But there is a commoner case than either of these; when the conflicting doctrines, instead of being one true and the other false, share the truth between them; and the nonconforming opinion is needed to supply the remainder of the truth, of which the received doctrine embodies only a part. Popular opinions, on subjects not palpable to sense, are often true, but seldom or never the whole truth. They are a part of the truth; sometimes a greater, sometimes a smaller part, but exaggerated, distorted, and disjointed from the truths by which they ought to be accompanied and limited. Heretical opinions, on the other hand, are generally some of these suppressed and neglected truths, bursting the bonds which kept them down, and either seeking reconciliation with the truth contained in the common opinion, or fronting it as enemies, and setting themselves up, with similar exclusiveness, as the whole truth. The latter case is hitherto the most frequent, as, in the human mind, one-sidedness has always been the rule, and many-sidedness the exception. Hence, even in revolutions of opinion, one part of the truth usually sets while another rises. Even progress, which ought to superadd, for the most part only substitutes, one partial and incomplete truth for another; improvement consisting chiefly in this, that the new fragment of truth is more wanted, more adapted to the needs of the time, than that which it displaces. Such being the partial character of prevailing opinions, even when resting on a true foundation, every opinion which embodies somewhat of the portion of truth which the common opinion omits, ought to be considered precious, with whatever amount of error and confusion that truth may be blended. No sober judge of human affairs will feel bound to be indignant because those who force on our notice truths which we should otherwise have overlooked, overlook some of those which we see. Rather, he will think that so long as popular truth is one-sided, it is more desirable than otherwise that unpopular truth should have one-sided assertors too; such being usually the most energetic, and the most likely to compel reluctant attention to the fragment of wisdom which they proclaim as if it were the whole.

Thus, in the eighteenth century, when nearly all the instructed, and all those of the uninstructed who were led by them, were lost in admiration of what is called civilisation, and of the marvels of modern science, literature, and philosophy, and while greatly overrating the amount of unlikeness between the men of modern and those of ancient times, indulged the belief that the whole of the difference was in their own favour;[3] with what a salutary shock did the paradoxes of Rousseau[4] explode like bombshells in the midst, dislocating the compact mass of one-sided opinion, and forcing its elements to recombine in a better form and with additional ingredients. Not that the current opinions were on the whole farther from the truth than Rousseau's were; on the contrary, they were nearer to it; they contained more of positive truth, and very much less of error. Nevertheless there lay in Rousseau's doctrine, and has floated down the stream of opinion along with it, a considerable amount of exactly those truths which the popular opinion wanted; and these

3. The battle between the Ancients, who believed that civilization, and in particular social and political philosophy, had declined since classical times, and the Moderns, who esteemed the contemporary as a marked advance over the classical world and its thought, lingers on into our own time. See the writings of Leo Strauss and his disciples today, e.g., Joseph Cropsey, ed., *Ancients and Moderns* (New York, 1964).

4. Jean-Jacques Rousseau (1712–78), French political philosopher and major contributor to the rise of Romanticism, attacked the corrupting influence of civilization on man's nature at a time when leading literary and philosophical voices were raised in praise of achievements of modern society. See in particular his *Discourse on the Arts and Sciences* (1750) and *The Social Contract* (1762).

are the deposit which was left behind when the flood subsided. The superior worth of simplicity of life, the enervating and demoralising effect of the trammels and hypocrisies of artificial society, are ideas which have never been entirely absent from cultivated minds since Rousseau wrote; and they will in time produce their due effect, though at present needing to be asserted as much as ever, and to be asserted by deeds, for words, on this subject, have nearly exhausted their power.

In politics, again, it is almost a commonplace, that a party of order or stability, and a party of progress or reform, are both necessary elements of a healthy state of political life; until the one or the other shall have so enlarged its mental grasp as to be a party equally of order and of progress, knowing and distinguishing what is fit to be preserved from what ought to be swept away. Each of these modes of thinking derives its utility from the deficiencies of the other; but it is in a great measure the opposition of the other that keeps each within the limits of reason and sanity. Unless opinions favourable to democracy and to aristocracy, to property and to equality, to co-operation and to competition, to luxury and to abstinence, to sociality and individuality, to liberty and discipline, and all the other standing antagonisms of practical life, are expressed with equal freedom, and enforced and defended with equal talent and energy, there is no chance of both elements obtaining their due; one scale is sure to go up, and the other down. Truth, in the great practical concerns of life, is so much a question of the reconciling and combining of opposites, that very few have minds sufficiently capacious and impartial to make the adjustment with an approach to correctness, and it has to be made by the rough process of a struggle between combatants fighting under hostile banners. On any of the great open questions just enumerated, if either of the two opinions has a better claim than the other, not merely to be tolerated, but to be encouraged and countenanced, it is the one which happens at the particular time and place to be in a minority. That is the opinion which, for the time being, represents the neglected interests, the side of human well-being which is in danger of obtaining less than its share. I am aware that there is not, in this country, any intolerance of differences of opinion on most of these topics. They are adduced to show, by admitted and multiplied examples, the universality of the fact, that only through diversity of opinion is there, in the existing state of human intellect, a chance of fair play to all sides of the truth. When there are persons to be found who form an exception to the apparent unanimity of the world on any subject, even if the world is in the right, it is always probable that dissentients have something worth hearing to say for themselves, and that truth would lose something by their silence.

It may be objected, "But *some* received principles, especially on the highest and most vital subjects, are more than half-truths. The Christian morality, for instance, is the whole truth on that subject, and if any one teaches a morality which varies from it, he is wholly in error." As this is of all cases the most important in practice, none can be fitter to test the general maxim. But before pronouncing what Christian morality is or is not, it would be desirable to decide what is meant by Christian morality. If it means the morality of the New Testament, I wonder that any one who derives his knowledge of this from the book itself, can suppose that it was announced, or intended, as a complete doctrine of morals. The Gospel always refers to a pre-existing morality, and confines its precepts to the particulars in which that morality was to be corrected, or superseded by a wider and higher; expressing itself, moreover, in terms most general, often impossible to be interpreted literally, and possessing rather the impressiveness of poetry or eloquence than the precision of legislation. To extract from it a body of ethical doctrine, has never been possible without eking it out from the Old Testament, that is, from a system elaborate indeed, but in many respects barbarous, and intended only for a barbarous people. St. Paul, a declared enemy to this Judaical mode of interpreting the doctrine and filling up the scheme of his Master, equally assumes a pre-existing morality, namely that of the Greeks and Romans; and his advice to Christians is in a great measure a system of accommodation to that; even to the extent of giving an apparent sanction to slavery. What is called Christian, but should rather be termed theological morality, was not the work of Christ or the Apostles, but is of much later origin, having been gradually built up by the Catholic church of the first five centuries, and though not implicitly adopted by moderns and Protestants, has been much less modified by them than might have been expected. For the most part, indeed, they have contented themselves with cutting off the additions which had been made to it in the Middle Ages, each sect supplying the place by fresh additions, adapted to its own character and tendencies. That mankind owe a great debt to this morality, and to its early teachers, I should be the last person to deny; but I do not scruple to say of it that it is, in many important points, incomplete and one-sided, and that unless ideas and feelings, not sanctioned by it, had contributed to the formation of European life and character, human affairs would have been in a worse condition than they now are. Christian morality (so called) has all the characters of a reaction; it is, in great part, a protest against Paganism. Its ideal is negative rather than positive; passive rather than active; Innocence rather than Nobleness; Abstinence from Evil, rather than energetic Pursuit of Good; in its precepts (as has been well said) "thou shall not" predominates unduly over "thou shalt." In its horror of sensuality, it made an idol of asceticism, which has been gradually compromised away into one of legality. It holds out the hope of heaven and the threat of hell, as the appointed and appropriate motives to a virtuous life: in this falling far below the best of the ancients, and doing what lies in it to give to human morality an essentially selfish character, by disconnecting each man's feelings of duty from the interests of his fellow-creatures, except so far as a self-interested inducement is offered to him for consulting them. It is essentially a doctrine of passive obedience; it inculcates submission to all authorities found established; who indeed are not to be actively obeyed when they command what religion forbids, but who are not to be resisted, far less rebelled against, for any amount of wrong to ourselves. And while, in the morality of the best Pagan nations,[5] duty to the State holds even a disproportionate place, infringing on the just liberty of the individual; in purely Christian ethics, that grand department of duty is scarcely noticed or acknowledged. It is in the Koran, not the New Testament, that we read the maxim—"A ruler who appoints any man to an office, when there is in his dominions another man better qualified for it, sins against God and against the State."[6] What little recognition the idea of obligation to the public obtains in modern morality is derived from Greek and Roman sources, not from Christian; as, even in the morality of private life, whatever exists of magnanimity, highmindedness, personal dignity, even the sense of honour, is derived from the purely human, not the religious part of our education, and never could have grown out of a standard of ethics in which the only worth, professedly recognised, is that of obedience.

I am as far as any one from pretending that these defects are necessarily inherent in the Christian ethics in every manner in which it can be conceived, or that the many requisites of a complete moral doctrine which it does not contain do not admit of being reconciled with it. Far less would I insinuate this of the doctrines and precepts of Christ himself. I believe that the sayings of Christ are all that I can see any evidence of their having been intended to be; that they are irreconcilable with nothing which a comprehensive morality requires; that everything which is excellent in ethics may be brought

---

5. E.g., Athens.
6. Mill is mistaken here. The quotation is not to be found in the Koran, accepted by believers as a sacred book containing the Revelations of God to the prophet Mohammed (570?–632). It may possibly be in the Hadit, compilations of the Sayings of Mohammed. (Unfortunately, it is one of the peculiarities of Oriental studies that one cannot trace a saying of the Prophet unless it is in Arabic.) The closest approximation to the quotation cited by Mill that I have been able to find in George Sale's translation of the Koran (London, 1734), the only English edition available to Mill, is the injunction that "when ye judge between men, that ye judge according to equity." Similar renderings will be found in the Everyman's edition, trans. Rodwell (London, 1909), p. 417 (Sura 4, 61), and in the Mentor edition, trans. Pickthall (New York, 1953), p. 85 (Sura 4, 58).

within them, with no greater violence to their language than has been done to it by all who have attempted to deduce from them any practical system of conduct whatever. But it is quite consistent with this to believe that they contain, and were meant to contain, only a part of the truth; that many essential elements of the highest morality are among the things which are not provided for, nor intended to be provided for, in the recorded deliverances of the Founder of Christianity, and which have been entirely thrown aside in the system of ethics erected on the basis of those deliverances by the Christian Church. And this being so, I think it a great error to persist in attempting to find in the Christian doctrine that complete rule for our guidance which its author intended it to sanction and enforce, but only partially to provide. I believe, too, that this narrow theory is becoming a grave practical evil, detracting greatly from the moral training and instruction which so many well-meaning persons are now at length exerting themselves to promote. I much fear that by attempting to form the mind and feelings on an exclusively religious type, and discarding those secular standards (as for want of a better name they may be called) which heretofore coexisted with and supplemented the Christian ethics, receiving some of its spirit, and infusing into it some of theirs, there will result, and is even now resulting, a low, abject, servile type of character, which, submit itself as it may to what it deems the Supreme Will, is incapable of rising to or sympathising in the conception of Supreme Goodness. I believe that other ethics than any which can be evolved from exclusively Christian sources, must exist side by side with Christian ethics to produce the moral regeneration of mankind; and that the Christian system is no exception to the rule, that in an imperfect state of the human mind the interests of truth require a diversity of opinions. It is not necessary that in ceasing to ignore the moral truths not contained in Christianity men should ignore any of those which it does contain. Such prejudice, or oversight, when it occurs, is altogether an evil; but it is one from which we cannot hope to be always exempt, and must be regarded as the price paid for an inestimable good. The exclusive pretension made by a part of the truth to be the whole, must and ought to be protested against; and if a reactionary impulse should make the protestors unjust in their turn, this one-sidedness, like the other, may be lamented, but must be tolerated. If Christians would teach infidels to be just to Christianity, they should themselves be just to infidelity. It can do truth no service to blink the fact, known to all who have the most ordinary acquaintance with literary history, that a large portion of the noblest and most valuable moral teaching has been the work, not only of men who did not know, but of men who knew and rejected, the Christian faith.

I do not pretend that the most unlimited use of the freedom of enunciating all possible opinions would put an end to the evils of religious or philosophical sectarianism. Every truth which men of narrow capacity are in earnest about, is sure to be asserted, inculcated, and in many ways even acted on, as if no other truth existed in the world, or at all events none that could limit or qualify the first. I acknowledge that the tendency of all opinions to become sectarian is not cured by the freest discussion, but is often heightened and exacerbated thereby; the truth which ought to have been, but was not, seen, being rejected all the more violently because proclaimed by persons regarded as opponents. But it is not on the impassioned partisan, it is on the calmer and more disinterested bystander, that this collision of opinions works its salutary effect. Not the violent conflict between parts of the truth, but the quiet suppression of half of it, is the formidable evil; there is always hope when people are forced to listen to both sides; it is when they attend only to one that errors harden into prejudices, and truth itself ceases to have the effect of truth, by being exaggerated into falsehood. And since there are few mental attributes more rare than that judicial faculty which can sit in intelligent judgment between two sides of a question, of which only one is represented by an advocate before it, truth has no chance but in proportion as every side of it, every opinion which embodies any fraction of the truth, not only finds advocates, but is so advocated as to be listened to.

We have now recognised the necessity to the mental well-being of mankind (on which all their other well-being depends) of freedom of opinion, and freedom of the expression of opinion, on four distinct grounds; which we will now briefly recapitulate.

First, if any opinion is compelled to silence, that opinion may, for aught we can certainly know, be true. To deny this is to assume our own infallibility.

Secondly, though the silenced opinion be an error, it may, and very commonly does, contain a portion of truth; and since the general or prevailing opinion on any subject is rarely or never the whole truth, it is only by the collision of adverse opinions that the remainder of the truth has any chance of being supplied.

Thirdly, even if the received opinion be not only true, but the whole truth; unless it is suffered to be, and actually is, vigorously and earnestly contested, it will, by most of those who receive it, be held in the manner of a prejudice, with little comprehension or feeling of its rational grounds. And not only this, but, fourthly, the meaning of the doctrine itself will be in danger of being lost, or enfeebled, and deprived of its vital effect on the character and conduct; the dogma becoming a mere formal profession, inefficacious for good, but cumbering the ground, and preventing the growth of any real and heartfelt conviction, from reason or personal experience.

Before quitting the subject of freedom of opinion, it is fit to take some notice of those who say that the free expression of all opinions should be permitted, on condition that the manner be temperate, and do not pass the bounds of fair discussion. Much might be said on the impossibility of fixing where these supposed bounds are to be placed; for if the test be offence to those whose opinions are attacked, I think experience testifies that this offence is given whenever the attack is telling and powerful, and that every opponent who pushes them hard, and whom they find it difficult to answer, appears to them, if he shows any strong feeling on the subject, an intemperate opponent. But this, though an important consideration in a practical point of view, merges in a more fundamental objection. Undoubtedly the manner of asserting an opinion, even though it be a true one, may be very objectionable, and may justly incur severe censure. But the principal offences of the kind are such as it is mostly impossible, unless by accidental self-betrayal, to bring home to conviction. The gravest of them is, to argue sophistically, to suppress facts or arguments, to misstate the elements of the case, or misrepresent the opposite opinion. But all this, even to the most aggravated degree, is so continually done in perfect good faith, by persons who are not considered, and in many other respects may not deserve to be considered, ignorant or incompetent, that it is rarely possible, on adequate grounds, conscientiously to stamp the misrepresentation as morally culpable; and still less could law presume to interfere with this kind of controversial misconduct. With regard to what is commonly meant by intemperate discussion, namely invective, sarcasm, personality, and the like, the denunciation of these weapons would deserve more sympathy if it were ever proposed to interdict them equally to both sides; but it is only desired to restrain the employment of them against the prevailing opinion: against the unprevailing they may not only be used without general disapproval, but will be likely to obtain for him who uses them the praise of honest zeal and righteous indignation. Yet whatever mischief arises from their use is greatest when they are employed against the comparatively defenceless; and whatever unfair advantage can be derived by any opinion from this mode of asserting it, accrues almost exclusively to received opinions. The worst offence of this kind which can be committed by a polemic is to stigmatise those who hold the contrary opinion as bad and immoral men. To calumny of this sort, those who hold any unpopular opinion are peculiarly exposed, because they are in general few and uninfluential, and nobody but themselves feels much interested in seeing justice done them; but this weapon is, from the nature of the case, denied to those who attack a prevailing opinion: they can neither use it with safety to themselves, nor, if they could, would it do anything but recoil on their own cause. In general, opinions contrary to those commonly received can only obtain a hearing by studied moderation of language, and the most cautious avoidance of unnecesary offence, from which they hardly ever deviate even in a slight degree without losing ground: while unmeasured vitupera-tion employed on the side of the prevailing opinion really does deter people from professing contrary opinions, and from listening to those who profess them. For the interest, therefore, of truth and justice, it is far more important to restrain this employment of vituperative language than the other; and, for example, if it were necessary to choose, there would be much more need to discourage offensive attacks on infidelity than on religion. It is, however, obvi-ous that law and authority have no business with restraining either, while opinion ought, in every instance, to determine its verdict by the circumstances of the individual case; condemning every one, on whichever side of the argument he places himself, in whose mode of advocacy either want of candour, or malignity, bigotry, or intoler-ance of feeling manifest themselves; but not inferring these vices from the side which a person takes, though it be the contrary side of the question to our own; and giving merited honour to every one, whatever opinion he may hold, who has calmness to see and honesty to state what his opponents and their opinions really are, exag-gerating nothing to their discredit, keeping nothing back which tells, or can be supposed to tell, in their favour. This is the real morality of public discussion: and if often violated, I am happy to think that there are many controversialists who to a great extent observe it, and a still greater number who conscientiously strive towards it.

Chapter III

Such being the reasons which make it imperative that human beings should be free to form opinions, and to express their opinions without reserve; and such the baneful consequences to the intellectual, and through that to the moral nature of man, unless this liberty is either conceded, or asserted in spite of prohibition; let us next examine whether the same reasons do not require that men should be free to act upon their opinions—to carry these out in their lives, without hindrance, either physical or moral, from their fellow-men, so long as it is at their own risk and peril. This last proviso is of course indispensable. No one pretends that actions should be as free as opinions. On the contrary, even opinions lose their immunity when the circumstances in which they are expressed are such as to constitute their expression a positive instigation to some mischievous act. An opinion that corn-dealers are starvers of the poor, or that private property is robbery, ought to be un-molested when simply circulated through the press, but may justly incur punishment when delivered orally to an excited mob as-sembled before the house of a corn-dealer, or when handed about among the same mob in the form of a placard.[2] Acts, of whatever kind, which, without justifiable cause, do harm to others, may be, and in the more important cases absolutely require to be, controlled by the unfavourable sentiments, and, when needful, by the active interference of mankind. The liberty of the individual must be thus far limited; he must not make himself a nuisance to other people. But if he refrains from molesting others in what concerns them, and merely acts according to his own inclination and judgment in things which concern himself, the same reasons which show that opinion should be free, prove also that he should be allowed, without molestation, to carry his opinions into practice at his own cost. That mankind are not infallible; that their truths, for the most part, are only half-truths; that unity of opinion, unless resulting from the fullest and freest comparison of opposite opinions, is not desirable, and diversity not an evil, but a good,

---

1. Despite this explicit wording, some of Mill's critics have alleged that he made individuality the only or ultimate legiti-mate value. See, for example, Gertrude Himmelfarb, *Lord Acton: A Study in Conscience and Politics* (Chicago, 1952), p. 75; and *contra* R. B. Friedman, "A New Exploration of Mill's Essay *On Liberty*," *Political Studies*, 14 (1966), 281–304, especially pp. 300ff.

2. Here, as in his discussion of tyranni-cide (chap. 2, p. 17, n. 2, above), Mill seems to anticipate Justice Holmes' cele-brated clear-and-present-danger doctrine in *Schenck* v. *United States*, 249 U.S. 47 (1919), i.e., that opinions may freely be expressed except where that expression creates a clear and present danger that violence, or unlawful action, may ensue.

until mankind are much more capable than at present of recognising all sides of the truth, are principles applicable to men's modes of action, not less than to their opinions. As it is useful that while mankind are imperfect there should be different opinions, so it is that there should be different experiments of living; that free scope should be given to varieties of character, short of injury to others; and that the worth of different modes of life should be proved practically, when any one thinks fit to try them. It is desirable, in short, that in things which do not primarily concern others, individuality should assert itself. Where, not the person's own character, but the traditions or customs of other people are the rule of conduct, there is wanting one of the principal ingredients of human happiness, and quite the chief ingredient of individual and social progress.

In maintaining this principle, the greatest difficulty to be encountered does not lie in the appreciation of means towards an acknowledged end, but in the indifference of persons in general to the end itself. If it were felt that the free development of individuality is one of the leading essentials of well-being; that it is not only a co-ordinate element with all that is designated by the terms civilisation, instruction, education, culture, but is itself a necessary part and condition of all those things; there would be no danger that liberty should be undervalued, and the adjustment of the boundaries between it and social control would present no extraordinary difficulty. But the evil is, that individual spontaneity is hardly recognised by the common modes of thinking as having any intrinsic worth, or deserving any regard on its own account. The majority, being satisfied with the ways of mankind as they now are (for it is they who make them what they are), cannot comprehend why those ways should not be good enough for everybody; and what is more, spontaneity forms no part of the ideal of the majority of moral and social reformers, but is rather looked on with jealousy, as a troublesome and perhaps rebellious obstruction to the general acceptance of what these reformers, in their own judgment, think would be best for mankind. Few persons, out of Germany, even comprehend the meaning of the doctrine which Wilhelm von Humboldt, so eminent both as a *savant*[3] and as a politician, made the text of a treatise—that "the end of man, or that which is prescribed by the eternal or immutable dictates of reason, and not suggested by vague and transient desires, is the highest and most harmonious development of his powers to a complete and consistent whole;" that, therefore, the object "towards which every human being must ceaselessly direct his efforts, and on which especially those who design to influence their fellow-men must ever keep their

---

3. Man of learning.

eyes, is the individuality of power and development;" that for this there are two requisites, "freedom, and variety of situations;" and that from the union of these arise "individual vigour and manifold diversity," which combine themselves in "originality."[4]

Little, however, as people are accustomed to a doctrine like that of Von Humboldt, and surprising as it may be to them to find so high a value attached to individuality, the question, one must nevertheless think, can only be one of degree. No one's idea of excellence in conduct is that people should do absolutely nothing but copy one another. No one would assert that people ought not to put into their mode of life, and into the conduct of their concerns, any impress whatever of their own judgment, or of their own individual character. On the other hand, it would be absurd to pretend that people ought to live as if nothing whatever had been known in the world before they came into it; as if experience had as yet done nothing towards showing that one mode of existence, or of conduct, is preferable to another. Nobody denies that people should be so taught and trained in youth as to know and benefit by the ascertained results of human experience. But it is the privilege and proper condition of a human being, arrived at the maturity of his faculties, to use and interpret experience in his own way. It is for him to find out what part of recorded experience is properly applicable to his own circumstances and character. The traditions and customs of other people are, to a certain extent, evidence of what their experience has taught *them*; presumptive evidence, and as such, have a claim to his deference: but, in the first place, their experience may be too narrow; or they may not have interpreted it rightly. Secondly, their interpretation of experience may be correct, but unsuitable to him. Customs are made for customary circumstances and customary characters; and his circumstances or his character may be uncustomary. Thirdly, though the customs be both good as customs, and suitable to him, yet to conform to custom, merely *as* custom, does not educate or develop in him any of the qualities which are the distinctive endowment of a human being. The human faculties of perception, judgment, discriminative feeling, mental activity, and even moral preference, are exercised only in making a choice. He who does anything because it is the custom makes no choice. He gains no practice either in discerning or in desiring what is best. The mental and moral, like the muscular powers, are improved only by being used. The faculties are called into no exercise by doing a thing merely because others do it, no more than by believing a thing only because others believe it. If the grounds of an opinion are not conclusive to the person's own

4. [Mill's note] *The Sphere and Duties of Government*, from the German of Baron Wilhelm von Humboldt, pp. 11–13.

reason, his reason cannot be strengthened, but is likely to be weakened, by his adopting it: and if the inducements to an act are not such as are consentaneous[5] to his own feelings and character (where affection, or the rights of others, are not concerned) it is so much done towards rendering his feelings and character inert and torpid, instead of active and energetic.

He who lets the world, or his own portion of it, choose his plan of life for him, has no need of any other faculty than the ape-like one of imitation. He who chooses his plan for himself, employs all his faculties. He must use observation to see, reasoning and judgment to foresee, activity to gather materials for decision, discrimination to decide, and when he has decided, firmness and self-control to hold to his deliberate decision. And these qualities he requires and exercises exactly in proportion as the part of his conduct which he determines according to his own judgment and feelings is a large one. It is possible that he might be guided in some good path, and kept out of harm's way, without any of these things. But what will be his comparative worth as a human being? It really is of importance, not only what men do, but also what manner of men they are that do it. Among the works of man, which human life is rightly employed in perfecting and beautifying, the first in importance surely is man himself. Supposing it were possible to get houses built, corn grown, battles fought, causes tried, and even churches erected and prayers said, by machinery—by automatons in human form—it would be a considerable loss to exchange for these automatons even the men and women who at present inhabit the more civilised parts of the world, and who assuredly are but starved specimens of what nature can and will produce. Human nature is not a machine to be built after a model, and set to do exactly the work prescribed for it, but a tree, which requires to grow and develop itself on all sides, according to the tendency of the inward forces which make it a living thing.[6]

It will probably be conceded that it is desirable people should exercise their understandings, and that an intelligent following of custom, or even occasionally an intelligent deviation from custom, is better than a blind and simply mechanical adhesion to it. To a certain extent it is admitted that our understanding should be our own: but there is not the same willingness to admit that our desires and impulses should be our own likewise; or that to possess impulses of our own, and of any strength, is anything but a peril and a

5. Agreeing, accordant.
6. In this oft-quoted paragraph (and succeeding passages), Mill spells out what has become the classic liberal conception of man's nature, in contradistinction (say) to deterministic theories.

For a currently fashionable variant of the deterministic school, see B. F. Skinner, *Beyond Freedom and Dignity* (New York, 1971), and *contra* David Spitz, "The Higher Reaches of the Lower Orders," *Dissent*, 20 (1973), 243–69.

snare. Yet desires and impulses are as much a part of a perfect human being as beliefs and restraints: and strong impulses are only perilous when not properly balanced; when one set of aims and inclinations is developed into strength, while others, which ought to co-exist with them, remain weak and inactive. It is not because men's desires are strong that they act ill; it is because their consciences are weak. There is no natural connection between strong impulses and a weak conscience. The natural connection is the other way. To say that one person's desires and feelings are stronger and more various than those of another, is merely to say that he has more of the raw material of human nature, and is therefore capable, perhaps of more evil, but certainly of more good. Strong impulses are but another name for energy. Energy may be turned to bad uses; but more good may always be made of an energetic nature, than of an indolent and impassive one. Those who have most natural feeling, are always those whose cultivated feelings may be made the strongest. The same strong susceptibilities which make the personal impulses vivid and powerful, are also the source from whence are generated the most passionate love of virtue, and the sternest self-control. It is through the cultivation of these that society both does its duty and protects its interests: not by rejecting the stuff of which heroes are made, because it knows not how to make them. A person whose desires and impulses are his own—are the expression of his own nature, as it has been developed and modified by his own culture—is said to have a character. One whose desires and impulses are not his own, has no character, no more than a steam-engine has a character. If, in addition to being his own, his impulses are strong, and are under the government of a strong will, he has an energetic character. Whoever thinks that individuality of desires and impulses should not be encouraged to unfold itself, must maintain that society has no need of strong natures—is not the better for containing many persons who have much character—and that a high general average of energy is not desirable.

In some early states of society, these forces might be, and were, too much ahead of the power which society then possessed of disciplining and controlling them. There has been a time when the element of spontaneity and individuality was in excess, and the social principle had a hard struggle with it. The difficulty then was to induce men of strong bodies or minds to pay obedience to any rules which required them to control their impulses. To overcome this difficulty, law and discipline, like the Popes struggling against the Emperors, asserted a power over the whole man, claiming to control all his life in order to control his character—which society had not found any other sufficient means of binding. But society has now fairly got the better of individuality; and the danger which threatens human nature is not the excess, but the deficiency, of personal impulses and preferences. Things are vastly changed since the passions of those who were strong by station or by personal endowment were in a state of habitual rebellion against laws and ordinances, and required to be rigorously chained up to enable the persons within their reach to enjoy any particle of security. In our times, from the highest class of society down to the lowest, every one lives as under the eye of a hostile and dreaded censorship. Not only in what concerns others, but in what concerns only themselves, the individual or the family do not ask themselves—what do I prefer? or, what would suit my character and disposition? or, what would allow the best and highest in me to have fair play, and enable it to grow and thrive? They ask themselves, what is suitable to my position? what is usually done by persons of my station and pecuniary circumstances? or (worse still) what is usually done by persons of a station and circumstances superior to mine? I do not mean that they choose what is customary in preference to what suits their own inclination. It does not occur to them to have any inclination, except for what is customary. Thus the mind itself is bowed to the yoke: even in what people do for pleasure, conformity is the first thing thought of; they like in crowds; they exercise choice only among things commonly done: peculiarity of taste, eccentricity of conduct, are shunned equally with crimes: until by dint of not following their own nature they have no nature to follow: their human capacities are withered and starved: they become incapable of any strong wishes or native pleasures, and are generally without either opinions or feelings of home growth, or properly their own. Now is this, or is it not, the desirable condition of human nature?

It is so, on the Calvinistic theory. According to that, the one great offence of man is self-will. All the good of which humanity is capable is comprised in obedience. You have no choice; thus you must do, and no otherwise: "whatever is not a duty, is a sin." Human nature being radically corrupt, there is no redemption for any one until human nature is killed within him. To one holding this theory of life, crushing out any of the human faculties, capacities, and susceptibilities, is no evil: man needs no capacity, but that of surrendering himself to the will of God: and if he uses any of his faculties for any other purpose but to do that supposed will more effectually, he is better without them. This is the theory of Calvinism; and it is held, in a mitigated form, by many who do not consider themselves Calvinists; the mitigation consisting in giving a less ascetic interpretation to the alleged will of God; asserting it to be his will that mankind should gratify some of their inclinations; of course not in the manner they themselves prefer, but in the way of obedience, that is, in a way prescribed to them by authority; and, therefore, by the necessary condition of the case, the same for all.

In some such insidious form there is at present a strong tendency to this narrow theory of life, and to the pinched and hidebound type of human character which it patronises. Many persons, no doubt, sincerely think that human beings thus cramped and dwarfed are as their Maker designed them to be; just as many have thought that trees are a much finer thing when clipped into pollards,[7] or cut out into figures of animals, than as nature made them. But if it be any part of religion to believe that man was made by a good Being, it is more consistent with that faith to believe that this Being gave all human faculties that they might be cultivated and unfolded, not rooted out and consumed, and that he takes delight in every nearer approach made by his creatures to the ideal conception embodied in them, every increase in any of their capabilities of comprehension, of action, or of enjoyment. There is a different type of human excellence from the Calvinistic: a conception of humanity as having its nature bestowed on it for other purposes than merely to be abnegated. "Pagan self-assertion" is one of the elements of human worth, as well as "Christian self-denial."[8] There is a Greek ideal of self-development, which the Platonic and Christian ideal of self-government blends with, but does not supersede. It may be better to be a John Knox than an Alicibiades, but it is better to be a Pericles than either; nor would a Pericles, if we had one in these days, be without anything good which belonged to John Knox.[9]

It is not by wearing down into uniformity all that is individual in themselves, but by cultivating it, and calling it forth, within the limits imposed by the rights and interests of others, that human beings become a noble and beautiful object of contemplation; and as the works partake the character of those who do them, by the same process human life also becomes rich, diversified, and animating, furnishing more abundant aliment to high thoughts and elevating feelings, and strengthening the tie which binds every individual to the race, by making the race infinitely better worth belonging to. In proportion to the development of his individuality, each person

7. A tree polled or cut back nearly to the trunk, so as to produce a dense growth of branches, forming a rounded head or mass.

8. [Mill's note] Sterling's *Essays*. [Editor: John Sterling (1806–44), one of Mill's close friends, whose article on Simonides, from which these phrases were taken, was much admired by Mill. See Mill's letter of September 12, 1838, in F. E. Mineka, ed., *The Earlier Letters of John Stuart Mill, 1812–1848, Collected Works* (Toronto, 1963), 13:387.]

9. Alcibiades (450?–404 B.C.), Athenian politician and general and a noted libertine, whose devotion to his own self-fulfillment is contrasted here both with the ascetic ideal of self-denial personified by John Knox, and with the combination of self-control and self-development exemplified by the great Athenian statesman Pericles (495?–429 B.C.).

becomes more valuable to himself, and is therefore capable of being more valuable to others. There is a greater fulness of life about his own existence, and when there is more life in the units there is more in the mass which is composed of them. As much compression as is necessary to prevent the stronger specimens of human nature from encroaching on the rights of others, cannot be dispensed with; but for this there is ample compensation even in the point of view of human development. The means of development which the individual loses by being prevented from gratifying his inclinations to the injury of others, are chiefly obtained at the expense of the development of other people. And even to himself there is a full equivalent in the better development of the social part of his nature, rendered possible by the restaint put upon the selfish part. To be held to rigid rules of justice for the sake of others, develops the feelings and capacities which have the good of others for their object. But to be restrained in things not affecting their good, by their mere displeasure, develops nothing valuable, except such force of character as may unfold itself in resisting the restraint. If acquiesced in, it dulls and blunts the whole nature. To give any fair play to the nature of each, it is essential that different persons should be allowed to lead different lives. In proportion as this latitude has been exercised in any age, has that age been noteworthy to posterity. Even despotism does not produce its worst effects, so long as individuality exists under it; and whatever crushes individuality is despotism, by whatever name it may be called, and whether it professes to be enforcing the will of God or the injunctions of men.

Having said that the individuality is the same thing with development, and that it is only the cultivation of individuality which produces, or can produce, well-developed human beings, I might here close the argument: for what more or better can be said of any condition of human affairs than that it brings human beings themselves nearer to the best things they can be? or what worse can be said of any obstruction to good than that it prevents this? Doubtless, however, these considerations will not suffice to convince those who most need convincing; and it is necessary further to show, that these developed human beings are of some use to the undeveloped —to point out to those who do not desire liberty, and would not avail themselves of it, that they may be in some intelligible manner rewarded for allowing other people to make use of it without hindrance.

In the first place, then, I would suggest that they might possibly learn something from them. It will not be denied by anybody, that originality is a valuable element in human affairs. There is always need of persons not only to discover new truths, and point out

when what were once truths are true no longer, but also to commence new practices, and set the example of more enlightened conduct, and better taste and sense in human life. This cannot well be
gainsaid by anybody who does not believe that the world has
already attained perfection in all its ways and practices. It is true
that this benefit is not capable of being rendered by everybody
alike: there are but few persons, in comparison with the whole of
mankind, whose experiments, if adopted by others, would be likely
to be any improvement on established practice. But these few are
the salt of the earth; without them, human life would become a
stagnant pool. Not only is it they who introduce good things which
did not before exist; it is they who keep the life in those which
already exist. If there were nothing new to be done, would human
intellect cease to be necessary? Would it be a reason why those who
do the old things should forget why they are done, and do them
like cattle, not like human beings? There is only too great a tendency in the best beliefs and practices to degenerate into the
mechanical; and unless there were a succession of persons whose
ever-recurring originality prevents the grounds of those beliefs and
practices from becoming merely traditional, such dead matter would
not resist the smaller shock from anything really alive, and there
would be no reason why civilisation should not die out, as in the
Byzantine Empire.[1] Persons of genius, it is true, are, and are always
likely to be, a small minority; but in order to have them, it is necessary to preserve the soil in which they grow. Genius can only
breathe freely in an *atmosphere* of freedom. Persons of genius are,
ex vi termini,[2] more individual than any other people—less capable,
consequently, of fitting themselves, without hurtful compression,
into any of the small number of moulds which society provides in
order to save its members the trouble of forming their own character. If from timidity they consent to be forced into one of these
moulds, and to let all that part of themselves which cannot expand
under the pressure remain unexpanded, society will be little the
better for their genius. If they are of a strong character, and break
their fetters, they become a mark for the society which has not succeeded in reducing them to commonplace, to point out with solemn
warning as "wild," "erratic," and the like; much as if one should
complain of the Niagara river for not flowing smoothly between its
banks like a Dutch canal.

I insist thus emphatically on the importance of genius, and the
necessity of allowing it to unfold itself freely both in thought and
in practice, being well aware that no one will deny the position in

1. The Eastern division of the Roman
Empire, having Byzantium (Constantino-
ple, now Istanbul) as its capital (395–
1453).
2. From the very meaning of the term
itself, by definition.

theory, but knowing also that almost every one, in reality, is totally indifferent to it. People think genius a fine thing if it enables a man to write an exciting poem, or paint a picture. But in its true sense, that of originality in thought and action, though no one says that it is not a thing to be admired, nearly all, at heart, think that they can do very well without it. Unhappily this is too natural to be wondered at. Originality is the one thing which unoriginal minds cannot feel the use of. They cannot see what it is to do for them: how should they? If they could see what it would do for them, it would not be originality. The first service which originality has to render them, is that of opening their eyes: which being once fully done, they would have a chance of being themselves original. Meanwhile, recollecting that nothing was ever yet done which some one was not the first to do, and that all good things which exist are the fruits of originality, let them be modest enough to believe that there is something still left for it to accomplish, and assure themselves that they are more in need of originality, the less they are conscious of the want.

In sober truth, whatever homage may be professed, or even paid, to real or supposed mental superiority, the general tendency of things throughout the world is to render mediocrity the ascendant power among mankind. In ancient history, in the Middle Ages, and in a diminishing degree through the long transition from feudality to the present time, the individual was a power in himself; and if he had either great talents or a high social position, he was a considerable power. At present individuals are lost in the crowd. In politics it is almost a triviality to say that public opinion now rules the world. The only power deserving the name is that of masses, and of governments while they make themselves the organ of the tendencies and instincts of masses. This is as true in the moral and social relations of private life as in public transactions. Those whose opinions go by the name of public opinion are not always the same sort of public: in America they are the whole white population; in England, chiefly the middle class. But they are always a mass, that is to say, collective mediocrity. And what is a still greater novelty, the mass do not now take their opinions from dignitaries in Church or State, from ostensible leaders, or from books. Their thinking is done for them by men much like themselves, addressing them or speaking in their name, on the spur of the moment, through the newspapers. I am not complaining of all this. I do not assert that anything better is compatible, as a general rule, with the present low state of the human mind. But that does not hinder the government of mediocrity from being mediocre government. No government by a democracy or a numerous aristocracy, either in its political acts or in the opinions, qualities, and tone of mind which it fosters, ever did or could rise above mediocrity, except in so far as the sovereign Many have let themselves be guided (which in their best times they always have done) by the counsels and influence of a more highly gifted and instructed One or Few.[3] The initiation of all wise or noble things comes and must come from individuals; generally at first from some one individual. The honour and glory of the average man is that he is capable of following that initiative; that he can respond internally to wise and noble things, and be led to them with his eyes open. I am not countenancing the sort of "hero-worship"[4] which applauds the strong man of genius for forcibly seizing on the government of the world and making it do his bidding in spite of itself. All he can claim is, freedom to point out the way. The power of compelling others into it is not only inconsistent with the freedom and development of all the rest, but corrupting to the strong man himself. It does seem, however, that when the opinions of masses of merely average men are everywhere become or becoming the dominant power, the counterpoise and corrective to that tendency would be the more and more pronounced individuality of those who stand on the higher eminences of thought. It is in these circumstances most especially, that exceptional individuals, instead of being deterred, should be encouraged in acting differently from the mass. In other times there was no advantage in their doing so, unless they acted not only differently but better. In this age, the mere example of non-conformity, the mere refusal to bend the knee to custom, is itself a service. Precisely because the tyranny of opinion is such as to make eccentricity a reproach, it is desirable, in order to break through that tyranny, that people should be eccentric. Eccentricity has always abounded when and where strength of character has abounded; and the amount of eccentricity in a society has generally been proportional to the amount of genius, mental vigour, and moral courage it contained. That so few now dare to be eccentric marks the chief danger of the time.

I have said that it is important to give the freest scope possible to uncustomary things, in order that it may in time appear which of these are fit to be converted into customs. But independence of action, and disregard of custom, are not solely deserving of encouragement for the chance they afford that better modes of action, and customs more worthy of general adoption, may be struck out; nor is it only persons of decided mental superiority who have a just claim

---

3. Critics have seized on this argument to contend that Mill is an elitist rather than a democratic thinker. See the discussion and citations in Spitz, "Freedom and Individuality: Mill's *Liberty* in Retrospect," pp. 183–87.

4. Here Mill explicitly breaks from the teaching of his long-time friend Thomas Carlyle, *Heroes and Hero-Worship* (1840).

to carry on their lives in their own way. There is no reason that all human existence should be constructed on some one or some small number of patterns. If a person possesses any tolerable amount of common sense and experience, his own mode of laying out his existence is the best, not because it is the best in itself, but because it is his own mode. Human beings are not like sheep; and even sheep are not undistinguishably alike. A man cannot get a coat or a pair of boots to fit him unless they are either made to his measure, or he has a whole warehouseful to choose from: and is it easier to fit him with a life than with a coat, or are human beings more like one another in their whole physical and spiritual conformation than in the shape of their feet? If it were only that people have diversities of taste, that is reason enough for not attempting to shape them all after one model. But different persons also require different conditions for their spiritual development; and can no more exist healthily in the same moral, than all the variety of plants can in the same physical, atmosphere and climate. The same things which are helps to one person towards the cultivation of higher nature are hindrances to another. The same mode of life is a healthy excitement to one, keeping all his faculties of action and enjoyment in their best order, while to another it is a distracting burthen, which suspends or crushes all internal life. Such are the differences among human beings in their sources of pleasure, their susceptibilities of pain, and the operation on them of different physical and moral agencies, that unless there is a corresponding diversity in their modes of life, they neither obtain their fair share of happiness, nor grow up to the mental, moral, and aesthetic stature of which their nature is capable. Why then should tolerance, as far as the public sentiment is concerned, extend only to tastes and modes of life which extort acquiescence by the multitude of their adherents? Nowhere (except in some monastic institutions) is diversity of taste entirely unrecognised; a person may, without blame, either like or dislike rowing, or smoking, or music, or athletic exercises, or chess, or cards, or study, because both those who like each of these things, and those who dislike them, are too numerous to be put down. But the man, and still more the woman, who can be accused either of doing "what nobody does," or of not doing "what everybody does," is the subject of as much depreciatory remark as if he or she had committed some grave moral delinquency. Persons require to possess a title, or some other badge of rank, or of the consideration of people of rank, to be able to indulge somewhat in the luxury of doing as they like without detriment to their estimation. To indulge somewhat, I repeat: for whoever allow themselves much of that indulgence, incur the risk of something worse than disparaging speeches—they are in peril of a commission *de lunatico*,[5] and of having their property taken from them and given to their relations.[6]

There is one characteristic of the present direction of public opinion peculiarly calculated to make it intolerant of any marked demonstration of individuality. The general average of mankind are not only moderate in intellect, but also moderate in inclinations: they have no tastes or wishes strong enough to incline them to do anything unusual, and they consequently do not understand those who have, and class all such with the wild and intemperate whom they are accustomed to look down upon. Now, in addition to this fact which is general, we have only to suppose that a strong movement has set in towards the improvement of morals, and it is evident what we have to expect. In these days such a movement has set in; much has actually been effected in the way of increased regularity of conduct and discouragement of excesses; and there is a philanthropic spirit abroad, for the exercise of which there is no more inviting field than the moral and prudential improvement of our fellow-creatures. These tendencies of the times cause the public to be more disposed than at most former periods to prescribe general rules of conduct, and endeavour to make every one conform to the approved standard. And that standard, express or tacit, is to desire nothing strongly. Its ideal of character is to be without any marked character; to maim by compression, like a Chinese lady's foot, every part of human nature which stands out prominently, and tends to make the person markedly dissimilar in outline to commonplace humanity.

As in usually the case with ideals which exclude one-half of what is desirable, the present standard of approbation produces only an inferior imitation of the other half. Instead of great energies guided

---

5. A commission to ascertain the presence of insanity.

6. [Mill's note] There is something both contemptible and frightful in the sort of evidence on which, of late years, any person can be judicially declared unfit for the management of his affairs; and after his death, his disposal of his property can be set aside, if there is enough of it to pay the expenses of litigation—which are charged on the property itself. All the minute details of his daily life are pried into, and whatever is found which, seen through the medium of the perceiving and describing faculties of the lowest of the low, bears an appearance unlike absolute commonplace, is laid before the jury as evidence of insanity, and often with success; the jurors being little, if at all, less vulgar and ignorant than the witnesses; while the judges, with that extraordinary want of knowledge of human nature and life which continually astonishes us in English lawyers, often help to mislead them. These trials speak volumes as to the state of feeling and opinion among the vulgar with regard to human liberty. So far from setting any value on individuality—so far from respecting the right of each individual to act, in things indifferent, as seems good to his own judgment and inclinations, judges and juries cannot even conceive that a person in a state of sanity can desire such freedom. In former days, when it was proposed to burn atheists, charitable people used to suggest putting them in a madhouse instead: it would be nothing surprising now-a-days were we to see this done, and the doers applauding themselves, because, instead of persecuting for religion, they had adopted so humane and Christian a mode of treating these unfortunates, not without a silent satisfaction at their having thereby obtained their deserts.

by vigorous reason, and strong feelings strongly controlled by a conscientious will, its result is weak feelings and weak energies, which therefore can be kept in outward conformity to rule without any strength either of will or of reason. Already energetic characters on any large scale are becoming merely traditional. There is now scarcely any outlet for energy in this country except business. The energy expended in this may still be regarded as considerable. What little is left from that employment is expended on some hobby; which may be a useful, even a philanthropic hobby, but is always some one thing, and generally a thing of small dimensions. The greatness of England is now all collective; individually small, we only appear capable of anything great by our habit of combining; and with this our moral and religious philanthropists are perfectly contented. But it was men of another stamp than this that made England what is has been; and men of another stamp will be needed to prevent its decline.

The despotism of custom is everywhere the standing hindrance to human advancement, being in unceasing antagonism to that disposition to aim at something better than customary, which is called, according to circumstances, the spirit of liberty, or that of progress or improvement. The spirit of improvement is not always a spirit of liberty, for it may aim at forcing improvements on an unwilling people; and the spirit of liberty, in so far as it resists such attempts, may ally itself locally and temporarily with the opponents of improvement; but the only unfailing and permanent source of improvement is liberty, since by it there are as many possible independent centres of improvement as there are individuals. The progressive principle, however, in either shape, whether as the love of liberty or of improvement, is antagonistic to the sway of Custom, involving at least emancipation from that yoke; and the contest between the two constitutes the chief interest of the history of mankind. The greater part of the world has, properly speaking, no history, because the despotism of Custom is complete. This is the case over the whole East. Custom is there, in all things, the final appeal; justice and right mean conformity to custom; the argument of custom no one, unless some tyrant intoxicated with power, thinks of resisting. And we see the result. Those nations must once have had originality; they did not start out of the ground populous, lettered, and versed in many of the arts of life; they made themselves all this, and were then the greatest and most powerful nations of the world. What are they now? The subjects or dependents of tribes whose forefathers wandered in the forests when theirs had magnificent palaces and gorgeous temples, but over whom custom exercised only a divided rule with liberty and progress. A people, it appears, may be progressive for a certain length of time, and then stop: when does it stop? When it ceases to possess individuality.[7] If a similar change should befall the nations of Europe, it will not be in exactly the same shape: the despotism of custom with which these nations are threatened is not precisely stationariness. It proscribes singularity, but it does not preclude change, provided all change together. We have discarded the fixed costumes of our forefathers; every one must still dress like other people, but the fashion may change once or twice a year. We thus take care that when there is a change, it shall be for change's sake, and not from any idea of beauty or convenience; for the same idea of beauty or convenience would not strike all the world at the same moment, and be simultaneously thrown aside by all at another moment. But we are progressive as well as changeable: we continually make new inventions in mechanical things, and keep them until they are again superseded by better; we are eager for improvement in politics, in education, even in morals, though in this last our idea of improvement chiefly consists in persuading or forcing other people to be as good as ourselves. It is not progress that we object to; on the contrary, we flatter ourselves that we are the most progressive people who ever lived. It is individuality that we war against: we should think we had done wonders if we had made ourselves all alike; forgetting that the unlikeness of one person to another is generally the first thing which draws the attention of either to the imperfection of his own type, and the superiority of another, or the possibility, by combining the advantages of both, of producing something better than either. We have a warning example in China—a nation of much talent, and, in some respects, even wisdom, owing to the rare good fortune of having been provided at an early period with a particularly good set of customs, the work, in some measure, of men to whom even the most enlightened European must accord, under certain limitations, the title of sages and philosophers. They are remarkable, too, in the excellence of their apparatus for impressing, as far as possible, the best wisdom they possess upon every mind in the community, and securing that those who have appropriated most of it shall occupy the posts of honour and power. Surely the people who did this have discovered the secret of human progressiveness, and must have kept themselves steadily at the head of the movement of the world. On the contrary, they have become stationary—have remained so for thousands of years; and if they are ever to be farther improved, it must be by foreigners. They have succeeded beyond all hope in what English philanthropists are so industriously working at—in making a people all alike, all governing

7. Compare Arnold J. Toynbee's thesis, in *A Study of History*, 2 vol. abridgment by D. C. Somervell (New York, 1946, 1957), that the shift from "creative" to "dominant" minorities is a primary cause of the decline of civilizations.

their thoughts and conduct by the same maxims and rules; and these are the fruits. The modern *régime* of public opinion is, in an unorganised form, what the Chinese educational and political systems are in an organised; and unless individuality shall be able successfully to assert itself against this yoke, Europe, notwithstanding its noble antecedents and its professed Christianity, will tend to become another China.

What is it that has hitherto preserved Europe from this lot? What has made the European family of nations an improving, instead of a stationary portion of mankind? Not any superior excellence in them, which, when it exists, exists as the effect, not as the cause; but their remarkable diversity of character and culture. Individuals, classes, nations, have been extremely unlike one another: they have struck out a great variety of paths, each leading to something valuable; and although at every period those who travelled in different paths have been intolerant of one another, and each would have thought it an excellent thing if all the rest could have been compelled to travel his road, their attempts to thwart each other's development have rarely had any permanent success, and each has in time endured to receive the good which the others have offered. Europe is, in my judgment, wholly indebted to this plurality of paths for its progressive and many-sided development. But it already begins to possess this benefit in a considerably less degree. It is decidedly advancing towards the Chinese ideal of making all people alike. M. de Tocqueville, in his last important work,[8] remarks how much more the Frenchmen of the present day resemble one another than did those even of the last generation. The same remark might be made of Englishmen in a far greater degree. In a passage already quoted from Wilhelm von Humboldt, he points out two things as necessary conditions of human development, because necessary to render people unlike one another; namely, freedom, and variety of situations. The second of these two conditions is in this country every day diminishing. The circumstances which surround different classes and individuals, and shape their characters, are daily becoming more assimilated. Formerly, different ranks, different neighbourhoods, different trades and professions, lived in what might be called different worlds; at present to a great degree in the same. Comparatively speaking, they now read the same things, listen to the same things, see the same things, go to the same places, have their hopes and fears directed to the same objects, have the same rights and liberties, and the same means of asserting them. Great as are the differences of position which remain, they are nothing to

8. Alexis de Tocqueville, *L'Ancien Régime et la revolution* (1856), translated by S. Gilbert as *The Old Régime and the French Revolution* (Garden City, N.Y.: Doubleday Anchor Books, 1955).

those which have ceased. And the assimilation is still proceeding. All the political changes of the age promote it, since they all tend to raise the low and to lower the high. Every extension of education promotes it, because education brings people under common influences, and gives them access to the general stock of facts and sentiments. Improvement in the means of communication promotes it, by bringing the inhabitants of distant places into personal contact, and keeping up a rapid flow of changes of residence between one place and another. The increase of commerce and manufactures promotes it, by diffusing more widely the advantages of easy circumstances, and opening all objects of ambition, even the highest, to general competition, whereby the desire of rising becomes no longer the character of a particular class, but of all classes. A more powerful agency than even all these, in bringing about a general similarity among mankind, is the complete establishment, in this and other free countries, of the ascendancy of public opinion in the State. As the various social eminences which enabled persons entrenched on them to disregard the opinion of the multitide gradually become levelled; as the very idea of resisting the will of the public, when it is positively known that they have a will, disappears more and more from the minds of practical politicians; there ceases to be any social support for nonconformity—any substantive power in society which, itself opposed to the ascendancy of numbers, is interested in taking under its protection opinions and tendencies at variance with those of the public.

The combination of all these causes forms so great a mass of influences hostile to Individuality, that it is not easy to see how it can stand its ground. It will do so with increasing difficulty, unless the intelligent part of the public can be made to feel its value—to see that it is good there should be differences, even though not for the better, even though, as it may appear to them, some should be for the worse. If the claims of individuality are ever to be asserted, the time is now, while much is still wanting to complete the enforced assimilation. It is only in the earlier stages that any stand can be successfully made against the encroachment. The demand that all other people shall resemble ourselves grows by what it feeds on. If resistance waits till life is reduced *nearly* to one uniform type, all deviations from that type will come to be considered impious, immoral, even monstrous and contrary to nature. Mankind speedily become unable to conceive diversity, when they have been for some time unaccustomed to see it.

Chapter IV

What, then, is the rightful limit to the sovereignty of the individual over himself? Where does the authority of society begin? How much of human life should be assigned to individuality, and how much to society?

Each will receive its proper share, if each has that which more particularly concerns it. To individuality should belong the part of life in which it is chiefly the individual that is interested; to society, the part which chiefly interests society.

Though society is not founded on a contract, and though no good purpose is answered by inventing a contract in order to deduce social obligations from it,[1] every one who receives the protection of society owes a return for the benefit, and the fact of living in society renders it indispensable that each should be bound to observe a certain line of conduct towards the rest. This conduct consists, first, in not injuring the interests of one another; or rather certain interests, which, either by express legal provision, or by tacit understanding, ought to be considered as rights; and secondly, in each person's bearing his share (to be fixed on some equitable principle) of the labours and sacrifices incurred for defending the society or its members from injury and molestation. These conditions society is justified in enforcing, at all costs to those who endeavour to withhold fulfilment. Nor is this all that society may do. The acts of an individual may be hurtful to others, or wanting in due consideration for their welfare, without going to the length of violating any of their constituted rights. The offender may then be justly punished by opinion, though not by law. As soon as any part of a person's conduct affects prejudicially the interests of others, society has jurisdiction over it, and the question whether the general welfare will or will not be promoted by interfering with it, becomes open to discussion. But there is no room for entertaining any such question when a person's conduct affects the interests of no persons besides himself, or needs not affect them unless they like (all the persons concerned being of full age, and the ordinary amount of understanding). In all such cases, there should be perfect freedom, legal and social, to do the action and stand the consequences.

It would be a great misunderstanding of this doctrine to suppose that it is one of selfish indifference, which pretends that human

1. Mill here dismisses the contract theories of Hobbes, Locke, and Rousseau.

beings have no business with each other's conduct in life, and that they should not concern themselves about the well-doing or well-being of one another, unless their own interest is involved.[2] Instead of any diminution, there is need of a great increase of disinterested exertion to promote the good of others. But disinterested benevolence can find other instruments to persuade people to their good than whips and scourges, either of the literal or the metaphorical sort. I am the last person to undervalue the self-regarding virtues; they are only second in importance, if even second, to the social. It is equally the business of education to cultivate both. But even education works by conviction and persuasion as well as by compulsion, and it is by the former only that, when the period of education is passed, the self-regarding virtues should be inculcated. Human beings owe to each other help to distinguish the better from the worse, and encouragement to choose the former and avoid the latter. They should be forever stimulating each other to increased exercise of their higher faculties, and increased direction of their feelings and aims towards wise instead of foolish, elevating instead of degrading, objects and contemplations. But neither one person, nor any number of persons, is warranted in saying to another human creature of ripe years, that he shall not do with his life for his own benefit what he chooses to do with it. He is the person most interested in his own well-being: the interest which any other person, except in cases of strong personal attachment, can have in it, is trifling, compared with that which he himself has; the interest which society has in him individually (except as to his conduct to others) is fractional, and altogether indirect; while with respect to his own feelings and circumstances, the most ordinary man or woman has means of knowledge immeasurably surpassing those that can be possessed by any one else. The interference of society to overrule his judgment and purposes in what only regards himself must be grounded on general presumptions; which may be altogether wrong, and even if right, are as likely as not to be misapplied to individual cases, by persons no better acquainted with the circumstances of such cases than those are who look at them merely from without. In this department, therefore, of human affairs, Individuality has its proper field of action. In the conduct of human beings towards one another it is necessary that general rules should for the most part be observed, in order that people may know what they have to expect: but in each person's own concerns his individual spontaneity is entitled to free exercise. Considerations to aid his judgment, exhortations to

2. Despite this explicit statement, critics of Mill continue to misunderstand him. See, for example, Robert Paul Wolff, "Beyond Tolerance," in R. P. Wolff *et al., A Critique of Pure Tolerance* (Boston, 1965), p. 29.

strengthen his will, may be offered to him, even obtruded on him, by others: but he himself is the final judge. All errors which he is likely to commit against advice and warning are far outweighed by the evil of allowing others to constrain him to what they deem his good.[3]

I do not mean that the feelings with which a person is regarded by others ought not to be in any way affected by his self-regarding qualities or deficiencies. This is neither possible nor desirable. If he is eminent in any of the qualities which conduce to his own good, he is, so far, a proper object of admiration. He is so much the nearer to the ideal perfection of human nature. If he is grossly deficient in those qualities, a sentiment the opposite of admiration will follow. There is a degree of folly, and a degree of what may be called (though the phrase is not unobjectionable) lowness or depravation of taste, which, though it cannot justify doing harm to the person who manifests it renders him necessarily and properly a subject of distaste, or, in extreme cases, even of contempt: a person could not have the opposite qualities in due strength without entertaining these feelings. Though doing no wrong to any one, a person may so act as to compel us to judge him, and feel to him, as a fool, or as a being of an inferior order: and since this judgment and feeling are a fact which he would prefer to avoid, it is doing him a service to warn him of it beforehand, as of any other disagreeable consequence to which he exposes himself. It would be well, indeed, if this good office were much more freely rendered than the common notions of politeness at present permit, and if one person could honestly point out to another that he thinks him in fault, without being considered unmannerly or presuming. We have a right, also, in various ways, to act upon our unfavourable opinion of any one, not to the oppression of his individuality, but in the exercise of ours. We are not bound, for example, to seek his society; we have a right to avoid it (though not to parade the avoidance), for we have a right to choose the society most acceptable to us. We have a right, and it may be our duty, to caution others against him, if we think his example or conversation likely to have a pernicious effect on those with whom he associates. We may give others a preference over him in optional good offices, except those which tend to his improvement. In these various modes a person may suffer very severe penalties at the hands of others for faults which directly concern only himself; but he suffers these penalties only in so far as they are the natural, and, as it were, the spontaneous consequences of the faults themselves, not because they are purposely inflicted on him for the sake of punishment. A person who shows rashness,

3. Here Mill resorts to a form of the Aristotelian principle that he whom the shoe pinches is best able to judge what is good for him.

obstinacy, self-conceit—who cannot live within moderate means—who cannot restrain himself from hurtful indulgences—who pursues animal pleasures at the expense of those of feeling and intellect—must expect to be lowered in the opinion of others, and to have a less share of their favourable sentiments; but of this he has no right to complain, unless he has merited their favour by special excellence in his social relations, and has thus established a title to their good offices, which is not affected by his demerits towards himself.

What I contend for is, that the inconveniences which are strictly inseparable from the unfavourable judgment of others, are the only ones to which a person should ever be subjected for that portion of his conduct and character which concerns his own good, but which does not affect the interest of others in their relations with him. Acts injurious to others require a totally different treatment. Encroachment on their rights; infliction on them of any loss or damage not justified by his own rights; falsehood or duplicity in dealing with them; unfair or ungenerous use of advantages over them; even selfish abstinence from defending them against injury—these are fit objects of moral reprobation, and, in grave cases, of moral retribution and punishment. And not only these acts, but the dispositions which lead to them, are properly immoral, and fit subjects of disapprobation which may rise to abhorrence. Cruelty of disposition; malice and ill-nature; that most anti-social and odious of all passions, envy; dissimulation and insincerity, irascibility on insufficient cause, and resentment disproportioned to the provocation; the love of domineering over others; the desire to engross more than one's share of advantages (the πλεονεξία[4] of the Greeks); the pride which derives gratification from the abasement of others; the egotism which thinks self and its concerns more important than everything else, and decides all doubtful questions in its own favour; —these are moral vices, and constitute a bad and odious moral character: unlike the self-regarding faults previously mentioned, which are not properly immoralities, and to whatever pitch they may be carried, do not constitute wickedness. They may be proofs of any amount of folly, or want of personal dignity and self-respect; but they are only a subject of moral reprobation when they involve a breach of duty to others, for whose sake the individual is bound to have care for himself. What are called duties to ourselves are not socially obligatory, unless circumstances render them at the same time duties to others. The term duty to oneself, when it means anything more than prudence, means self-respect or self-development, and for none of these is any one accountable to his fellow creatures, because for none of them is it for the good of mankind that he be held accountable to them.

4. Pleonexia: Covetousness, avarice, greed.

The distinction between the loss of consideration which a person may rightly incur by defect of prudence or of personal dignity, and the reprobation which is due to him for an offence against the rights of others, is not a merely nominal distinction. It makes a vast difference both in our feelings and in our conduct towards him whether he displeases us in things in which we think we have a right to control him, or in things in which we know that we have not. If he displeases us, we may express our distaste, and we may stand aloof from a person as well as from a thing that displeases us; but we shall not therefore feel called on to make his life uncomfortable. We shall reflect that he already bears, or will bear, the whole penalty of his error; if he spoils his life by mismanagement, we shall not, for that reason, desire to spoil it still further: instead of wishing to punish him, we shall rather endeavour to alleviate his punishment, by showing him how he may avoid or cure the evils his conduct tends to bring upon him. He may be to us an object of pity, perhaps of dislike, but not of anger or resentment; we shall not treat him like an enemy of society: the worst we shall think ourselves justified in doing is leaving him to himself, if we do not interfere benevolently by showing interest or concern for him. It is far otherwise if he has infringed the rules necessary for the protection of his fellow-creatures, individually or collectively. The evil consequences of his acts do not then fall on himself, but on others; and society, as the protector of all its members, must retaliate on him; must inflict pain on him for the express purpose of punishment, and must take care that it be sufficiently severe. In the one case, he is an offender at our bar, and we are called on not only to sit in judgment on him, but, in one shape or another, to execute our own sentence: in the other case, it is not our part to inflict any suffering on him, except what may incidentally follow from our using the same liberty in the regulation of our own affairs, which we allow to him in his.

The distinction here pointed out between the part of a person's life which concerns only himself, and that which concerns others, many persons will refuse to admit. How (it may be asked) can any part of the conduct of a member of society be a matter of indifference to the other members? No person is an entirely isolated being; it is impossible for a person to do anything seriously or permanently hurtful to himself, without mischief reaching at least to his near connections, and often far beyond them. If he injures his property, he does harm to those who directly or indirectly derived support from it, and usually diminishes, by a greater or less amount, the general resources of the comunity. If he deteriorates his bodily or mental faculties, he not only brings evil upon all who depended on him for any portion of their happiness, but disqualifies himself for

rendering the services which he owes to his fellow-creatures generally; perhaps becomes a burthen on their affection or benevolence;
and if such conduct were very frequent, hardly any offence that is
committed would detract more from the general sum of good.
Finally, if by his vices or follies a person does no direct harm to
others, he is nevertheless (it may be said) injurious by his example;
and ought to be compelled to control himself, for the sake of those
whom the sight or knowledge of his conduct might corrupt or mislead.

And even (it will be added) if the consequences of misconduct
could be confined to the vicious or thoughtless individual, ought
society to abandon to their own guidance those who are manifestly
unfit for it? If protection against themselves is confessedly due to
children and persons under age, is not society equally bound to
afford it to persons of mature years who are equally incapable of
self-government? If gambling, or drunkenness, or incontinence, or
idleness, or uncleanliness, are as injurious to happiness, and as great
a hindrance to improvement, as many or most of the acts prohibited by law, why (it may be asked) should not law, so far as is consistent with practicability and social convenience, endeavour to
repress these also? And as a supplement to the unavoidable imperfections of law, ought not opinion at least to organise a powerful
police against these vices, and visit rigidly with social penalties those
who are known to practise them? There is no question here (it may
be said) about restricting individuality, or impeding the trial of new
and original experiments in living. The only things it is sought to
prevent are things which have been tried and condemned from the
beginning of the world until now; things which experience has
shown not to be useful or suitable to any person's individuality.
There must be some length of time and amount of experience after
which a moral or prudential truth may be regarded as established:
and it is merely desired to prevent generation after generation from
falling over the same precipice which has been fatal to their predecessors.

I fully admit that the mischief which a person does to himself
may seriously affect, both through their sympathies and their interests, those nearly connected with him and, in a minor degree,
society at large. When, by conduct of this sort, a person is led to
violate a distinct and assignable obligation[5] to any other person or
persons, the case is taken out of the self-regarding class, and
becomes amenable to moral disapprobation in the proper sense of

---

5. Whether this notion of "a distinct
and assignable obligation" is an adequate principle for distinguishing self-regarding from other-regarding activities
has been much discussed in the literature. See, for example, R. M. MacIver,
The Modern State (London, 1926), pp.
457–58.

the term. If, for example, a man, through intemperance or extravagance, becomes unable to pay his debts, or, having undertaken the
moral responsibility of a family, becomes from the same cause
incapable of supporting or educating them, he is deservedly reprobated, and might be justly punished; but it is for the breach of duty
to his family or creditors, not for the extravagance. If the resources
which ought to have been devoted to them, had been diverted
from them for the most prudent investment, the moral culpability
would have been the same. George Barnwell[6] murdered his uncle
to get money for his mistress, but if he had done it to set himself
up in business, he would equally have been hanged. Again, in the
frequent case of a man who causes grief to his family by addiction
to bad habits, he deserves reproach for his unkindness or ingratitude; but so he may for cultivating habits not in themselves vicious, if they are painful to those with whom he passes his life, or
who from personal ties are dependent on him for their comfort.
Whoever fails in the consideration generally due to the interests
and feelings of others, not being compelled by some more imperative duty, or justified by allowable self-preference, is a subject of
moral disapprobation for that failure, but not for the cause of it,
nor for the errors, merely personal to himself, which may have remotely led to it. In like manner, when a person disables himself, by
conduct purely self-regarding, from the performance of some definite duty incumbent on him to the public, he is guilty of a social
offence. No person ought to be punished simply for being drunk;
but a soldier or a policeman should be punished for being drunk
on duty. Whenever, in short, there is a definite damage, or a definite risk of damage, either to an individual or to the public, the
case is taken out of the province of liberty, and placed in that of
morality or law.

But with regard to the merely contingent, or, as it may be called,
constructive injury which a person causes to society, by conduct
which neither violates any specific duty to the public, nor occasions
perceptible hurt to any assignable individual except himself; the
inconvenience is one which society can afford to bear, for the sake
of the greater good of human freedom. If grown persons are to be
punished for not taking proper care of themselves, I would rather it
were for their own sake, than under pretence of preventing them
from imparing their capacity of rendering to society benefits which
society does not pretend it has a right to exact. But I cannot consent to argue the point as if society had no means of bringing its

6. The protagonist of a well-known English ballad, "George Barnwell," and of
George Lillo's bourgeois prose tragedy,
*The London Merchant; or, The History
of George Barnwell* (1731).

weaker members up to its ordinary standard of rational conduct, except waiting till they do something irrational, and then punishing them, legally or morally, for it. Society has had absolute power over them during all the early portion of their existence: it has had the whole period of childhood and nonage in which to try whether it could make them capable of rational conduct in life. The existing generation is master both of the training and the entire circumstances of the generation to come; it cannot indeed make them perfectly wise and good, because it is itself so lamentably deficient in goodness and wisdom; and its best efforts are not always, in individual cases, its most successful ones; but it is perfectly well able to make the rising generation, as a whole, as good as, and a little better than, itself. If society lets any considerable number of its members grow up mere children, incapable of being acted on by rational consideration of distant motives, society has itself to blame for the consequences. Armed not only with all the powers of education, but with the ascendancy which the authority of a received opinion always exercises over the minds who are least fitted to judge for themselves; and aided by the *natural* penalties which cannot be prevented from falling on those who incur the distaste or the contempt of those who know them; let not society pretend that it needs, besides all this, the power to issue commands and enforce obedience in the personal concerns of individuals, in which, on all principles of justice and policy, the decision ought to rest with those who are to abide the consequences. Nor is there anything which tends more to discredit and frustrate the better means of influencing conduct than a resort to the worse. If there be among those whom it is attempted to coerce into prudence or temperance any of the material of which vigorous and independent characters are made, they will infallibly rebel against the yoke. No such person will ever feel that others have a right to control him in his concerns, such as they have to prevent him from injuring them in theirs; and it easily comes to be considered a mark of spirit and courage to fly in the face of such usurped authority, and do with ostentation the exact opposite of what it enjoins; as in the fashion of grossness which succeeded, in the time of Charles II.,[7] to the fanatical moral intolerance of the Puritans. With respect to what is said of the necessity of protecting society from the bad example set to others by the vicious or the self-indulgent; it is true that bad example may have a pernicious effect, especially the example of doing wrong to others with impunity to the wrong-doer. But we are now speaking

7. **Charles II** (1630–85), pleasure-loving English king whose reign, after the restoration of the monarchy in 1660, was marked by a reaction against the strictness of Puritan rule.

of conduct which, while it does no wrong to others, is supposed to do great harm to the agent himself: and I do not see how those who believe this can think otherwise than that the example, on the whole, must be more salutary than hurtful, since, if it displays the misconduct, it displays also the painful or degrading consequences which, if the conduct is justly censured, must be supposed to be in all or most cases attendant on it.

But the strongest of all the arguments against the interference of the public with purely personal conduct is that, when it does interfere, the odds are that it interferes wrongly, and in the wrong place. On questions of social morality, of duty to others, the opinion of the public, that is, of an overruling majority, though often wrong, is likely to be still oftener right; because on such questions they are only required to judge of their own interests; of the manner in which some mode of conduct, if allowed to be practised, would affect themselves. But the opinion of a similar majority, imposed as a law on the minority, on questions of self-regarding conduct, is quite as likely to be wrong as right; for in these cases public opinion means, at the best, some people's opinion of what is good or bad for other people; while very often it does not even mean that; the public, with the most perfect indifference, passing over the pleasure or convenience of those whose conduct they censure, and considering only their own preference. There are many who consider as an injury to themselves any conduct which they have a distaste for, and resent it as an outrage to their feelings; as a religious bigot, when charged with disregarding the religious feelings of others, has been known to retort that they disregard his feelings, by persisting in their abominable worship or creed. But there is no parity between the feeling of a person for his own opinion, and the feeling of another who is offended at his holding it; no more than between the desire of a thief to take a purse, and the desire of the right owner to keep it. And a person's taste is as much his own peculiar concern as his opinion or his purse. It is easy for any one to imagine an ideal public which leaves the freedom and choice of individuals in all uncertain matters undisturbed, and only requires them to abstain from modes of conduct which universal experience has condemned. But where has there been seen a public which set any such limit to its censorship? or when does the public trouble itself about universal experience? In its interferences with personal conduct it is seldom thinking of anything but the enormity of acting or feeling differently from itself; and this standard of judgment, thinly disguised, is held up to mankind as the dictate of religion and philosophy, by nine-tenths of all moralists and speculative writers. These teach that things are right because they are right; because we feel them to be so.[8] They tell us to search in our own minds and hearts for laws of conduct binding on ourselves and on all others. What can the poor public do but apply these instructions, and make their own personal feelings of good and evil, if they are tolerably unanimous in them, obligatory on all the world?

The evil here pointed out is not one which exists only in theory; and it may perhaps be expected that I should specify the instances in which the public of this age and country improperly invests its own preferences with the character of moral laws. I am not writing an essay on the aberrations of existing moral feeling. That is too weighty a subject to be discussed parenthetically, and by way of illustration. Yet examples are necessary to show that the principle I maintain is of serious and practical moment, and that I am not endeavouring to erect a barrier against imaginary evils. And it is not difficult to show, by abundant instances, that to extend the bounds of what may be called moral police, until it encroaches on the most unquestionably legitimate liberty of the individual, is one of the most universal of all human propensities.

As a first instance, consider the antipathies which men cherish on no better grounds than that persons whose religious opinions are different from theirs do not practise their religious observances, especially their religious abstinences. To cite a rather trivial example, nothing in the creed or practice of Christians does more to envenom the hatred of Mahomedans against them than the fact of their eating pork. There are few acts which Christians and Europeans regard with more unaffected disgust than Mussulmans[9] regard this particular mode of satisfying hunger. It is, in the first place, an offence against their religion; but this circumstance by no means explains either the degree or the kind of their repugnance; for wine also is forbidden by their religion, and to partake of it is by all Mussulmans accounted wrong, but not disgusting. Their aversion to the flesh of the "unclean beast" is, on the contrary, of that peculiar character, resembling an instinctive antipathy, which the idea of uncleanness, when once it thoroughly sinks into the feelings, seems always to excite even in those whose personal habits are anything but scrupulously cleanly, and of which the sentiment of religious impurity, so intense in the Hindoos, is a remarkable example. Suppose now that in a people, of whom the majority were Mussulmans, that majority should insist upon not permitting pork to be eaten within the limits of the country. This would be nothing new in

8. Mill apparently refers here to natural law and intuitionist doctrines.

9. Mohammedans, or Moslems.

Mahomedan countries.[1] Would it be a legitimate exercise of the moral authority of public opinion? and if not, why not? The practice is really revolting to such a public. They also sincerely think that it is forbidden and abhorred by the Deity. Neither could the prohibition be censured as religious persecution. It might be religious in its origin, but it would not be persecution for religion, since nobody's religion makes it a duty to eat pork. The only tenable ground of condemnation would be that with the personal tastes and self-regarding concerns of individuals the public has no business to interfere.

To come somewhat nearer home: the majority of Spaniards consider it a gross impiety, offensive in the highest degree to the Supreme Being, to worship him in any other manner than the Roman Catholic; and no other public worship is lawful on Spanish soil. The people of all Southern Europe look upon a married clergy as not only irreligious, but unchaste, indecent, gross, disgusting. What do Protestants think of these perfectly sincere feelings, and of the attempt to enforce them against non-Catholics? Yet, if mankind are justified in interfering with each other's liberty in things which do not concern the interests of others, on what principle is it possible consistently to exclude these cases? or who can blame people for desiring to suppress what they regard as a scandal in the sight of God and man? No stronger case can be shown for prohibiting anything which is regarded as a personal immorality, than is made out for suppressing these practices in the eyes of those who regard them as impieties; and unless we are willing to adopt the logic of persecutors, and to say that we may persecute others because we are right, and that they must not persecute us because they are wrong, we must beware of admitting a principle of which we should resent as a gross injustice the application to ourselves.

The preceding instances may be objected to, although unreasonably, as drawn from contingencies impossible among us: opinion, in this country, not being likely to enforce abstinence from meats, or to interfere with people for worshipping, and for either marrying or not marrying, according to their creed or inclination. The next example, however, shall be taken from an interference with liberty which we have by no means passed all danger of. Wherever the

---

1. [Mill's note] The case of the Bombay Parsees [Editor: A Zoroastrian sect.] is a curious instance in point. When this industrious and enterprising tribe, the descendants of the Persian fire-worshippers, flying from their native country before the Caliphs, arrived in Western India, they were admitted to toleration by the Hindoo sovereigns, on condition of not eating beef. When those regions afterwards fell under the dominion of Mahomedan conquerors, the Parsees obtained from them a continuance of indulgence, on condition of refraining from pork. What was at first obedience to authority became a second nature, and the Parsees to this day abstain both from beef and pork. Though not required by their religion, the double abstinence has had time to grow into a custom of their tribe; and custom, in the East, is a religion.

Puritans have been sufficiently powerful, as in New England, and in Great Britain at the time of the Commonwealth, they have endeavoured, with considerable success, to put down all public, and nearly all private, amusements: especially music, dancing, public games, or other assemblages for purposes of diversion, and the theatre. There are still in this country large bodies of persons by whose notions of morality and religion these recreations are condemned; and those persons belonging chiefly to the middle class, who are the ascendant power in the present social and political condition of the kingdom, it is by no means impossible that persons of these sentiments may at some time or other command a majority in Parliament. How will the remaining portion of the community like to have the amusements that shall be permitted to them regulated by the religious and moral sentiments of the stricter Calvinists and Methodists?[2] Would they not, with considerable peremptoriness, desire these intrusively pious members of society to mind their own business? This is precisely what should be said to every government and every public, who have the pretension that no person shall enjoy any pleasure which they think wrong. But if the principle of the pretension be admitted, no one can reasonably object to its being acted on in the sense of the majority, or other preponderating power in the country; and all persons must be ready to conform to the idea of a Christian commonwealth, as understood by the early settlers in New England, if a religious profession similar to theirs should ever succeed in regaining its lost ground, as religions supposed to be declining have so often been known to do.

To imagine another contingency, perhaps more likely to be realised than the one last mentioned. There is confessedly a strong tendency in the modern world towards a democratic constitution of society, accompanied or not by popular political institutions. It is affirmed that in the country where this tendency is most completely realised—where both society and the government are most democratic—the United States—the feeling of the majority, to whom any appearance of a more showy or costly style of living than they can hope to rival is disagreeable, operates as a tolerably effectual sumptuary law,[3] and that in many parts of the Union it is really difficult for a person possessing a very large income to find any mode of spending it which will not incur popular disapprobation. Though such statements as these are doubtless much exaggerated as a representation of existing facts, the state of things they describe is not only a conceivable and possible, but a probable result of democratic feeling, combined with the notion that the public has a right

2. Followers of the British preacher John Wesley (1703–91), who broke from the Church of England and founded an evangelistic movement characterized by strictness of piety and morality.

3. Laws regulating personal habits and extravagant expenditure for food, dress, equipage, entertainment, etc., which offend the conscience of the community.

to a veto on the manner in which individuals shall spend their incomes. We have only further to suppose a considerable diffusion of Socialist opinions,[4] and it may become infamous in the eyes of the majority to possess more property than some very small amount, or any income not earned by manual labour. Opinions similar in principle to these already prevail widely among the artisan class, and weigh oppressively on those who are amenable to the opinion chiefly of that class, namely, its own members. It is known that the bad workmen who form the majority of the operatives in many branches of industry, are decidedly of opinion that bad workmen ought to receive the same wages as good, and that no one ought to be allowed, through piecework or otherwise, to earn by superior skill or industry more than others can without it. And they employ a moral police, which occasionally becomes a physical one, to deter skillful workmen from receiving, and employers from giving, a larger remuneration for a more useful service. If the public have any juris-diction over private concerns, I cannot see that these people are in fault, or that any individuals's particular public can be blamed for asserting the same authority over his individual conduct which the general public asserts over people in general.

But, without dwelling upon supposititious[5] cases, there are, in our own day, gross usurpations upon the liberty of private life actually practised, and still greater ones threatened with some expectation of success, and opinions propounded which assert an unlimited right in the public not only to prohibit by law everything which it thinks wrong, but, in order to get at what it thinks wrong, to prohibit a number of things which it admits to be innocent.

Under the name of preventing intemperance, the people of one English colony, and of nearly half the United States, have been interdicted by law from making any use whatever of fermented drinks, except for medical purposes: for prohibition of their sale is in fact, as it is intended to be, prohibition of their use. And though the impracticability of executing the law has caused its repeal in several of the States which had adopted it, including the one from which it derives its name,[6] an attempt has notwithstanding been commenced, and is prosecuted with considerable zeal by many of the professed philanthropists, to agitate for a similar law in this

4. By Socialist opinions Mill had in mind not the doctrines of Karl Marx, with whose writings he does not seem to have been acquainted, but those of Louis Blanc (1811–82), Etienne Cabet (1788–1856), Charles Fourier (1772-1837), Robert Owen (1771–1858), and the Comte de Saint-Simon (1760–1825). Mill's own view of socialism was a mixture of sympathy and antagonism. See his *Principles of Political Economy*,

Collected Works (Toronto, 1965), vols. 2–3, and "Chapters on Socialism," in his *Essays on Economics and Society, Collected Works* (Toronto, 1967), 5: 703–53.
5. Fancied, imaginary, hypothetical.
6. Maine; a reference to the Maine Liquor Law (1815), which interdicted the manufacture, sale, and use of most alcoholic beverages.

country. The association, or "Alliance"[7] as it terms itself, which has been formed for this purpose, has acquired some notoriety through the publicity given to a correspondence between its secretary and one of the very few English public men who hold that a politician's opinions ought to be founded on principles. Lord Stanley's[8] share in this correspondence is calculated to strengthen the hopes already built on him, by those who know how rare such qualities as are manifested in some of his public appearances unhappily are among those who figure in political life. The organ of the Alliance, who would "deeply deplore the recognition of any principle which could be wrested to justify bigotry and persecution," undertakes to point out the "broad and impassable barrier" which divides such principles from those of the association. "All matters relating to thought, opinion, conscience, appear to me," he says, "to be without the sphere of legislation; all pertaining to social act, habit, relation, subject only to a discretionary power vested in the State itself, and not in the individual, to be within it." No mention is made of a third class, different from either of these, viz., acts and habits which are not social, but individual; although it is to this class, surely, that the act of drinking fermented liquors belongs. Selling fermented liquors, however, is trading, and trading is a social act. But the infringement complained of is not on the liberty of the seller, but on that of the buyer and consumer; since the State might just as well forbid him to drink wine as purposely make it impossible for him to obtain it. The secretary, however, says, "I claim, as a citizen, a right to legislate whenever my social rights are invaded by the social act of another." And now for the definition of these "social rights." "If anything invades my social rights, certainly the traffic in strong drink does. It destroys my primary right of security, by constantly creating and stimulating social disorder. It invades my right of equality, by deriving a profit from the creation of a misery I am taxed to support. It impedes my right to free moral and intellectual development, by surrounding my path with dangers, and by weakening and demoralising society, from which I have a right to claim mutual aid and intercourse." A theory of "social rights" the like of which probably never before found its way into distinct language: being nothing short of this—that it is the absolute social right of every individual, that every other individual shall act in every respect exactly as he ought; that whosoever fails thereof in the smallest particular violates my social right, and entitles me to demand from the legislature the removal of the grievance. So monstrous a principle is far more dangerous than any single interference

7. The United Kingdom Alliance for the Legislative Suppression of the Sale of Intoxicating Liquors, founded in 1853.

8. Edward Henry Stanley (1826–93), Earl of Derby, British parliamentarian and the first Secretary of State for India.

with liberty; there is no violation of liberty which it would not justify; it acknowledges no right to any freedom whatever, except perhaps to that of holding opinions in secret, without ever disclosing
them: for, the moment an opinion which I consider noxious passes
any one's lips, it invades all the "social rights" attributed to me by
the Alliance. The doctrine ascribes to all mankind a vested interest
in each other's moral, intellectual, and even physical perfection, to
be defined by each claimant according to his own standard.

Another important example of illegitimate interference with the
rightful liberty of the individual, not simply threatened, but long
since carried into triumphant effect, is Sabbatarian legislation.[9]
Without doubt, abstinence on one day in the week, so far as the
exigencies of life permit, from the usual daily occupation, though in
no respect religiously binding on any except Jews, is a highly beneficial custom. And inasmuch as this custom cannot be observed without a general consent to that effect among the industrious classes,
therefore, in so far as some persons by working may impose the
same necessity on others, it may be allowable and right that the law
should guarantee to each the observance by others of the custom,
by suspending the greater operations of industry on a particular day.
But this justification, grounded on the direct interest which others
have in each individual's observance of the practice, does not apply
to the self-chosen occupations in which a person may think fit to
employ his leisure; nor does it hold good, in the smallest degree, for
legal restrictions on amusements. It is true that the amusement of
some is the day's work of others; but the pleasure, not to say the
useful recreation, of many, is worth the labour of a few, provided
the occupation is freely chosen, and can be freely resigned. The
operatives are perfectly right in thinking that if all worked on
Sunday, seven days' work would have to be given for six days'
wages; but so long as the great mass of employments are suspended,
the small number who for the enjoyment of others must still work,
obtain a proportional increase of earnings; and they are not obliged
to follow those occupations if they prefer leisure to emolument. If a
further remedy is sought, it might be found in the establishment
by custom of a holiday on some other day of the week for those
particular classes of persons. The only ground, therefore, on which
restrictions on Sunday amusements can be defended, must be that
they are religiously wrong; a motive of legislation which can never
be too earnestly protested against. "Deorum injuriæ Diis curæ."[1]
It remains to be proved that society or any of its officers holds a commission from on high to avenge any supposed offence to Omnipo-
tence, which is not also a wrong to our fellow-creatures. The notion

---

9. Laws prohibiting or strictly regulating
various kinds of conduct with regard to
Sunday observance.
1. "The Gods can take care of themselves." (Literally, "Injuries to the gods
can be cured by the gods.") Tacitus,
Annals, 1. 73.

that it is one man's duty that another should be religious, was the foundation of all the religious persecutions ever perpetrated, and, if admitted, would fully justify them. Though the feeling which breaks out in the repeated attempts to stop railway travelling on Sunday, in the resistance to the opening of Museums, and the like, has not the cruelty of the old persecutors, the state of mind indicated by it is fundamentally the same. It is a determination not to tolerate others in doing what is permitted by their religion, because it is not permitted by the persecutor's religion. It is a belief that God not only abominates the act of the misbeliever, but will not hold us guiltless if we leave him unmolested.

I cannot refrain from adding to these examples of the little account commonly made of human liberty, the language of downright persecution which breaks out from the press of this country whenever it feels called on to notice the remarkable phenomenon of Mormonism.[2] Much might be said on the unexpected and instructive fact that an alleged new revelation, and a religion founded on it, the product of palpable imposture, not even supported by the *prestige* of extraordinary qualities in its founder, is believed by hundreds of thousands, and has been made the foundation of a society, in the age of newspapers, railways, and the electric telegraph. What here concerns us is, that this religion, like other and better religions, has its martyrs: that its prophet and founder was, for his teaching, put to death by a mob; that others of its adherents lost their lives by the same lawless violence; that they were forcibly expelled, in a body, from the country in which they first grew up; while, now that they have been chased into a solitary recess in the midst of a desert, many in this country openly declare that it would be right (only that it is not convenient) to send an expedition against them, and compel them by force to conform to the opinions of other people. The article of the Mormonite doctrine which is the chief provocative to the antipathy which thus breaks through the ordinary restraints of religious tolerance, is its sanction of polygamy; which, though permitted to Mahomedans, and Hindoos, and Chinese, seems to excite unquenchable animosity when practised by persons who speak English and profess to be a kind of Christians. No one has a deeper disapprobation than I have of this Mormon institution; both for other reasons, and because, far from being in any way countenanced by the principle of liberty, it is a direct infraction of that principle, being a mere riveting of the chains of one half of the community, and an emancipation of the other from reciprocity of obligation towards them. Still, it must be remembered that this relation is as much voluntary on the part of the women

2. Doctrine of the Mormons, or Church of Jesus Christ of Latter-Day Saints, founded by Joseph Smith (1805–44) in 1830 in New York. To escape persecution, primarily for their practice of polygamy, the Mormons, led by Brigham Young (1801–77), fled to Salt Lake City, Utah.

concerned in it, and who may be deemed the sufferers by it, as is the case with any other form of the marriage institution; and however surprising this fact may appear, it has its explanation in the common ideas and customs of the world, which teaching women to think marriage the one thing needful, make it intelligible that many a woman should prefer being one of several wives, to not being a wife at all. Other countries are not asked to recognise such unions, or release any portion of their inhabitants from their own laws on the score of Mormonite opinions. But when the dissentients have conceded to the hostile sentiments of others far more than could justly be demanded; when they have left the countries to which their doctrines were unacceptable, and established themselves in a remote corner of the earth, which they have been the first to render habitable to human beings; it is difficult to see on what principles but those of tyranny they can be prevented from living there under what laws they please, provided they commit no aggression on other nations, and allow perfect freedom of departure to those who are dissatisfied with their ways. A recent writer,[3] in some respects of considerable merit, proposes (to use his own words) not a crusade, but a *civilisade*,[4] against this polygamous community, to put an end to what seems to him a retrograde step in civilisation. It also appears so to me, but I am not aware that any community has a right to force another to be civilised. So long as the sufferers by the bad law do not invoke assistance from other communities, I cannot admit that persons entirely unconnected with them ought to step in and require that a condition of things with which all who are directly interested appear to be satisfied, should be put an end to because it is a scandal to persons some thousands of miles distant, who have no part or concern in it. Let them send missionaries, if they please, to preach against it; and let them, by any fair means (of which silencing the teachers is not one), oppose the progress of similar doctrines among their own people. If civilisation has got the better of barbarism when barbarism had the world to itself, it is too much to profess to be afraid lest barbarism, after having been fairly got under, should revive and conquer civilisation. A civilisation that can thus succumb to its vanquished enemy, must first have become so degenerate, that neither its appointed priests and teachers, nor anybody else, has the capacity, or will take the trouble, to stand up for it. If this be so, the sooner such a civilisation receives notice to quit the better. It can only go on from bad to worse, until destroyed and regenerated (like the Western Empire)[5] by energetic barbarians.

---

3. Unknown to this Editor.
4. Presumably a crusade in behalf of civilization.

5. The Western portion of the Roman Empire, overrun by barbarian invasions in the fifth century.

Chapter V

The principles asserted in these pages must be more generally admitted as the basis for discussion of details, before a consistent application of them to all the various departments of government and morals can be attempted with any prospect of advantage. The few observations I propose to make on questions of detail are designed to illustrate the principles, rather than to follow them out to their consequences. I offer, not so much applications, as specimens of application; which may serve to bring into greater clearness the meaning and limits of the two maxims which together form the entire doctrine of this Essay, and to assist the judgment in holding the balance between them, in the cases where it appears doubtful which of them is applicable to the case.

The maxims are, first, that the individual is not accountable to society for his actions, in so far as these concern the interests of no person but himself. Advice, instruction, persuasion, and avoidance by other people if thought necessary by them for their own good, are the only measures by which society can justifiably express its dislike or disapprobation of his conduct. Secondly, that for such actions as are prejudicial to the interests of others, the individual is accountable, and may be subjected either to social or to legal punishment, if society is of opinion that the one or the other is requisite for its protection.

In the first place, it must by no means be supposed, because damage, or probability of damage, to the interests of others, can alone justify the interference of society, that therefore it always does justify such interference. In many cases, an individual, in pursuing a legitimate object, necessarily and therefore legitimately causes pain or loss to others, or intercepts a good which they had a reasonable hope of obtaining. Such oppositions of interest between individuals often arise from bad social institutions, but are unavoidable while those institutions last; and some would be unavoidable under any institutions. Whoever succeeds in an overcrowded profession, or in a competitive examination; whoever is preferred to another in any contest for an object which both desire, reaps benefit from the loss of others, from their wasted exertion and their disappointment. But it is, by common admission, better for the general interest of mankind, that persons should pursue their objects undeterred by this sort of consequences. In other words, society admits no right, either legal or moral, in the disappointed competitors to immunity from this kind of suffering; and feels called on to interfere, only when means of success have been employed which it is contrary to the general interest to permit—namely, fraud or treachery, and force.

Again, trade is a social act. Whoever undertakes to sell any description of goods to the public, does what affects the interest of other persons, and of society in general; and thus his conduct, in principle, comes within the jurisdiction of society: accordingly, it was once held to be the duty of governments, in all cases which were considered of importance, to fix prices, and regulate the processes of manufacture. But it is now recognised, though not till after a long struggle, that both the cheapness and the good quality of commodities are most effectually provided for by leaving the producers and sellers perfectly free, under the sole check of equal freedom to the buyers for supplying themselves elsewhere. This is the so-called doctrine of Free Trade,[1] which rests on grounds different from, though equally solid with, the principle of individual liberty asserted in this Essay. Restrictions on trade, or on production for purposes of trade, are indeed restraints; and all restraint, *quâ* restraint, is an evil: but the restraints in question affect only that part of conduct which society is competent to restrain, and are wrong solely because they do not really produce the results which it is desired to produce by them. As the principle of individual liberty is not involved in the doctrine of Free Trade, so neither is it in most of the questions which arise respecting the limits of that doctrine; as, for example, what amount of public control is admissible for the prevention of fraud by adulteration; how far sanitary precautions, or arrangements to protect workpeople employed in dangerous occupations, should be enforced on employers. Such questions involve considerations of liberty, only in so far as leaving people to themselves is always better, *cæteris paribus*,[2] than controlling them: but that they may be legitimately controlled for these ends is in principle undeniable.[3] On the other hand, there are questions relating to interference with trade which are essentially questions of liberty; such as the Maine Law, already touched upon; the prohibition of the importation of opium into China;[4] the restriction of the sale of poisons; all cases, in short, where the object of the interference is to make it impossible or difficult to obtain a particular commodity. These interferences are objectionable, not as infringements on the liberty of the producer or seller, but on that of the buyer.

1. That there should be no restrictions on the buying and selling or exchange of commodities between nations; a doctrine generally associated with the Scottish economist and moral philosopher Adam Smith (1723–90), and the British economist David Ricardo (1772–1823).
2. Other things being equal.
3. Though generally regarded as a neo-classical economist, Mill here differentiates his position from those who defend a more thoroughgoing version of laissez-faire. See p. 101, n. 6, below.
4. China's prohibition of the importation of opium by the British in 1834 led to the so-called Opium War with Britain, and then to the Tientsin Treaty of 1858, which compromised the conflict by giving China the right to establish a duty on the importation.

One of these examples, that of the sale of poisons,[5] opens a new question; the proper limits of what may be called the functions of police; how far liberty may legitimately be invaded for the prevention of crime, or of accident. It is one of the undisputed functions of government to take precautions against crime before it has been committed, as well as to detect and punish it afterwards. The preventive function of government, however, is far more liable to be abused, to the prejudice of liberty, than the punitory function; for there is hardly any part of the legitimate freedom of action of a human being which would not admit of being represented, and fairly too, as increasing the facilities for some form or other of delinquency. Nevertheless, if a public authority, or even a private person, sees any one evidently preparing to commit a crime, they are not bound to look on inactive until the crime is committed, but may interfere to prevent it. If poisons were never bought or used for any purpose except the commission of murder, it would be right to prohibit their manufacture and sale. They may, however, be wanted not only for innocent but for useful purposes, and restrictions cannot be imposed in the one case without operating in the other. Again, it is a proper office of public authority to guard against accidents. If either a public officer or any one else saw a person attempting to cross a bridge which had been ascertained to be unsafe, and there were no time to warn him of his danger, they might seize him and turn him back, without any real infringement of his liberty; for liberty consists in doing what one desires, and he does not desire to fall into the river.[6] Nevertheless, when there is not a certainty, but only a danger of mischief, no one but the person himself can judge of the sufficiency of the motive which may prompt him to incur the risk: in this case, therefore (unless he is a child, or delirious, or in some state of excitement or absorption incompatible with the full use of the reflecting faculty), he ought, I conceive, to be only warned of the danger; not forcibly prevented from exposing himself to it. Similar considerations, applied to such a question as the sale of poisons, may enable us to decide which among the possible modes of regulation are or are not contrary to principle. Such a precaution, for example, as that of labelling the drug with some word expressive of its dangerous character, may be enforced without violation of liberty: the buyer cannot wish not to

5. This particular application of Mill's principles has occasioned considerable debate, most recently in connection with the use of drugs for other than medicinal purposes, especially by the young.
6. This example has received great attention in the literature because it seems to entail Mill's acceptance of the Idealist distinction between the real and the actual will, i.e., between what one ought to desire (what he "really" wills) and what he says (at the moment, unreflectively) he desires. So Bernard Bosanquet, *The Philosophical Theory of the State*, 4th ed. (London, 1923), pp. 64–65. For an objection to this interpretation, see Spitz, "Freedom and Individuality: Mill's *Liberty* in Retrospect," pp. 210–15.

know that the thing he possesses has poisonous qualities. But to require in all cases the certificate of a medical practitioner would make it sometimes impossible, always expensive, to obtain the article for legitimate uses. The only mode apparent to me, in which difficulties may be thrown in the way of crime committed through this means, without any infringement worth taking into account upon the liberty of those who desire the poisonous substance for other purposes, consists in providing what, in the apt language of Bentham,[7] is called "pre-appointed evidence." This provision is familiar to every one in the case of contracts. It is usual and right that the law, when a contract is entered into, should require as the condition of its enforcing performance, that certain formalities should be observed, such as signatures, attestation of witnesses, and the like, in order that in case of subsequent dispute there may be evidence to prove that the contract was really entered into, and that there was nothing in the circumstances to render it legally invalid: the effect being to throw great obstacles in the way of fictitious contracts, or contracts made in circumstances which, if known, would destroy their validity. Precautions of a similar nature might be enforced in the sale of articles adapted to be instruments of crime. The seller, for example, might be required to enter in a register the exact time of the transaction, the name and address of the buyer, the precise quality and quantity sold; to ask the purpose for which it was wanted, and record the answer he received. When there was no medical prescription, the presence of some third person might be required to bring home the fact to the purchaser, in case there should afterwards be reason to believe that the article had been applied to criminal purposes. Such regulations would in general be no material impediment to obtaining the article, but a very considerable one to making an improper use of it without detection.

The right inherent in society, to ward off crimes against itself by antecedent precautions, suggests the obvious limitations to the maxim, that purely self-regarding misconduct cannot properly be meddled with in the way of prevention or punishment. Drunkenness, for example, in ordinary cases, is not a fit subject for legislative interference; but I should deem it perfectly legitimate that a person, who had once been convicted of any act of violence to others under the influence of drink, should be placed under a special legal restriction, personal to himself; that if he were afterwards found drunk, he should be liable to a penalty, and that if when in that state he committed another offence, the punishment to which he would be liable for that other offence should be increased in severity. The making himself drunk, in a person whom drunkenness excites to do

---

7. British utilitarian, philosopher, and reformer. Mill was for many years Bentham's student and disciple.

harm to others, is a crime against others. So, again, idleness, except in a person receiving support from the public, or except when it constitutes a breach of contract, cannot without tyranny be made a subject of legal punishment; but if, either from idleness or from any other avoidable cause, a man fails to perform his legal duties to others, as for instance to support his children, it is no tyranny to force him to fulfil that obligation, by compulsory labour, if no other means are available.

Again, there are many acts which, being directly injurious only to the agents themselves, ought not to be legally interdicted, but which, if done publicly, are a violation of good manners, and coming thus within the category of offences against others, may rightly be prohibited. Of this kind are offences against decency; on which it is unnecessary to dwell, the rather as they are only connected indirectly with our subject, the objection to publicity being equally strong in the case of many actions not in themselves condemnable, nor supposed to be so.

There is another question to which an answer must be found, consistent with the principles which have been laid down. In cases of personal conduct supposed to be blameable, but which respect for liberty precludes society from preventing or punishing, because the evil directly resulting falls wholly on the agent; what the agent is free to do, ought other persons to be equally free to counsel or instigate? This question is not free from difficulty. The case of a person who solicits another to do an act is not strictly a case of self-regarding conduct. To give advice or offer inducements to any one is a social act, and may, therefore, like actions in general which affect others, be supposed amenable to social control. But a little reflection corrects the first impression, by showing that if the case is not strictly within the definition of individual liberty, yet the reasons on which the principle of individual liberty is grounded are applicable to it. If people must be allowed, in whatever concerns only themselves, to act as seems best to themselves, at their own peril, they must equally be free to consult with one another about what is fit to be so done; to exchange opinions, and give and receive suggestions. Whatever it is permitted to do, it must be permitted to advise to do. The question is doubtful only when the instigator derives a personal benefit from his advice; when he makes it his occupation, for subsistence or pecuniary gain, to promote what society and the State consider to be an evil. Then, indeed, a new element of complication is introduced; namely, the existence of classes of persons with an interest opposed to what is considered as the public weal, and whose mode of living is grounded on the counteraction of it. Ought this to be interfered with, or not? Fornication, for example, must be tolerated, and so must gambling; but should a person be free to be a pimp, or to keep a gambling-house? The case is one of those which lie on the exact boundary line between two principles, and it is not at once apparent to which of the two it properly belongs. There are arguments on both sides. On the side of toleration it may be said that the fact of following anything as an occupation, and living or profiting by the practice of it, cannot make that criminal which would otherwise be admissible; that the act should either be consistently permitted or consistently prohibited; that if the principles which we have hitherto defended are true, society has no business, *as* society, to decide anything to be wrong which concerns only the individual; that it cannot go beyond dissuasion, and that one person should be as free to persuade as another to dissuade. In opposition to this it may be contended, that although the public, or the State, are not warranted in authoritatively deciding, for purposes of repression or punishment, that such or such conduct affecting only the interests of the individual is good or bad, they are fully justified in assuming, if they regard it as bad, that its being so or not is at least a disputable question: That, this being supposed, they cannot be acting wrongly in endeavouring to exclude the influence of solicitations which are not disinterested, of instigators who cannot possibly be impartial—who have a direct personal interest on one side, and that side the one which the State believes to be wrong, and who confessedly promote it for personal objects only. There can surely, it may be urged, be nothing lost, no sacrifice of good, by so ordering matters that persons shall make their election, either wisely or foolishly, on their own prompting, as free as possible from the arts of persons who stimulate their inclinations for interested purposes of their own. Thus (it may be said) though the statutes respecting unlawful games are utterly indefensible —though all persons should be free to gamble in their own or each other's houses, or in any place of meeting established by their own subscriptions, and open only to the members and their visitors—yet public gambling-houses should not be permitted. It is true that the prohibition is never effectual, and that whatever amount of tyrannical power may be given to the police, gambling-houses can always be maintained under other pretences; but they may be compelled to conduct their operations with a certain degree of secrecy and mystery, so that nobody knows anything about them but those who seek them; and more than this society ought not to aim at. There is considerable force in these arguments. I will not venture to decide whether they are sufficient to justify the moral anomaly of punishing the accessary, when the principal is (and must be) allowed to go free; of fining or imprisoning the procurer, but not the fornicator—the gambling-house keeper, but not the gambler. Still less ought the common operations of buying and selling to be interfered with on analogous grounds. Almost every article which is bought and sold may be used in excess, and the sellers have a pecuniary interest in encouraging that excess; but no argument can be founded on this, in favour, for instance, of the Maine Law; because the class of dealers in strong drinks, though interested in their abuse, are indispensably required for the sake of their legitimate use. The interest, however, of these dealers in promoting intemperance is a real evil, and justifies the State in imposing restrictions and requiring guarantees which, but for that justification, would be infringements of legitimate liberty.

A further question is, whether the State, while it permits, should nevertheless indirectly discourage conduct which it deems contrary to the best interests of the agent; whether, for example, it should take measures to render the means of drunkenness more costly, or add to the difficulty of procuring them by limiting the number of the places of sale. On this as on most other practical questions, many distinctions require to be made. To tax stimulants for the sole purpose of making them more difficult to be obtained, is a measure differing only in degree from their entire prohibition; and would be justifiable only if that were justifiable. Every increase of cost is a prohibition, to those whose means do not come up to the augmented price; and to those who do, it is a penalty laid on them for gratifying a particular taste. Their choice of pleasures, and their mode of expending their income, after satisfying their legal and moral obligations to the State and to individuals, are their own concern, and must rest with their own judgment. These considerations may seem at first sight to condemn the selection of stimulants as special subjects of taxation for the purposes of revenue. But it must be remembered that taxation for fiscal purposes is absolutely inevitable; that in most countries it is necessary that a considerable part of that taxation should be indirect; that the State, therefore, cannot help imposing penalties, which to some persons may be prohibitory, on the use of some articles of consumption. It is hence the duty of the State to consider, in the imposition of taxes, what commodities the consumers can best spare; and *à fortiori*,[8] to select in preference those of which it deems the use, beyond a very moderate quantity, to be positively injurious. Taxation, therefore, of stimulants, up to the point which produces the largest amount of revenue (supposing that the State needs all the revenue which it yields) is not only admissible, but to be approved of.

The question of making the sale of these commodities a more or less exclusive privilege, must be answered differently, according to the purposes to which the restriction is intended to be subservient.

---

8. With stronger reason, still more conclusively.

All places of public resort require the restraint of a police, and places of this kind peculiarly, because offences against society are especially apt to originate there. It is, therefore, fit to confine the power of selling these commodities (at least for consumption on the spot) to persons of known or vouched-for respectability of conduct; to make such regulations respecting hours of opening and closing as may be requisite for public surveillance, and to withdraw the licence if breaches of the peace repeatedly take place through the conniv- ance or incapacity of the keeper of the house, or if it becomes a ren- dezvous for concocting and preparing offences against the law. Any further restriction I do not conceive to be, in principle, justifiable. The limitation in number, for instance, of beer and spirit houses, for the express purpose of rendering them more difficult of access, and diminishing the occasions of temptation, not only exposes all to an inconvenience because there are some by whom the facility would be abused, but is suited only to a state of society in which the labouring classes are avowedly treated as children or savages, and placed under an education of restraint, to fit them for future admission to the privileges of freedom. This is not the principle on which the labouring classes are professedly governed in any free country; and no person who sets due value on freedom will give his adhesion to their being so governed, unless after all efforts have been exhausted to educate them for freedom and govern them as freemen, and it has been definitively proved that they can only be governed as children. The bare statement of the alternative shows the absurdity of supposing that such efforts have been made in any case which needs be considered here. It is only because the institu- tions of this country are a mass of inconsistencies, that things find admittance into our practice which belong to the system of des- potic, or what is called paternal, government, while the general free- dom of our institutions precludes the exercise of the amount of con- trol necessary to render the restraint of any real efficacy as a moral education.

It was pointed out in an early part of this Essay, that the liberty of the individual, in things wherein the individual is alone con- cerned, implies a corresponding liberty in any number of individuals to regulate by mutual agreement such things as regard them jointly, and regard no persons but themselves. This question presents no difficulty, so long as the will of all the persons implicated remains unaltered; but since that will may change, it is often necessary, even in things in which they alone are concerned, that they should enter into engagements with one another; and when they do, it is fit, as a general rule, that those engagements should be kept. Yet, in the laws, probably, of every country, this general rule has some excep- tions. Not only persons are not held to engagements which violate the rights of third parties, but it is sometimes considered a sufficient reason for releasing them from an engagement, that it is injurious to themselves. In this and most other civilised countries, for example, an engagement by which a person should sell himself, or allow himself to be sold, as a slave, would be null and void; neither enforced by law nor by opinion.[9] The ground for thus limiting his power of voluntarily disposing of his own lot in life, is apparent, and is very clearly seen in this extreme case. The reason for not interfering, unless for the sake of others, with a person's voluntary acts, is consideration for his liberty. His voluntary choice is evidence that what he so chooses is desirable, or at least endurable, to him, and his good is on the whole best provided for by allowing him to take his own means of pursuing it. But by selling himself for a slave, he abdicates his liberty; he foregoes any future use of it beyond that single act. He therefore defeats, in his own case, the very purpose which is the justification of allowing him to dispose of himself. He is no longer free; but is thenceforth in a position which has no longer the presumption in its favour, that would be afforded by his voluntarily remaining in it. The principle of freedom cannot require that he should be free not to be free. It is not freedom to be allowed to alienate his freedom. These reasons, the force of which is so conspicuous in this peculiar case, are evidently of far wider application; yet a limit is everywhere set to them by the necessities of life, which continually require, not indeed that we should resign our freedom, but that we should consent to this and the other limitation of it. The principle, however, which demands uncontrolled freedom of action in all that concerns only the agents themselves, requires that those who have become bound to one another, in things which concern no third party, should be able to release one another from the engagement: and even without such voluntary release there are perhaps no contracts or engagements, except those that relate to money or money's worth, of which one can venture to say that there ought to be no liberty whatever of retractation.[1] Baron Wilhelm von Humboldt, in the excellent essay from which I have already quoted, states it as his conviction, that engagements which involve personal relations or services should never be legally binding beyond a limited duration of time; and that the most important of these engagements, marriage, having the peculiarity that its objects are frustrated unless the feelings of both the parties are in harmony with it, should require nothing more than the declared will of either party to dissolve it. This subject is too impor-

9. The example of slavery has generated much controversy. See, for example, Bosanquet, *op. cit.*, pp. 64–65, 110–11. For Mill's earlier comments on the invalidity of such a contract, see his *Principles of Political Economy, Collected Works*, 3:801–2, 953–54.

1. Generally, retraction, i.e., withdrawal from an engagement or promise.

tant, and too complicated, to be dicussed in a parenthesis, and I touch on it only so far as is necessary for purposes of illustration. If the conciseness and generality of Baron Humboldt's dissertation had not obliged him in this instance to content himself with enunciating his conclusion without discussing the premises, he would doubtless have recognised that the question cannot be decided on grounds so simple as those to which he confines himself. When a person, either by express promise or by conduct, has encouraged another to rely upon his continuing to act in a certain way—to build expectations and calculations, and stake any part of his plan of life upon that supposition—a new series of moral obligations arises on his part towards that person, which may possibly be overruled, but cannot be ignored. And again, if the relation between two contracting parties has been followed by consequences to others; if it has placed third parties in any peculiar position, or, as in the case of marriage, has even called third parties into existence, obligations arise on the part of both the contracting parties towards those third persons, the fulfilment of which, or at all events the mode of fulfilment, must be greatly affected by the continuance or disruption of the relation between the original parties to the contract. It does not follow, nor can I admit, that these obligations extend to requiring the fulfilment of the contract at all costs to the happiness of the reluctant party; but they are a necessary element in the question; and even if, as Von Humboldt maintains, they ought to make no difference in the *legal* freedom of the parties to release themselves from the engagement (and I also hold that they ought not to make *much* difference), they necessarily make a great difference in the *moral* freedom. A person is bound to take all these circumstances into account before resolving on a step which may affect such important interests of others; and if he does not allow proper weight to those interests, he is morally responsible for the wrong. I have made these obvious remarks for the better illustration of the general principle of liberty, and not because they are at all needed on the particular question, which, on the contrary, is usually discussed as if the interest of children was everything, and that of grown persons nothing.

I have already observed that, owing to the absence of any recognised general principles, liberty is often granted where it should be withheld, as well as withheld where it should be granted; and one of the cases in which, in the modern European world, the sentiment of liberty is the strongest, is a case where in my view, it is altogether misplaced. A person should be free to do as he likes in his own concerns; but he ought not to be free to do as he likes in acting for another, under the pretext that the affairs of the other are his own affairs. The State, while it respects the liberty of each in what specially regards himself, is bound to maintain a vigilant control over his exercise of any power which it allows him to possess over others. This obligation is almost entirely disregarded in the case of the family relations, a case, in its direct influence on human happiness, more important than all others taken together. The almost despotic power of husbands over wives needs not be enlarged upon here, because nothing more is needed for the complete removal of the evil than that wives should have the same rights, and should receive the protection of law in the same manner, as all other persons; and because, on this subject, the defenders of established injustice do not avail themselves of the plea of liberty, but stand forth openly as the champions of power.[2] It is in the case of children that misapplied notions of liberty are a real obstacle to the fulfilment by the State of its duties. One would almost think that a man's children were supposed to be literally, and not metaphorically, a part of himself, so jealous is opinion of the smallest interference of law with his absolute and exclusive control over them; more jealous than of almost any interference with his own freedom of action: so much less do the generality of mankind value liberty than power. Consider, for example, the case of education. Is it not almost a self-evident axiom, that the State should require and compel the education, up to a certain standard, of every human being who is born its citizen? Yet who is there that is not afraid to recognise and assert this truth? Hardly any one indeed will deny that it is one of the most sacred duties of the parents (or, as law and usage now stand, the father), after summoning a human being into the world, to give to that being an education fitting him to perform his part well in life towards others and towards himself. But while this is unanimously declared to be the father's duty, scarcely anybody, in this country, will bear to hear of obliging him to perform it. Instead of his being required to make any exertion or sacrifice for securing education to his child, it is left to his choice to accept it or not when it is provided gratis! It still remains unrecognised, that to bring a child into existence without a fair prospect of being able, not only to provide food for its body, but instruction and training for its mind, is a moral crime, both against the unfortunate offspring and against society; and that if the parent does not fulfil this obligation, the State ought to see it fulfilled, at the charge, as far as possible, of the parent.

Were the duty of enforcing universal education once admitted

2. Mill was throughout his life a champion of the emancipation of women. He may well have been the first legislator in modern times to have proposed in Parliament (in 1867) the extension of the suffrage to women—by moving to replace the word "man" by the word "person" in the debate on the Reform Bill—a proposal then greeted by ridicule. See, among his many writings on this theme, the essay *The Subjection of Women* (1869).

there would be an end to the difficulties about what the State should teach, and how it should teach, which now convert the subject into a mere battlefield for sects and parties, causing the time and labour which should have been spent in educating, to be wasted in quarrelling about education. If the government would make up its mind to require for every child a good education, it might save itself the trouble of providing one.[3] It might leave to parents to obtain the education where and how they pleased, and content itself with helping to pay the school fees of the poorer classes of children, and defraying the entire school expenses of those who have no one else to pay for them. The objections which are urged with reason against State education do not apply to the enforcement of education by the State, but to the State's taking upon itself to direct that education; which is a totally different thing. That the whole or any large part of the education of the people should be in State hands, I go as far as any one in deprecating. All that has been said of the importance of individuality of character, and diversity in opinions and modes of conduct, involves, as of the same unspeakable importance, diversity of education. A general State education is a mere contrivance for moulding people to be exactly like one another: and as the mould in which it casts them is that which pleases the predominant power in the government, whether this be a monarch, a priesthood, an aristocracy, or the majority of the existing generation; in proportion as it is efficient and successful, it establishes a despotism over the mind, leading by natural tendency to one over the body. An education established and controlled by the State should only exist, if it exist at all, as one among many competing experiments, carried on for the purpose of example and stimulus, to keep the others up to a certain standard of excellence. Unless, indeed, when society in general is in so backward a state that it could not or would not provide for itself any proper institutions of education unless the government undertook the task: then, indeed, the government may, as the less of two great evils, take upon itself the business of schools and universities, as it may that of joint stock companies, when private enterprise, in a shape fitted for undertaking great works of industry, does not exist in the country. But in general, if the country contains a sufficient number of persons qualified to provide education under government auspices, the same persons would be able and willing to give an equally good education on the voluntary principle, under the assurance of remuneration afforded by a law rendering educa-

3. This sentence has been taken by some of Mill's critics (e.g., Bosanquet, *op. cit.*, p. 63) to imply that Mill opposed state support of and provision for education. The full text of the passages here, as well as Mill's statements on the subject elsewhere (see, for example, his *Principles of Political Economy*), suggest a contrary reading.

tion compulsory, combined with State aid to those unable to defray the expense.

The instrument for enforcing the law could be no other than public examinations, extending to all children, and beginning at an early age. An age might be fixed at which every child must be examined, to ascertain if he (or she) is able to read. If a child proves unable, the father, unless he has some sufficient ground of excuse, might be subjected to a moderate fine, to be worked out, if necessary, by his labour, and the child might be put to school at his expense. Once in every year the examination should be renewed, with a gradually extending range of subjects, so as to make the universal acquisition, and what is more, retention, of a certain minimum of general knowledge virtually compulsory. Beyond that minimum there should be voluntary examinations on all subjects, at which all who come up to a certain standard of proficiency might claim a certificate. To prevent the State from exercising, through these arrangements, an improper influence over opinion, the knowledge required for passing an examination (beyond the merely instrumental parts of knowledge, such as languages and their use) should, even in the higher classes of examinations, be confined to facts and positive science exclusively. The examinations on religion, politics, or other disputed topics, should not turn on the truth or falsehood of opinions, but on the matter of fact that such and such an opinion is held, on such grounds, by such authors, or schools, or churches. Under this system, the rising generation would be no worse off in regard to all disputed truths than they are at present; they would be brought up either churchmen or dissenters as they now are, the State merely taking care that they should be instructed churchmen, or instructed dissenters. There would be nothing to hinder them from being taught religion, if their parents chose, at the same schools where they were taught other things. All attempts by the State to bias the conclusions of its citizens on disputed subjects are evil; but it may very properly offer to ascertain and certify that a person possesses the knowledge requisite to make his conclusions, on any given subject, worth attending to. A student of philosophy would be the better for being able to stand an examination both in Locke and in Kant,[4] whichever of the two he takes up with, or even if with neither: and there is no reasonable objecton to examining an atheist in the evidences of Christianity, provided he is not required to profess a belief in them. The examinations, however, in the higher branches of knowledge should, I conceive, be entirely voluntary. It would be giving too dangerous a power to gov-

4. The polarity here is between two schools of philosophical thought: British empiricism, represented by John Locke, and German idealism, represented by Immanuel Kant.

ernments were they allowed to exclude any one from professions, even from the profession of teacher, for alleged deficiency of qualifications: and I think, with Wilhelm von Humboldt, that degrees, or other public certificates of scientific or professional acquirements, should be given to all who present themselves for examination, and stand the test; but that such certificates should confer no advantage over competitors other than the weight which may be attached to their testimony by public opinion.

It is not in the matter of education only that misplaced notions of liberty prevent moral obligations on the part of parents from being recognised, and legal obligations from being imposed, where there are the strongest grounds for the former always, and in many cases for the latter also. The fact itself, of causing the existence of a human being, is one of the most responsible actions in the range of human life. To undertake this responsibility—to bestow a life which may be either a curse or a blessing—unless the being on whom it is to be bestowed will have at least the ordinary chances of a desirable existence, is a crime against that being. And in a country either over-peopled, or threatened with being so, to produce children, beyond a very small number, with the effect of reducing the reward of labour by their competition, is a serious offence against all who live by the remuneration of their labour. The laws which, in many countries on the Continent, forbid marriage unless the parties can show that they have the means of supporting a family, do not exceed the legitimate powers of the State: and whether such laws be expedient or not (a question mainly dependent on local circumstances and feelings), they are not objectionable as violations of liberty. Such laws are interferences of the State to prohibit a mischievous act—an act injurious to others, which ought to be a subject of reprobation, and social stigma, even when it is not deemed expedient to superadd legal punishment.[5] Yet the current ideas of liberty, which bend so easily to real infringements of the freedom of the individual in things which concern only himself, would repel the attempt to put any restraint upon his inclinations when the consequence of their indulgence is a life or lives of wretchedness and depravity to the offspring, with manifold evils to those sufficiently within reach to be in any way affected by their actions. When we compare the strange respect of mankind for liberty, with their

5. Mill held strong views against the bearing of children who could not be adequately fed and educated. As a young man he was arrested and perhaps held in jail for a day or two on a charge of distributing obscene literature, by a Lord Mayor who (he later said) was unable to discriminate between an attempt to prevent infanticide and the promotion of obscenity. This little known incident is recounted in Packe, *op. cit.*, pp. 56–59. See, further, Mill's discussion of the problem, and of laws and customs in various countries restraining marriage and population, in his *Principles of Political Economy, Collected Works,* 2:346–54.

strange want of respect for it, we might imagine that a man had an indispensable right to do harm to others, and no right at all to please himself without giving pain to any one.

I have reserved for the last place a large class of questions respecting the limits of government interference, which, though closely connected with the subject of this Essay, do not, in strictness, belong to it. These are cases in which the reasons against interference do not turn upon the principle of liberty: the question is not about restraining the actions of individuals, but about helping them; it is asked whether the government should do, or cause to be done, something for their benefit, instead of leaving it to be done by themselves, individually or in voluntary combination.[6]

The objection to government interference, when it is not such as to involve infringement of liberty, may be of three kinds.

The first is, when the thing to be done is likely to be better done by individuals than by the government. Speaking generally, there is no one so fit to conduct any business, or to determine how or by whom it shall be conducted, as those who are personally interested in it. This principle condemns the interferences, once so common, of the legislature, or the officers of government, with the ordinary processes of industry. But this part of the subject has been sufficiently enlarged upon by political economists, and is not particularly related to the principles of this Essay.

The second objection is more nearly allied to our subject. In many cases, though individuals may not do the particular thing so well, on the average, as the officers of government, it is nevertheless desirable that it should be done by them, rather than by the government, as a means to their own mental education—a mode of strengthening their active faculties, exercising their judgment, and giving them a familiar knowledge of the subjects with which they are thus left to deal. This is a principal, though not the sole, recommendation of jury trial (in cases not political); of free and popular local and municipal institutions; of the conduct of industrial and philanthropic enterprises by voluntary associations. These are not questions of liberty, and are connected with that subject only by remote tendencies; but they are questions of development. It belongs to a different occasion from the present to dwell on these things as parts of national education; as being, in truth, the peculiar training of a citizen, the practical part of the political education of a free people, taking them out of the narrow circle of personal and family selfishness, and accustoming them to the comprehension of joint interests, the management of joint concerns—habituating them to act from public or semi-public motives, and guide their

---

6. Mill discusses the proper role and influence of government interference more fully in his *Principles of Political Economy*, Book 5, chaps. 10–11.

conduct by aims which unite instead of isolating them from one another. Without these habits and powers, a free constitution can neither be worked nor preserved;[7] as is exemplified by the too-often transitory nature of political freedom in countries where it does not rest upon a sufficient basis of local liberties. The management of purely local business by the localities, and of the great enterprises of industry by the union of those who voluntarily supply the pecuniary means, is further recommended by all the advantages which have been set forth in this Essay as belonging to individuality of development, and diversity of modes of action. Government operations tend to be everywhere alike. With individuals and voluntary associations, on the contrary, there are varied experiments, and endless diversity of experience. What the State can usefully do is to make itself a central depository, and active circulator and diffuser, of the experience resulting from many trials. Its business is to enable each experimentalist to benefit by the experiments of others; instead of tolerating no experiments but its own.

The third and most cogent reason for restricting the interference of government is the great evil of adding unnecessarily to its power. Every function superadded to those already exercised by the government causes its influence over hopes and fears to be more widely diffused, and converts, more and more, the active and ambitious part of the public into hangers-on of the government, or of some party which aims at becoming the government. If the roads, the railways, the banks, the insurance offices, the great joint-stock companies, the universities, and the public charities, were all of them branches of the government; if, in addition, the municipal corporations and local boards, with all that now devolves on them, became departments of the central administration; if the employés[8] of all these different enterprises were appointed and paid by the government, and looked to the government for every rise in life; not all the freedom of the press and popular constitution of the legislature would make this or any other country free otherwise than in name. And the evil would be greater, the more efficiently and scientifically the administrative machinery was constructed—the more skilful the arrangements for obtaining the best qualified hands and heads with which to work it. In England it has of late been proposed that all the members of the civil service of government should be selected by competitive examination, to obtain for these employments the most intelligent and instructed persons procurable; and much has been said and written for and against this proposal. One of the arguments most insisted on by its opponents is that the occupation of a permanent official servant of the State does not hold out sufficient prospects of emolument and importance to attract the

7. Mill develops this theme at greater length in his *Representative Government*, especially chaps. 1–6.

8. Employees.

highest talents, which will always be able to find a more inviting career in the professions, or in the service of companies and other public bodies. One would not have been surprised if this argument had been used by the friends of the proposition, as an answer to its principal difficulty. Coming from the opponents it is strange enough. What is urged as an objection is the safety-valve of the proposed system. If indeed all the high talent of the country *could* be drawn into the service of the government, a proposal tending to bring about that result might well inspire uneasiness. If every part of the business of society which required organised concert, or large and comprehensive views, were in the hands of the government, and if government offices were universally filled by the ablest men, all the enlarged culture and practised intelligence in the country, except the purely speculative, would be concentrated in a numerous bureaucracy, to whom alone the rest of the community would look for all things: the multitude for direction and dictation in all they had to do; the able and aspiring for personal advancement. To be admitted into the ranks of this bureaucracy, and when admitted, to rise therein, would be the sole objects of ambition. Under this régime, not only is the outside public ill-qualified, for want of practical experience, to criticise or check the mode of operation of the bureaucracy, but even if the accidents of despotic or the natural working of popular institutions occasionally raise to the summit a ruler or rulers of reforming inclinations, no reform can be effected which is contrary to the interest of the bureaucracy. Such is the melancholy condition of the Russian empire, as shown in the accounts of those who have had sufficient opportunity of observation. The Czar himself is powerless against the bureaucratic body; he can send any one of them to Siberia, but he cannot govern without them, or against their will. On every decree of his they have a tacit veto, by merely refraining from carrying it into effect. In countries of more advanced civilisation and of a more insurrectionary spirit, the public, accustomed to expect everything to be done for them by the State, or at least to do nothing for themselves without asking from the State not only leave to do it, but even how it is to be done, naturally hold the State responsible for all evil which befalls them, and when the evil exceeds their amount of patience, they rise against the government, and make what is called a revolution; whereupon somebody else, with or without legitimate authority from the nation, vaults into the seat, issues his orders to the bureaucracy, and everything goes on much as it did before; the bureaucracy being unchanged, and nobody else being capable of taking their place.

A very different spectacle is exhibited among a people accustomed to transact their own business. In France, a large part of the people, having been engaged in military service, many of whom have held at least the rank of non-commissioned officers, there are in every popular insurrection several persons competent to take the lead, and improvise some tolerable plan of action. What the French are in military affairs, the Americans are in every kind of civil business; let them be left without a government, every body of Americans is able to improvise one, and to carry on that or any other public business with a sufficient amount of intelligence, order, and decision. This is what every free people ought to be: and a people capable of this is certain to be free; it will never let itself be enslaved by any man or body of men because these are able to seize and pull the reins of the central administration. No bureaucracy can hope to make such a people as this do or undergo anything that they do not like. But where everything is done through the bureaucracy, nothing to which the bureaucracy is really adverse can be done at all. The constitution of such countries is an organisation of the experience and practical ability of the nation into a disciplined body for the purpose of governing the rest; and the more perfect that organisation is in itself, the more successful in drawing to itself and educating for itself the persons of greatest capacity from all ranks of the community, the more complete is the bondage of all, the members of the bureaucracy included. For the governors are as much the slaves of their organisation and discipline as the governed are of the governors. A Chinese mandarin[9] is as much the tool and creature of a despotism as the humblest cultivator. An individual Jesuit[1] is to the utmost degree of abasement the slave of his order, though the order itself exists for the collective power and importance of its members.

It is not, also, to be forgotten, that the absorption of all the principal ability of the country into the governing body is fatal, sooner or later, to the mental activity and progressiveness of the body itself. Banded together as they are—working a system which, like all systems, necessarily proceeds in a great measure by fixed rules—the official body are under the constant temptation of sinking into indolent routine, or, if they now and then desert that mill-horse round, of rushing into some half-examined crudity which has struck the fancy of some leading member of the corps; and the sole check to these closely allied, though seemingly opposite, tendencies, the only stimulus which can keep the ability of the body itself up to a high

9. In Chinese, *Kwan*; a member of the educated class; more specifically, any of the nine ranks or grades of public officials in the Chinese Empire.
1. A member of the Society of Jesus, a Roman Catholic order founded by Ignatius Loyola in 1533, to defend the Church against the sixteenth-century Reformers. Its secret power and casuistical principles (maintained by many of its representatives and generally ascribed to the order as a whole) have brought the name into opprobrium in some circles. With respect to the issue of intellectual obedience rather than of trickery, however, it must be borne in mind that the Jesuit constitutions explicitly state that while orders of superiors are always to be obeyed, what is commanded must not be sinful; if sinful, such orders are not, presumably, to be obeyed.

standard, is liability to the watchful criticism of equal ability out-side the body. It is indispensable, therefore, that the means should exist, independently of the government, of forming such ability, and furnishing it with the opportunities and experience necessary for a correct judgment of great practical affairs. If we would possess per-manently a skilful and efficient body of functionaries—above all, a body able to originate and willing to adopt improvements; if we would not have our bureaucracy degenerate into a pedantocracy,[2] this body must not engross all the occupations which form and cul-tivate the faculties required for the government of mankind.

To determine the point at which evils, so formidable to human freedom and advancement, begin, or rather at which they begin to predominate over the benefits attending the collective application of the force of society, under its recognised chiefs, for the removal of the obstacles which stand in the way of its well-being; to secure as much of the advantages of centralised power and intelligence as can be had without turning into governmental channels too great a pro-portion of the general activity—is one of the most difficult and com-plicated questions in the art of government. It is, in a great meas-ure, a question of detail, in which many and various considerations must be kept in view, and no absolute rule can be laid down. But I believe that the practical principle in which safety resides, the ideal to be kept in view, the standard by which to test all arrangements intended for overcoming the difficulty, may be conveyed in these words: the greatest dissemination of power consistent with efficiency; but the greatest possible centralisation of information, and diffusion of it from the centre. Thus, in municipal administra-tion, there would be, as in the New England States, a very minute division among separate officers, chosen by the localities, of all busi-ness which is not better left to the persons directly interested; but besides this, there would be, in each department of local affairs, a central superintendence, forming a branch of the general govern-ment. The organ of this superintendence would concentrate, as in a focus, the variety of information and experience derived from the conduct of that branch of public business in all the localities, from everything analogous which is done in foreign countries, and from the general principles of political science. This central organ should have a right to know all that is done, and its special duty should be that of making the knowledge acquired in one place available for others. Emancipated from the petty prejudices and narrow views of a locality by its elevated position and comprehensive sphere of obser-vation, its advice would naturally carry much authority; but its actual power, as a permanent institution, should, I conceive, be lim-ited to compelling the local officers to obey the laws laid down for

2. A system of government by pedants, i.e., those who have mere learning with-out practical wisdom, who slavishly ad-here to trifling details and formal rules.

their guidance. In all things not provided for by general rules, those officers should be left to their own judgment, under responsibility to their constituents. For the violation of rules, they should be responsible to law, and the rules themselves should be laid down by the legislature; the central administrative authority only watching over their execution, and if they were not properly carried into effect, appealing, according to the nature of the case, to the tribunals to enforce the law, or to the constituencies to dismiss the functionaries who had not executed it according to its spirit. Such, in its general conception, is the central superintendence which the Poor Law Board[3] is intended to exercise over the administrators of the Poor Rate throughout the country. Whatever powers the Board exercises beyond this limit, were right and necessary in that peculiar case, for the cure of rooted habits of maladministration in matters deeply affecting not the localities merely, but the whole community; since no locality has a moral right to make itself by mismanagement a nest of pauperism, necessarily overflowing into other localities, and impairing the moral and physical condition of the whole labouring community. The powers of administrative coercion and subordinate legislation possessed by the Poor Law Board (but which, owing to the state of opinion on the subject, are very scantily exercised by them), though perfectly justifiable in a case of first-rate national interest, would be wholly out of place in the superintendence of interests purely local. But a central organ of information and instruction for all the localities, would be equally valuable in all departments of administration. A government cannot have too much of the kind of activity which does not impede, but aids and stimulates, individual exertion and development. The mischief begins when, instead of calling forth the activity and powers of individuals and bodies, it substitutes its own activity for theirs; when, instead of informing, advising, and, upon occasion, denouncing, it makes them work in fetters, or bids them stand aside and does their work instead of them. The worth of a State, in the long run, is the worth of the individuals composing it; and a State which postpones the interests of *their* mental expansion and elevation, to a little more of administrative skill, or of that semblance of it which practice gives, in the details of business; a State which dwarfs its men, in order that they may be more docile instruments in its hands even for beneficial purposes—will find that with small men no great thing can really be accomplished; and that the perfection of machinery to which it has sacrificed everything, will in the end avail it nothing, for want of the vital power which, in order that the machine might work more smoothly, it has preferred to banish.

---

3. An administrative unit set up under the Poor Law of 1834 to supervise those in charge of local taxes collected for support of the local poor.

Sources and Background

JOHN STUART MILL

[The Writing of "On Liberty"]†

* * * It is in this way that all my books have been composed. They were always written at least twice over; a first draft of the entire work was completed to the very end of the subject, then the whole begun again *de novo*; but incorporating, in the second writing, all sentences and parts of sentences of the old draft, which appeared as suitable to my purpose as anything which I could write in lieu of them. I have found great advantages in this system of double redaction. It combines, better than any other mode of composition, the freshness and vigour of the first conception, with the superior precision and completeness resulting from prolonged thought. In my own case, moreover, I have found that the patience necessary for a careful elaboration of the details of composition and expression, costs much less effort after the entire subject has been once gone through, and the substance of all that I find to say has in some manner, however imperfect, been got upon paper. The only thing which I am careful, in the first draft, to make as perfect as I am able, is the arrangement. If that is bad, the whole thread on which the ideas string themselves becomes twisted; thoughts placed in a wrong connexion are not expounded in a manner that suits the right, and a first draft with this original vice is next to useless as a foundation for the final treatment.

* * *

During the two years which immediately preceded the cessation of my official life, my wife and I were working together at the "Liberty." I had first planned and written it as a short essay in 1854. It was in mounting the steps of the Capitol,[1] in January, 1855, that the thought first arose of converting it into a volume. None of my writings have been either so carefully composed, or so sedulously corrected as this. After it had been written as usual twice over, we kept it by us, bringing it out from time to time, and going through it *de novo*, reading, weighing, and criticizing every sentence. Its final revision was to have been a work of the winter of 1858–9, the first after my retirement, which we had arranged to pass in the South of Europe. That hope and every other were frustrated by the most unexpected and bitter calamity of her death—at Avignon, on our way to Montpellier, from a sudden attack of pulmonary congestion.

†From *The Autobiography of John Stuart Mill* (New York: Columbia University Press, 1924), pp. 155–56, 170–73, 175–80.
1. In Rome.

Since then I have sought for such alleviation as my state admitted of, by the mode of life which most enabled me to feel her still near me. I bought a cottage as close as possible to the place where she is buried, and there her daughter (my fellow-sufferer and now my chief comfort) and I, live constantly during a great portion of the year. My objects in life are solely those which were hers; my pursuits and occupations those in which she shared, or sympathized, and which are indissolubly associated with her. Her memory is to me a religion, and her approbation the standard by which, summing up as it does all worthiness, I endeavour to regulate my life.

In resuming my pen some years after closing the preceding narrative, I am influenced by a desire not to have incomplete the record, for the sake of which chiefly this biographical sketch was undertaken, of the obligations I owe to those who have either contributed essentially to my own mental development or had a direct share in my writings and in whatever else of a public nature I have done. In the preceding pages, this record, so far as it relates to my wife, is not so detailed and precise as it ought to be; and since I lost her, I have had other help, not less deserving and requiring acknowledgment.

When two persons have their thoughts and speculations completely in common; when all subjects of intellectual or moral interest are discussed between them in daily life, and probed to much greater depths than are usually or conveniently sounded in writings intended for general readers; when they set out from the same principles, and arrive at their conclusions by processes pursued jointly, it is of little consequence in respect to the question of originality, which of them holds the pen; the one who contributes least to the composition may contribute most to the thought; the writings which result are the joint product of both, and it must often be impossible to disentangle their respective parts, and affirm that this belongs to one and that to the other. In this wide sense, not only during the years of our married life, but during many of the years of confidential friendship which preceded it, all my published writings were as much my wife's work as mine; her share in them constantly increasing as years advanced. But in certain cases, what belongs to her can be distinguished, and specially identified. Over and above the general influence which her mind had over mine, the most valuable ideas and features in these joint productions—those which have been most fruitful of important results, and have contributed most to the success and reputation of the works themselves—originated with her, were emanations from her mind, my part in them being no greater than in any of the thoughts which I found in previous writers, and made my own only by incorporating them with my own system of thought. During the greater part of my literary life I have performed the office in relation to her, which from a rather early period I had considered as the most useful part that I was qualified to take in the domain of thought, that of an interpreter of original thinkers, and mediator between them and the public; for I had always a humble opinion of my own powers as an original thinker, except in abstract science (logic, metaphysics, and the theoretic principles of political economy and politics), but thought myself much superior to most of my contemporaries in willingness and ability to learn from everybody; as I found hardly any one who made such a point of examining what was said in defence of all opinions, however new or however old, in the conviction that even if they were errors there might be a substratum of truth underneath them, and that in any case the discovery of what it was that made them plausible, would be a benefit to truth. I had, in consequence, marked out this as a sphere of usefulness in which I was under a special obligation to make myself active: the more so, as the acquaintance I had formed with the ideas of the Coleridgians, of the German thinkers, and of Carlyle, all of them fiercely opposed to the mode of thought in which I had been brought up, had convinced me that along with much error they possessed much truth, which was veiled from minds otherwise capable of receiving it by the transcendental and mystical phraseology in which they were accustomed to shut it up, and from which they neither cared, nor knew how, to disengage it; and I did not despair of separating the truth from the error, and expressing it in terms which would be intelligible and not repulsive to those on my own side in philosophy. Thus prepared, it will easily be believed that when I came into close intellectual communion with a person of the most eminent faculties, whose genius, as it grew and unfolded itself in thought, continually struck out truths far in advance of me, but in which I could not, as I had done in those others, detect any mixture of error, the greatest part of my mental growth consisted in the assimilation of those truths, and the most valuable part of my intellectual work was in building the bridges and clearing the paths which connected them with my general system of thought.[2]

* * *

2. [Mill's note] The steps in my mental growth for which I was indebted to her were far from being those which a person wholly uninformed on the subject would probably suspect. It might be supposed, for instance, that my strong convictions on the complete equality in all legal, political, social and domestic relations, which ought to exist between men and women, may have been adopted or learnt from her. This was so far from being the fact, that those convictions were among the earliest results of the application of my mind to political subjects, and the strength with which I held them was, as I believe, more than anything else, the originating cause of the interest she felt in me. What is true is, that until I knew her, the opinion was in my mind, little more than an abstract principle. I saw no more reason why women should be held in legal subjection to other people, than why men should. I was certain that their interests required fully as much protection as those of men, and were quite as little likely to obtain it without an equal voice in making the laws by which they are to be bound. But that perception of the vast practical bearings of women's disabilities

* * * What was abstract and purely scientific was generally mine; the properly human element came from her: in all that concerned the application of philosophy to the exigencies of human society and progress, I was her pupil, alike in boldness of speculation and cautiousness of practical judgment. For, on the one hand, she was much more courageous and far-sighted than without her I should have been, in anticipations of an order of things to come, in which many of the limited generalizations now so often confounded with universal principles will cease to be applicable. Those parts of my writings, and especially of the Political Economy, which contemplate possibilities in the future such as, when affirmed by Socialists, have in general been fiercely denied by political economists, would, but for her, either have been absent, or the suggestions would have been made much more timidly and in a more qualified form. But while she thus rendered me bolder in speculation on human affairs, her practical turn of mind, and her almost unerring estimate of practical obstacles, repressed in me all tendencies that were really visionary. Her mind invested all ideas in a concrete shape, and formed to itself a conception of how they would actually work: and her knowledge of the existing feelings and conduct of mankind was so seldom at fault, that the weak point in any unworkable suggestion seldom escaped her.[3]

The "Liberty" was more directly and literally our joint production than anything else which bears my name, for there was not a sentence of it that was not several times gone through by us together, turned over in many ways, and carefully weeded of any faults, either in thought or expression, that we detected in it. It is in consequence of this that, although it never underwent her final revision, it far surpasses, as a mere specimen of composition, anything which has proceeded from me either before or since. With regard to the thoughts, it is difficult to identify any particular part or element as being more hers than all the rest. The whole mode of thinking of which the book was the expression, was emphatically hers. But I also was so thoroughly imbued with it, that the same

---

which found expression in the book on the "Subjection of Women" was acquired mainly through her teaching. But for her rare knowledge of human nature and comprehension of moral and social influences, though I should doubtless have held my present opinions, I should have had a very insufficient perception of the mode in which the consequences of the inferior position of women intertwine themselves with all the evils of existing society and with all the difficulties of human improvement. I am indeed painfully conscious how much of her best thoughts on the subject I have

failed to reproduce, and how greatly that little treatise falls short of what would have been if she had put on paper her entire mind on this question, or had lived to revise and improve, as she certainly would have done, my imperfect statement of the case.

3. [Mill's note] A few dedicatory lines acknowledging what the book owed to her, were prefixed to some of the presentation copies of the Political Economy on its first publication. Her dislike of publicity alone prevented their insertion in the other copies of the work.

thoughts naturally occurred to us both. That I was thus penetrated with it, however, I owe in a great degree to her. There was a moment in my mental progress when I might easily have fallen into a tendency towards over-government, both social and political; as there was also a moment when, by reaction from a contrary excess, I might have become a less thorough radical and democrat than I am. In both these points, as in many others, she benefited me as much by keeping me right where I was right, as by leading me to new truths, and ridding me of errors. My great readiness and eagerness to learn from everybody, and to make room in my opinions for every new acquisition by adjusting the old and the new to one another, might, but for her steadying influence, have seduced me into modifying my early opinions too much. She was in nothing more valuable to my mental development than by her just measure of the relative importance of different considerations, which often protected me from allowing to truths I had only recently learnt to see, a more important place in my thoughts than was properly their due.

The "Liberty" is likely to survive longer than anything else that I have written (with the possible exception of the "Logic"), because the conjunction of her mind with mine has rendered it a kind of philosophic text-book of a single truth, which the changes progressively taking place in modern society tend to bring out into ever stronger relief: the importance, to man and society, of a large variety in types of character, and of giving full freedom to human nature to expand itself in innumerable and conflicting directions. Nothing can better show how deep are the foundations of this truth, than the great impression made by the exposition of it at a time which, to superficial observation, did not seem to stand much in need of such a lesson. The fears we expressed, lest the inevitable growth of social equality and of the government of public opinion, should impose on mankind an oppressive yoke of uniformity in opinion and practice, might easily have appeared chimerical to those who looked more at present facts than at tendencies; for the gradual revolution that is taking place in society and institutions has, thus far, been decidedly favourable to the development of new opinions, and has procured for them a much more unprejudiced hearing than they previously met with. But this is a feature belonging to periods of transition, when old notions and feelings have been unsettled, and no new doctrines have yet succeeded to their ascendancy. At such times people of any mental activity, having given up many of their old beliefs, and not feeling quite sure that those they still retain can stand unmodified, listen eagerly to new opinions. But this state of things is necessarily transitory: some particular body of doctrine in time rallies the majority round it, organizes social institutions and modes of action conformably to itself, education impresses this new creed upon the new generations without the mental processes that have led to it, and by degrees it acquires the very same power of compression, so long exercised by the creeds of which it had taken the place. Whether this noxious power will be exercised, depends on whether mankind have by that time become aware that it cannot be exercised without stunting and dwarfing human nature. It is then that the teachings of the "Liberty" will have their greatest value. And it is to be feared that they will retain that value a long time.

As regards originality, it has of course no other than that which every thoughtful mind gives to its own mode of conceiving and expressing truths which are common property. The leading thought of the book is one which though in many ages confined to insulated thinkers, mankind have probably at no time since the beginning of civilization been entirely without. To speak only of the last few generations, it is distinctly contained in the vein of important thought respecting education and culture, spread through the European mind by the labours and genius of Pestalozzi. The unqualified championship of it by Wilhelm von Humboldt is referred to in the book; but he by no means stood alone in his own country. During the early part of the present century the doctrine of the rights of individuality, and the claim of the moral nature to develop itself in its own way, was pushed by a whole school of German authors even to exaggeration; and the writings of Goethe, the most celebrated of all German authors, though not belonging to that or to any other school, are penetrated throughout by views of morals and of conduct in life, often in my opinion not defensible, but which are incessantly seeking whatever defence they admit of in the theory of the right and duty of self-development. In our own country, before the book "On Liberty" was written, the doctrine of Individuality had been enthusiastically asserted, in a style of vigorous declamation sometimes reminding one of Fichte, by Mr. William Maccall, in a series of writings of which the most elaborate is entitled "Elements of Individualism:" and a remarkable American, Mr. Warren, had framed a System of Society, on the foundation of "the Sovereignty of the Individual," had obtained a number of followers, and had actually commenced the formation of a Village Community (whether it now exists I know not), which, though bearing a superficial resemblance to some of the projects of Socialists, is diametrically opposite to them in principle, since it recognizes no authority whatever in Society over the individual, except to enforce equal freedom of development for all individualities. As the book which bears my name claimed no originality for any of its doctrines, and was not intended to write their history, the only author who had preceded me in their assertion, of whom I thought it appropriate to say anything, was Humboldt, who furnished the motto to the work; although in one passage I borrowed from the Warrenites their phrase, the sovereignty of the individual. It is hardly necessary here to remark that there are abundant differences in detail, between the conception of the doctrine by any of the predecessors I have mentioned, and that set forth in the book.

After my irreparable loss,[4] one of my earliest cares was to print and publish the treatise, so much of which was the work of her whom I had lost, and consecrate it to her memory. I have made no alteration or addition to it, nor shall I ever. Though it wants the last touch of her hand, no substitute for that touch shall ever be attempted by mine.

HARRIET TAYLOR

[An Early Essay on Toleration]†

More than two hundred years ago, Cecil said 'Tenderness & sympathy are not enough cultivated by any of us; no one is kind enough, gentle enough, forbearing and forgiving enough'. In this two centuries in how many ways have we advanced and improved, yet could the speaker of those words now 'revisit the glimpses of the moon', he would find us but at the point he left us on the ground of toleration: his lovely lament is to the full as applicable now, as it was in the days of the hard-visaged and cold-blooded Puritans. Our faults of uncharitableness have rather changed their objects than their degree. The root of all intolerance, the spirit of conformity, remains; and not until that is destroyed, will envy, hatred and all uncharitableness, with their attendant hypocrisies, be destroyed too. Whether it would be religious conformity, Political conformity, moral conformity or Social conformity, no matter which the species, the spirit is the same: all kinds agree in this one point, of hostility to individual character, and individual character if it exists at all, can rarely declare itself openly while there is, on all topics of importance a standard of conformity raised by the indolent minded many and guarded by a [?] of opinion which, though composed individually of the weakest twigs, yet makes up collectively a mass which is not to be resisted with impunity.

What is called the opinion of Society is a phantom power, yet as is often the case with phantoms, of more force over the minds of

4. Harriet Taylor Mill died at Avignon after a brief illness, November 3, 1858.
† From F. A. Hayek, *John Stuart Mill* *and Harriet Taylor* (Chicago, 1951), pp. 275–79.

the unthinking than all the flesh and blood arguments which can be brought to bear against it. It is a combination of the many weak, against the few strong; an association of the mentally listless to punish any manifestation of mental independance. The remedy is, to make all strong enough to stand alone; and whoever has once known the pleasure of self-dependance, will be in no danger of relapsing into subserviency. Let people once suspect that their leader *is* a phantom, the next step will be, to cease to be led, altogether and each mind guide itself by the light of as much knowledge as it can acquire for itself by means of unbiased experience.

We have always been an aristocracy-ridden people, which may account for the fact of our being so peculiarly a propriety-ridden people. The aim of our life seems to be, not our own happiness, nor the happiness of others unless it happens to come in as an accident of our great endeavour to attain some standard of right or duty erected by some or other of the sets into which society is divided like a net—to catch gudgeons.

Who are the people who talk most about doing their duty? always those who for their life could give no intelligible theory of duty? What are called people of principle, are often the most unprincipled people in the world, if by principle is intended the only useful meaning of the word, accordance of the individual's conduct with the individual's self-formed opinion. Grant this to be the definition of principle, then eccentricity should be prima facie evidence for the existence of principle. So far from this being the case, 'it is odd' therefore it is wrong is the feeling of society; while they whom it distinguishes par excellence as people of principle, are almost invariably the slaves of some dicta or other. They have been taught to think, and accustomed to think, so and so right—others think so and so right—therefore it must be right. This is the logic of the world's good sort of people; and if, as is often the case their right should prove indisputably wrong, they can but plead those good intentions which make a most slippery and uneven pavement.

To all such we would say, think for yourself, and act for yourself, but whether you have strength to do either the one or the other, attempt not to impede, much less to resent the genuine expression of the others.

Were the spirit of toleration abroad, the name of toleration would be unknown. The name implies the existence of its opposites. Toleration can not even rank with those strangely named qualities a 'negative virtue'; while we can be conscious that we tolerate there must remain some vestige of *intolerance*—not being virtuous it is possible also not to be vicious: not so in this—not to be charitable is to be uncharitable. To tolerate is to abstain from unjust interference, a quality which will surely one day not need a place in

any catalogue of virtues. Now, alas, its spirit is not even compre-
hended by many, 'The quality of mercy is strained', and by the education for its opposite which most of us receive becomes if ever it
be attained, a praiseworthy faculty, instead of an unconscious and
almost intuitive state.

'Evil-speaking, lying and slandering' as the catechism formulary
has it, is accounted a bad thing by every one. Yet how many do not
hesitate about the evil-speaking as long as they avoid the lying and
slandering—making what they call Truth a mantle to cover a multitude of injuries. 'Truth must not be spoken at all times' is the
vulgar maxim. We would have the Truth, and if possible all the
Truth, certainly nothing but the Truth said and acted universally.
But we would never lose sight of the important fact that what is
truth to one mind is often not truth to another. That no human
being ever did or ever will comprehend the whole mind of any
other human being. It would perhaps not be possible to find two
minds accustomed to think for themselves whose thoughts on any
identical subject should take in their expression the same form of
words. Who shall say that the very same order of ideas is conveyed
to another mind, by those words which to him perfectly represent
his thought? It is probable that innumerable shades of variety,
modify in each instance, the conception of every expression of
thought; for which variety the imperfections of language offer no
measure, and the differences of organization no proof. To an honest
mind what a lesson of tolerance is included in this knowledge. To
such not a living heart and brain but is like the planet 'whose
worth's unknown although his height *be* taken, and feeling that one
touch of nature makes the whole world kin' finds something that is
admirable in all, and something to interest and respect in each. In
this view we comprehend that

> All thoughts, all creeds, all dreams are true,
> All visions wild and strange—

to those who believe them, for after all we must come to that fine
saying of the poet-philosopher,

> Man is the measure of all Truth
> Unto himself

of the same signification is that thought, as moral as profound,
which has been often in different ways expressed, yet which the universal practice of the world disproves its comprehension of, 'Toute
la moralité de nos actions est dans le jugement que nous en portons
nous-meme'—'dangerous' may exclaim the blind followers of that
sort of conscience, which is the very opposite of consciousness;
would but people give up that sort of conscience which depends on

conforming they would find the judgement of an enlightened consciousness proved by its results the voice of God:

> Our acts our angels are, or good or ill,
> Our fatal shadows that walk by us still

and to make them pleasant companions we must get rid, not only
of error, but of the moral sources from which it springs. As the
study of the mind of others is the only way in which effectually to
improve our own, the endeavour to approximate as nearly as possible towards a complete knowledge of, and sympathy with another
mind, is the spring and the food of all fineness of heart and mind.
There seems to be this great distinction between physical and moral
science: that while the degree of perfection which the first has
attained is marked by the progressive completeness and exactness of
its rules, that of the latter is in the state most favourable to, and
most showing healthfulness as it advances beyond all classification
except on the widest and most universal principles. The science of
morals should rather be called an art: to do something towards its
improvement is in the power of every one, for every one may at
least show truly their own page in the volume of human history,
and be willing to allow that no two pages of it are alike.

Were everyone to seek only the beauty and the good which
might be found in every object, and to pass by defect lightly where
it could not but be evident—if evil would not cease to exist, it
would surely be greatly mitigated, for half the power of outward ill
may be destroyed by inward strength, and half the beauty of outward objects is shown by the light within. The admiring state of
mind is like a refracting surface which while it receives the rays of
light, and is illuminated by them gives back an added spendour; the
critical state is the impassive medium which cannot help
[   ]1 the sun's beams, but can neither transmit nor increase
them. It is indeed much easier to discern the errors and blemishes
of things than their good, for the same reason that we observe more
quickly privation than enjoyment. Suffering is the exception to the
extensive rule of good, and so stands out distinctly and vividly. It
should be remembered by the critically-minded, that the habit of
noting deficiencies before we observe beauties, does really for themselves lessen the amount of the latter.

Whoever notes a fault in the right spirit will surely find some
beauty too. He who appreciates the one is the fittest judge of the
other also. The capability of even serious error, proves the capacity
for proportionate good. For if anything may be called a principle of
nature this seems to be one, that force of any kind has an intuitive
tendency towards good.

---

1. A gap left in the manuscript for one word later to be filled in.

We believe that a child of good physical organization who were never to hear of evil, would not know from its own nature that evil existed in the mental or moral world. We would place before the minds of children no examples but of good and beautiful, and our strongest effort should be, to prevent individual emulation. The spirit of Emulation in childhood and of competition in manhood are the fruitful sources of selfishness and misery. They are a part of the conformity plan, making each persons idea of goodness and happiness a thing of comparison with some received mode of being good and happy. But this is not the Creed of Society, for Society abhors individual character. It asks the sacrifice of body heart and mind. This is the summary of its cardinal virtues: would that such virtues were as nearly extinct as the diginitaries who are their namesakes.

At this present time the subject of social morals is in a state of most lamentable neglect. It is a subject so deeply interesting to all, yet so beset by prejudice, that the mere approach to it is difficult, if not dangerous. Yet there are 'thunders heard afar' by quick senses, and we firmly believe that many years will not pass before the clearest intellects of the time will expound, and the multitude have wisdom to receive reverently the exposition of the great moral paradoxes with which Society is hemmed in on all sides. Meanwhile they do something who in ever so small a circle or in ever so humble a guise, have courage to declare the evil they see.

Criticism

The Case Against Mill

[ANON.]

Mill on Liberty†

Mr. John Stuart Mill's essay on Liberty is a very melancholy book on a great subject. It is written in the sincere foreboding that the strong individualities of the old types of English character are in imminent danger of being swallowed up in those political and social influences which emanate from large masses of men. It might almost, indeed, have come from the prison-cell of some persecuted thinker bent on making one last protest against the growing tyranny of the public mind, though conscious that his appeal will be in vain,—instead of from the pen of a writer who has perhaps exercised more influence over the formation of the philosophical and social principles of cultivated Englishmen than any other man of his generation. While agreeing with Mr. Mill, as most thoughtful politicians must, in some at least of the most important practical conclusions at which he eventually arrives as to the fitting limits of legislative interference, and the proper bounds to the jurisdiction of that secondary tribunal which we call public opinion, we differ from him widely and fundamentally with regard to the leading assumptions from which he starts, and the main principle which he takes with him as his clue in the inquiry. * * * But before we follow him into his political philosophy, we must explain why we think him totally wrong in the most important of his preliminary assumptions.

We differ widely from Mr. Mill as to the *truth* of the painful conviction which has evidently given rise to this essay. We do not for a moment doubt that English "public opinion" is a much more intelligible and homogeneous thing in our own day than it has ever been at any previous time; that it comprehends much fewer conflicting types of thought, much fewer distinctly divergent social tendencies, much less honest and sturdy controversy between diametrical opposites in intellectual theory. Sectarian lines are fading away, political bonds are sundering, even social attractions and repulsions are less marked than they used to be; and to this extent we willingly concede to Mr. Mill that considerable progress is rapidly making towards that universal assimilation of the social conditions of life. * * * But to what do these facts point? Mr. Mill be-

† From *The National Review*, 8 (1859), 393–424.

lieves that they point to an increasing despotism of social and political masses over the moral and intellectual freedom of individuals. To us his conclusion appears singularly hasty, and utterly unsustained by the premises he lays down. If, indeed, Mr. Mill still holds, as many passages in his earlier works would seem to indicate, that there is no such thing as an inherent difference in the original constitution of human minds,—that the varieties in the characters of men are due entirely to the varieties of physical, moral, and social influence to which they are exposed,—then, no doubt, he must argue that the great assimilation of outward circumstances which civilisation necessarily brings, will naturally end in producing a fatal monotony in human character. But * * * we would suggest that any moral monotony which springs exclusively from the assimilation of social conditions is not only inevitable, but a necessary result of social and political *liberty*, instead of a menace to it.

And what *are* the varieties of character which disappear as the process of social assimilation goes on? Surely *not* individual varieties of character,—varieties, that is, proper to the natural development of an individual character; but simply class types,—the varieties due to well-marked sectional groups,—to widely-severed phases of custom,—to the exclusive occupations of separate *castes*,—in short, to some local or social organisation, the sharp boundary of which is gradually becoming softened or altogether dissolved by the blending and fusing influences of civilisation. That this process has been going on very rapidly during the last century, we believe. But so far from holding, with Mr. Mill, that it is a process fatal to the due development of individualities of character, we conceive that it has not contracted, but rather enlarged, the sphere of individual freedom. The country gentleman stands out no longer in that marked contrast to the tradesman or the man of letters which was observable in the days of Sir Robert Walpole; the dissenter is no longer a moral foil to the churchman; and the different shades of English religious opinion can not any more be mapped out as distinctly as the different counties in a map of England. But what individual freedom has any one lost by the fading away of those well-defined local and moral groups? That there has been a loss of social *intensity* of character in consequence, we admit. The exclusive association of people of the same habits of life and thought has no doubt a tendency to intensify the peculiarities thus associated, and to steep the character thoroughly with that one influence, to the exclusion of all others. But this intensification of local, or social, or religious one-sidedness is as far as possible from the development of that individuality of character for which Mr. Mill pleads so eagerly. Rather must the impressed force of such social moulds or stamps have tended to overpower all forms of individual originality which were not consistent with those special moulds or stamps. No doubt if there were any remarkable element of character in the individual which also belongs specially to the group or caste, we might expect that it would be fostered by such association into excessive energy. But any peculiarly individual element of character, on the other hand, would have been in danger of being overwhelmed. And it is therefore mere assumption to say that because there are now fewer striking varieties of type and class than there were in former generations, there is less scope for individual freedom. The very reverse must be the case, unless the assimilated public opinion of a whole nation be supposed to be more minute, more exigent and irritating in its despotism, than the sectarian opinion of small local bodies or social castes.

* * *

But Mr. Mill may perhaps say that there is much more danger of tyranny from the unchecked power of a single homogeneous body of "public opinion" than there is from the local prejudices or conflicting political sects which formerly contended for the mastery. But this depends entirely on the mode in which this body of public opinion is generated,—whether it arise, as in England, from the genuine assimilation of opposite schools of thought, or, as in the United States, from the mere forcible triumph of a single class-creed, which in consequence of democratic institutions, is unhappily able to drown by sheer violence the voice of all higher and more cultivated schools of thought. When people come to think more and more alike, simply because the same influences are extending from class to class, and the same set of reasons recommend themselves to the intellects of moderate men in all classes,—when this is the way in which a "public opinion" is formed, it is obvious that the restraint exercised by such public opinion, gathered up as it is from a *very wide social range*, is far less oppressive than the narrower and intenser type of opinion which pervades a single social class or political sect. In the United States, on the other hand, there has been nothing of this gradual assimilation of the different political convictions of different classes. Knowledge and civilising influences have not been the agents in giving predominance to that tyrannical type of thought which there goes by the name of "public opinion." The despotism of public opinion in America is not due to the gradual disappearance of local types of opinion and sectional habits of mind, and the natural fusion of political creeds which thus results,—but to the complete political victory which a false constitutional system has given to the largest and most ignorant class of the community over all those whose wishes and judgment were entitled to greater weight. A public opinion which is really only a special class-opinion, accidentally enabled to *silence* all higher elements of thought *instead of* assimilating them, is no fair specimen of that assimilation of view which is confessedly due mainly to the freer interchange of thought between class and class. And yet it is a public opinion formed, as he admits, in the latter fashion, which Mr. Mill thinks so much more menacing to individual liberty than those narrower and straiter forms of class-opinion and conviction which preceded it, and have been absorbed into it.

* * * Though we believe that never at any previous time were Englishmen at large so free to think and act as they deem right in all important matters, without even the necessity of rendering any account of their actions to the social circles in which they move,— we believe also that the intensity of character lost in this process is sometimes not counterbalanced by the gain in freedom. Mr. Mill has got into inextricable confusion between the strength or intensity of a well-marked type of character encouraged by every social influence to grow *out* prominently in certain directions,—and that individuality which is simply left at liberty to find and follow out its own perhaps not very defined bent. Massiveness and strong outline in character are certainly less promoted by the *laissez-faire* system Mr. Mill recommends than by the predominance of certain tyrannical and one-sided customs, and motives, and restraints, and schools of thought, in the moral atmosphere by which men are surrounded. Mr. Mill is probably right when he complains that the character of the present age is to be "without any marked character;" but for our parts, instead of ascribing it to that exigeant commonplace with which our author wages so internecine a war, we ascribe it in the main to the exactly opposite cause,—the dissolution of various stringent codes of social opinion and custom, which extended the variety of well-marked types of character *at the expense* of the individuality of those who were subject to their influence. * * *

Holding as we do that Mr. Mill ascribes this dead level of character to a cause nearly the reverse of the true cause, it is not surprising that we differ from him still more widely when he suggests his remedy. Mr. Mill sees no means of stimulating the individual mind to assert its own right to rebel against the tyrannous desire of average men "that all other people shall resemble" themselves. And so he sets himself to persuade average men that, whether with regard to their influence over legislation, or with regard to their share in forming the public opinion of the day, they must steadily resist the temptation of interfering at all to regulate the standard of individual morality, except so far as it touches social rights. This is the one object of his essay. It is not at present half so important, he says, to purify the public conscience, as to break down once and for ever its right to intrude its impressions on individuals. * * * He is so anxious to secure free action for human individualities, that he would interdict the "public mind" from expressing any opinion at all on some of the gravest topics that can be submitted to human discussion. He would, in short, emasculate public opinion, in order to remove one principal stumbling-block in the way of those who tremble to assert their own individual convictions in the face of that terrible tribunal.

Now we are far from denying that the power of public opinion is often a real and painful stumbling-block to men in the discharge of their duty. It is often hasty, and often ignorant, and often cruel. It sometimes crushes the weak, while it spares altogether the strong and the shameless. It continually "judges according to appearance and not righteous judgment." Its standard is conventional, and is yet generally applied with most rigour where it is, in fact, inapplicable altogether. All this is true, but is certainly no truer of that section of public opinion which regards individual duty than of that which regards social duty; and the remedy does not lie in the artificial proposal to warn Government and Society off the former field altogether. This, however, is exactly the position which Mr. Mill has written his book to defend. * * * His essay is an inquiry into the "nature and limits of the power which can be legitimately exercised by society over the individual;" and he does not confine it to investigating the legitimate degree of *State* interference, but, assuming that the principle on which society may claim to interfere with individual self-government by the infliction of social penalties is identical in kind, though not necessarily equally applicable in all cases, with that which warrants legislative interference, he makes it his object to establish that "the sole end for which mankind are warranted, individually or collectively, in interfering with the liberty of action of any of their number is self-protection," or "to prevent harm to others."

Before we follow Mr. Mill into his able exposition and defence of this principle, we wish to call attention to the new light thrown upon it by the position we have attempted to establish. We have affirmed that the loss of power and intensity which is observable in the typical characters of the present day arises not, as Mr. Mill affirms, from that galling slavery to Commonplace, under the name of Public Opinion, into which men, as it is said, have recently fallen; but from the partial disappearance of those narrow religious, social, and political organisations which formerly gave a more definite outline, and lent a more constant sustaining power, in the shape of strong class-sympathy, to the minds of those who were formed under their influence. But if this be so, * * * then it would seem that the effect of even much stricter codes of social custom, and much narrower sectarian and political prejudices, than any now prevalent tended to sharpen rather than obliterate that edge, and flavour, and intensity which Mr. Mill so much admires and which he misnames "individuality." Suppose for a moment Mr. Mill could have emasculated the various petty "public opinions," confined to special castes and classes, which produced the well-marked characters of the last century, as he would now emasculate the wider and less definite public opinion of modern English society, what would have been the result? The very pith of every strong class-opinion was and is its ideal of *personal* excellence, that touchstone by which it proves the mettle of all its members, and by reference to which it accords its popular judgment of favour or censure. And not only is this true, but it is equally true that no qualities of character enter more deeply into such class-ideals of excellence than those termed by Mr. Mill purely "self-regarding qualities,"—self-possession, courage, firmness, self-restraint,—which, according to our author, should be confined to the most solitary chambers of the imagination. Moreover, once admit that such virtues may and must enter into the very essence of popular standards of character, and you cannot prevent that severity of popular condemnation on the corresponding vices which Mr. Mill regards as a violation of the principle of individual freedom. Suppose, for instance, the country gentlemen of the last century had been induced, in anticipation of Mr. Mill's philosophy, sternly to discourage all tyrannical social prejudices as to the so-called "self-regarding" excellences of the country gentleman; they would of course have discouraged any attempt to affix a social stigma on avarice, meanness, timidity in field-sports, and so forth. But how could this have been possible without destroying entirely the strength, freshness, and clearness of outline, which has engraved that type of character so deeply in the English imagination? * * * In fact, nothing is more remarkable as regards popular English standards of character than a certain undue esteem for purely personal gifts and excellences, and a deeper detestation of those deformities which imply a want of self-respect than even of those which imply a want of respect for others.

* * * Mr. Mill's proposal to encourage the growth of moral individuality by entirely warning off the conscience of a society or a class from any responsible criticism of this interior world, would have exactly the opposite effect to that which he desires. A strong type of character may be the result either of vivid sympathy or keen collision with the social morality it finds around it; but where the social conscience practically ignores altogether any sphere of universal morality, it will seldom be the case that individual characters will dwell with any intensity upon it. Social indifference will result, not in individual vitality, but in individual indifference. Personal morality, once conscious that society has suspended its judgment, will grow up as colourless as a flower excluded from the light. And

if society do not suspend its judgment, it cannot but take leave to mark its approval and disapproval, to praise its heroes and to brand its outlaws. In spite of Mr. Mill's authority, we hold that if his object be, as he states, to encourage the growth of those more bold and massive types of character which he mourns over as extinct, it will be more wise, as well as more practicable, to select as his means to that end the purifying of social judgments from their one-sidedness than to attempt the complete suspension of them on certain tabooed subjects; to seek to infuse into them a truer justice and a deeper charity in estimating individual principles of conduct than to lecture society on the impropriety of passing any opinion on them at all. The "liberty of indifference" is the only kind of liberty which Mr. Mill's proposal would be likely to confer; and that is scarcely consistent with the massive and defined strength of purpose he wishes to restore.

* * * Mr. Mill begins by disclaiming, as a utilitarian must, any appeal to abstract right. "I regard utility," he says, "as the ultimate appeal on all ethical questions; but it must be utility in the largest sense, grounded on the permanent interests of man as a progressive being." And the influence of this theory is marked throughout the book. For, starting with the assumption that there is no inward standard of right or wrong, no standard except that which is attained by studying the *results* of conduct, he is led to divide actions into two great classes,—those which affect exclusively or mainly the agents, which are therefore beyond the reach of any external criticism, since no one can know the full consequences except the agent; and actions which affect directly or at least necessarily the interests of others, which can be classified into right and wrong according as they would, if generally permitted, satisfy or interfere with the claims of others.

* * *

Accordingly he classes cruelty, malice, envy, dissimulation, insincerity, love of domineering, as *immoral*; while cowardice, self-conceit, prodigality, and sensuality, so long as they infringe no one else's rights, he regards as beyond the bounds of morality proper. Their evil, he maintains, depends on their evil consequences. Those consequences, we may think, indeed, that we discern, but they are really experienced only by the mind of the agent; while the evil consequences of the former class of dispositions, on the other hand, are directly measurable by the disturbing influence they exert on the well-being of others. Mr. Mill is consistent, therefore, as a utilitarian, in drawing the broadest distrinction between the faults and crimes which aggrieve others, and those which directly hurt, or are supposed to hurt, none except those who commit them.

Mr. Mill is perfectly consistent, we say; but what conscience can acquiesce? Insincerity, he says, is an immorality; lying is a *vice* properly visited by an extreme social penalty; and a fraud is a *crime* properly requited by a severe legal penalty; for lying and fraud invade the rights of others; it is an obligation to others to tell the truth and to act the truth, for others are relying upon you. But sensuality, unless it trespasses on the rights of others, is a "folly," a "want of self-respect," a carelessness as to "self-development;" but, "to whatever pitch" it may be carried, it "does not constitute wickedness." We cannot wonder at this inference from the utilitarian ethics; but we do wonder that so marvellous a result should not stagger any great thinker as to the justice of his premises. The truth is, that Mr. Mill is deceived by the epithet of "self-regarding," which he assigns to the various evil dispositions and actions thus intended to be exempted from social criticism. "Prudence," "self-respect," and "self-development," against which alone he considers them to be transgressions, convey no sense of obligation. A man may sacrifice his own good, indulge little in self-respect, or even have erroneous notions as to the best direction of self-development, without any sense of guilt. None of these phrases in the least describe the origin of the self-reproach which accompanies any kind of evil self-indulgence, moral or sensual. The reason why the term "self-regarding" is so misleading, is not because there is any error in supposing that these things do primarily affect ourselves, but because it seems to indicate that there is a real distinction in kind, which there is not, between the inward moral conditions of this kind of evil disposition or action and those of dispositions or actions which affect primarily others than ourselves. Were Mr. Mill's theory, and the special epithet of "self-regarding" which represents it, a copy of any characteristic inward feeling,—then any habit of self-indulgence, such as that of anger or envy for example, which directly tends to infringe the rights of others, would be separated by a broad moral chasm in our own minds from any other habit of self-indulgence, moral or sensual, which directly tends only to affect our own nature. But this, as Mr. Mill knows, is not the case. The consideration as to whom any guilty act will mainly strike is an *arrière pensée* of the mind, not the least involved in the primary sense of guilt. The classification may be important to the politician, but to the moralist it is utterly artificial. There is as much, and usually far more, sense of a violated claim in the first impurity of thought, which does not seem to go forth into the external world at all, than in the first passionate blow or the first malignant insinuation, which are clear self-indulgences at the expense of another. However important, therefore, may be the distinction between what Mr. Mill calls "self-regarding" faults and what he calls immoralities affecting others in result, it is simply an error to suppose that it is a *natural* distinction, which is recognised by the self-accusing and self-condemning power in man. In both classes of moral evils alike the sting of self-reproach is entirely inward; and is not removed by any demonstration that no *injury* to society has resulted, or is likely to result. Of neither class of evils, again, is it a true account of the matter to say that they lie absolutely within us; for, quite apart from any theological conviction, in both classes of offences alike there is the same sense of transgression of some deep invisible claim on us, which we have no power to release as we can release any mere right of property of our own. * * * Mr. Mill's classification is in no sense a classification of wrong dispositions and actions according to the kind, or even degree, of guilt with which they universally impress men, in no sense a moral, but only a political classification. In this, of course, we are at direct issue with Mr. Mill; since, as we have seen, he applies the word "immoral" to the one class, and entirely excludes the other class from any share in that epithet.

But notwithstanding this broad distinction in our ethical theory, it is clear that Mr. Mill's case may be argued, as, indeed, he generally argues it, without any explicit logical reference to his utilitarian creed. For the object of the essay is not to discuss the amount of moral penalty to the individual which different classes of faults ought to entail, but only that portion of it which social custom or political law is justified in *inflicting* for the purpose either of retribution or restraint. Now, even for those who hold that Mr. Mill's classification of "self-regarding" and non-self-regarding faults is morally an artificial one, it is quite a tenable position that the only legitimate ground for social or political penalty ought to be an injury to society or the state. This, accordingly, is Mr. Mill's position; he denies to society the right to intimidate by any intentional combination, even by the combined expression of moral opinion, those whose practice evinces a great divergence of moral principle from the accepted standard, so long as the practice at issue has no bearing on the rights of any other than the offending persons. We have a right, he says, to choose our own society according to our own tastes, and we may therefore avoid the society of a man who offends those tastes; but we have no right to inflict any social penalty upon him by inducing others to do the same, unless his offence be one which threatens the social rights of others.

* * *

This contains, we believe, the substance of Mr. Mill's argument. First, an injury to society is the only legitimate ground of social or political punishment; since any other fault or vice expiates itself, and we can only claim to inflict penalty from that principle of

social resentment which is implied in the right to self-protection.
Next, if society does transgress this rule at all, the chances are that
it will be on the wrong side; since society is some judge of its own
interests, but will judge simply by accidental liking or prejudice as
to things which do not affect its own interests. Again, the individual
is the best judge of his own self-development; and to fetter him by
social restraints in what does not affect society is to menace the
principle of free self-government. And finally, to the argument that
every thing which hurts the inward life and purity of the individual
necessarily reacts on society, Mr. Mill replies that he does not deny
it, but that the principle of mere authority has had at least an adequate trial during the period of early education, when no one would
argue for absolute liberty, even in "self-regarding" acts: but there
must be some limit to interference; and if society is to interfere
with the self-government of the mature, on the ground only of the
infectious nature of all moral evil, there will be no secure sphere of
individual freedom at all.

We must keep in mind, in discussing this argument, that Mr.
Mill applies it as much to any combination of social opinion which
tends to prevent or to render painful the assertion of individual
freedom as to political legislation. His tests of what such social combination is, seems to be this: any act of which it is the intention to
discourage a social heresy of this kind, is a social persecution if the
heresy menace the rights of no one but the heretics. Individual disapproval may show itself, as a mere offended taste would show
itself; but if you try to put an end to it at all, if you do more than
simply withdraw your own countenance, and express your own opinion when natural occasion offers, you are guilty of a social persecution. You may disapprove of gambling or fornication,—you may
even perhaps punish those who live by offering inducements to
these vices, for that is a social act, which may possibly, at least,
trench on the rights of others; but you may not (even socially)
punish those who commit them in the exercise of their mature discretion; for the evil falls on themselves, and not (except through
the moral infection) on society. You may avoid them yourself; you
are bound not to do any thing with the intention of discouraging
such a life, except by expressing temperately your individual opinion
and regulating your individual conduct. You may not try to excite
public censure against these things,—to bring them under the ban
of society; as you might a furious temper or an envious and dishonest tongue. In the latter case, the heavier the social penalty you
bring down the better. Society must be protected against it. But the
evil of "errors" which are visited exclusively on the head of those
who commit them ought not to be increased, but if possible alle-
viated, by lookers-on: and they may not be errors, after all; there is

no worse judge than a society on whose rights they do not trench, and which is actuated only by prejudiced "likings" or "dislikings" of its own.

We have done our best to state Mr. Mill's case. * * * Still it seems to us to fail miserably in furnishing even the ground-plan of a sound political philosophy. * * * There is no element so utterly absent, from the first page to the last, as any indication of sympathy with the free play of a national or social character in its natural organic action. Mr. Mill's essay regards "liberty" from first to last in its negative rather than its positive significance. But in that sense in which the very word "liberty" is apt to excite the deepest enthusiasm of which human nature is capable, it means a great deal more than the mere absence of restraints on the individual; it implies that fresh and unconstrained play of national character, that fullness of social life and vivacity of public energy, which it is one of the worst results of such constraint to subdue or extinguish. But any sympathy with a full social life or fresh popular impulses is exactly the element in which Mr. Mill's book is most deficient. The only liberty he would deny the nation is the liberty to be a nation. He distrusts social and political freedom. There is a depressed and melancholy air about his essay in treating of social and political organisms. He thinks strongly that individuals should be let alone, but virtually on condition that they shall not coalesce into a society and have a social or political life that may react strongly on the principles of individual action. * * * An aggregate of individually free minds, if they are to be held asunder from natural social combinations by the stiff framework of such a doctrine as Mr. Mill's, would not make in any true or deep sense a free society or a free nation. For any thing this essay contains to the contrary, a nation might be held to possess the truest freedom though there were no indication in it of a common life, no sign of a united society, no vestige of a national will. It is strange that, while Mr. Mill lays so much and such just stress on the liberty of individual thought and expression, he should quite ignore the equally sacred liberty of social and national thought and expression, and even invent a canon for the express purpose of discouraging any action of society at all on topics where he would think it dangerous to the liberty of the individual. In England we should regard the mere absence of interference with individual opinions and actions as a poor sort of liberty, unless there were also due provision for the free play of social opinion, a suitable organ for the expression of those characteristic thoughts which elicit a response from the whole nation, a fit instrument for the timely assertion of England's antipathies and sympathies, hopes and will. If it be in reality a far truer mode of thinking to conceive individuals as members of a society, rather than society

as pieced together of individuals, it is certain that true liberty
demands for the deepest forms of social thought and life as free and
characteristic an expression as it demands for the deepest forms of
individual thought and life.

But, says Mr. Mill, what business has society to interfere with
actions which do not in any way infringe on the rights of others?
* * * We reply that, even if the consequences of what Mr. Mill calls
"self-regarding errors" can be admitted to be individual only, yet
that it is not by the consequences that even the agent himself
judges his own action, and therefore not by the consequences that
the society of which he is a member can judge it. Both the individual and society feel that the inward principle which is violated in
many of these "self-regarding errors" is of infinitely more importance
in estimating their relation both to the individual character and to
the constitution of society, than the immediate consequences can
ever be. The distinction between "self-regarding" consequences and
consequences to society is not usually a distinction naturally suggested to the agent, but a distinction taken afterwards on his behalf
by astute advocates. And if not a distinction which the individual
conscience can always recognise as morally important, then also not
a distinction which the social conscience—if a society may be permitted a conscience—can recognise either. Mr. Mill speaks as if
those who violate the laws of social morality could properly be conceived as *outside* the social body, as mere invaders of society, and
their guilt estimated by the amount of immediate social confusion
it tends to produce upon others than themselves. * * * Now this is
a completely artificial and deceptive mode of thought. Individuals
who in any special point reject the moral authority of the society in
which they live, are none the less members of that society. Their
act is not an invasion, but a rebellion. In other words, it has a
double influence, which the aggressive acts of mere invaders never
have,—the external and the internal,—the directly injurious results,
which, even though they fall exclusively upon their own heads, still
fall upon living members of a society who cannot suffer without
injury to the whole; and again, the still more important influence of
the practical protest put forth by living members of a society
against the social principle they have violated. If that principle be
one really essential either to social unity or social purity, it is clear
that society cannot treat either the immediate ill consequences or
the practical protest as if it came from an external source.

If there be any transgressions of social morality which are conceived, as well by the individual as the social conscience, as momen-
tous, not nearly so much because of their immediate results as
because they soon extinguish that sense of the inviolable sanctity of
social life which is its best and most distinctly religious bond, then

surely society, if it have an inward life and constitution and conscience at all, has even more right to express itself in open resentment and displeasure, than in the case of offences which happen to
affect the external lot of others of its members. Mr. Mill will not
deny that there are offences not trenching on the rights of any
other member of society, which yet do more to relax the strength
of that spiritual tie which holds society together, than many offences which are direct aggressions upon the rights of others. * * *
Yet because offences of the former class are, in the first instance,
sins only against that hidden conscience, or rather that overshadow-
ing power, which constitutes the true spiritual bond of society,
while offences of the latter class are also visibly traced in unjust violence or defrauded claims, Mr. Mill would call an organic expression
of social displeasure towards sins of the one class a tyranny, and
towards sins of the other class a needful and justifiable resentment.
It is, we suppose, because Mr. Mill denies the existence of any
moral standard of action, except consequences, in the individual,
that he is also unwilling to admit the existence of any inward social
principles apart from consequences against which members of a
society can offend. Were it not so, he would see as clearly as we see
that the danger of severing the spiritual roots of social purity and
unity is the true danger to society, and needs even more sedulous
and organised protest in cases where there is no one person specially
interested in raising it, than even in those cases where some one is
directly wronged, and therefore certain to call in the aid of others in
his own behalf. Social liberty, or liberty for the free play of social
character, is quite as sacred as individual liberty; and it cannot exist
at all if the deepest principles which form that character are to be
kept in abeyance out of respect for the liberty of those who infringe
them. How far the individual should be compelled, *otherwise* than
by the free expression of social opinion, to respect such moral laws,
is quite another question, which involves a large class of new considerations. But to propose that social opinion should spontaneously
put itself under unnatural restrictions, with regard to principles
which go to the very root of social life, in deference to individual liberty, is to ask that society should renounce its best impulses, in
order that individuals may indulge their worst.

We shall not, we trust, be understood to deny that such a thing
as social tyranny—quite apart from legislative enactment—is very
common and very dangerous. No doubt society often does interfere
with the proper sphere of private individual liberty. We only maintain that Mr. Mill's principle altogether fails properly to distinguish
the two spheres, and practically denies any inward life and character
to society altogether; turning it into a mere *arbiter* between individuals, instead of regarding it as an organised body, in the common

life of which all its members partake. Mr. Mill thinks society a competent judge of its own *external interests*; but that its moral likings and dislikings are mere tyrannical sentiments, which it will impose at pleasure on any unfortunate minority within its control. No doubt societies, like individuals, are disposed to bigotry. No doubt majorities will at times strive to impose their coarser tastes and poor commonplace thoughts on minorities, instead of desiring to know and try the principle opposed to theirs. But what is the true check upon social bigotry? According to Mr. Mill, the only guarantee against it is to erect, by common consent, every individual human mind into an impregnable and independent fortress, within the walls of which social authority shall have no jurisdiction; the functions of the latter being strictly limited to arbitrating questions at issue between all such independent lords, and prohibiting mutual encroachments. Now we do not deny that such a total withdrawal of individual duty and morality from the circle of social questions might secure against bigotry; but at what expense? At the sacrifice, we believe, of that mediating body of social faith and conviction which connects together the more marked individualities of different minds, interprets them, and renders them mutually intelligible and useful,—at the cost of that social unity of spirit which alone renders the diversity of individual gifts capable of profiting by each other. Mr. Mill's essay may be said to be one long *éloge* on individuality—its importance in itself, and its paramount importance to society. This we accept as strongly as Mr. Mill. But individuality may suffer in either of two ways: from the too great rigour or from the too great looseness of the social bond,—from the tyrannical domination of custom and commonplace over the individual; or from that paralysis of social life which permits individual modes of thought and conduct to diverge too widely for mutual influence and aid. What is it that really makes strong individualities of character and thought so important to society, but their real power of increasing the moral and intellectual experience of general society? And how could this be, if they were not kept constantly in living relation with general society by the sense of social authority over them? It is this moral authority exercised by social opinion, and this alone, which obliges the innovator to remember, and, if he can, to appreciate, the body of diffused social conviction, even while modifying, deviating from, and expanding it. People of strong one-sided individualities are always in danger of losing their full and fair influence on society; nay, of losing even the full advantage of their special characteristics, from want of adequate sympathy with the society which they wish to influence. * * *

And what is true of intellectual characteristics is far more uniformly true of moral characteristics. Those who ignore entirely the restraints of the code of social morality under which they live, are never likely to deepen, widen, or elevate it. Moral heretics may often render a great service to the world, but only where they feel acutely where it is that their creed diverges from that of the world, and on what grounds it thus diverges; only if they recognise the moral authority of the social creed to the full so far as it is sound, and dispute it on the one point on which they have tested its unsoundness. Mere groundless eccentricity,—which Mr. Mill, with less than his usual good sense, goes into a special digression to extol, —has more effect, we believe, in aggravating the social bigotry of Commonplace, and rendering men suspicious of all genuine individuality, than any other influence. Proper individuality is any thing but eccentricity; it is a development—one-sided perhaps, but still a development—of convictions and characteristics the germs of which are common to all men. * * *

If now Mr. Mill asks us what we regard as the true check upon that oppressive social bigotry which so often gives rise to weakness and moral cowardice on the one hand, and to unjust social excommunications on the other, we should reply, that there is the same check on the tyrannical treatment by society of what he calls "self-regarding" heresies as there is on similar social tyrannies towards what he admits to be justly punishable social immoralities. * * * That society is an imperfect judge of right and wrong, is true enough. Is it likely to improve under the exhortation to give up thinking of right and wrong altogether, and to calculate instead the tendency of human actions to produce external social disturbance? Is it likely to be more charitable and less unjust when told that it must no longer try human action by a practical human standard; that it must take pains to distinguish between actions with evil social consequences and actions with evil individual consequences only; and while disregarding the latter altogether, it should administer the unwritten law of social instinct upon the former with all the deterrent rigour it can command? * * * He thinks that if society would but confess that is has no social right to set up any concrete standard of moral duty, if it could but be persuaded to confine its criticisms to that abstract idea of his, "social man," and to plead absolute incompetence to deal with the "self-regarding" duties of human life,—that then individual minds would begin to play freely, and health to return to the whole social system. We believe, on the contrary, that if Mr. Mill's prescription could be carried out at all, which it cannot, the result would be exactly opposite. The individuality of individual life would be paralysed by this artificial indifference on the part of Society to its proceedings. The social morality of social life would lose all depth and seriousness by being thus unnaturally dissevered from the deeper judgments of the individual conscience. Social morality, striving to judge of actions simply by their effects on the rights of others, and ostentatiously excluding all the natural canons of moral criticism, would become arbitrary, conventional, formal. In proportion as it relaxed its hold on the individual conscience, it would become pharisaic in its anxiety about the rights of others. Professing to judge men only by this rigid test-formula, 'What is the net social result of your action?' instead of by any natural human conception of good or evil, social morality would wander farther and farther from the natural principles of justice, and soon substitute a *doctrinaire* social bigotry of its own, in the place of that moral bigotry in judging of individual conduct from which Mr. Mill hopes to redeem it.

* * *

Mr. Mill is well aware that the principal recommendation of his social theory to ordinary minds is not likely to consist in its inherent strength half so much as in its inviting logical affinity to one very important and very direct application, which English thought has already, on other grounds, heartily accepted; we mean the perfect liberty of individual opinion, and the evil of any sort of social excommunication of mere heresy. * * * Accordingly he spends the first half of his essay on reconsidering this principle, and developing it beyond its already familiar political aspects into its purely social bearings. He sees that there is much chronic social intolerance left which ought to be eradicated, and he perhaps justly thinks his theory of society well adapted to educe an extension of this principle, to prove the inadmissibility of those social excommunications which religious heresy still frequently draws down. If society has no further right than to protect itself againt practical transgressors of social duties and claims, how clear that it has no right to stir up any sort of social resentment or arm prejudice against a man who has simply used his own individual liberty of thought to form his own individual convictions! And what theory of society but that of self-protection would be likely to leave the sphere of individual thought so inviolable? * * *

Unfortunately, however, for his social theory, he ought to separate the right to form individual convictions from the right to *propagate* them. The two rights, he freely concedes, are practically inseparable; yet the two certainly do not bear the same relation to his social theory. So long, indeed, as the convictions formed have no direct bearing on the admitted rights of others,—so long as they are religious, or belong only to the "self-regarding" class of moral duties,—so long his theory would justify their free propagation as well as their free formation. But once let them have a revolutionary tendency in their bearing on social life,—once let their adoption have evil consequence which would fall primarily on *others*,—and he feels at once that the "self-protecting" theory of society would justify both government and social opinion in interfering to punish or to excommunicate the propagandist. Mr. Mill does not attempt to get over this difficulty. He knows that government ought to interfere only with evil actions, not with dangerous opinions. He knows that social feeling itself ought to draw a broad distinction between evil actions and those opinions which merely encourage and impel to evil actions; but his theory will not admit this distinction. If "self-protection" be the duty of society, it ought surely to discourage in the germ those views which endanger its existence, and not to wait till the risk has borne fruits of serious evil.

Mr. Mill is obliged to draw a distinction between opinions so expressed "as to constitute a positive instigation to some mischievous act," and abstract opinions with the same tendency: "An opinion that corn-dealers are starvers of the poor, or that private property is robbery, ought to be unmolested when simply circulated through the press; but may justly incur punishment when delivered orally to an excited mob assembled before the house of a corn-dealer, or when handed about by the same mob in the form of a placard."

With this doctrine we entirely agree; but if it be taken absolutely, what does it really amount to except a complete abandonment of Mr. Mill's own theory, and a virtual admission of our position that, after all, it is the judgment of the social conscience, and not any technical formula derived from a right to protect itself against external disorders, which justifies society in the infliction of political and social penalties, and the expression of social resentment? For if, as Mr. Mill contends, society is the best and only proper judge of what is inimical to its own interest, and is bound to watch over and protect them without regard to the principles of individual morality involved, how can he regard as any thing but positively praiseworthy its attempt to stifle at once,—if not by law, at least by the expression of stern displeasure on the part of the public,—all teaching that would directly tend to subversive actions? On the principle that prevention is better than cure, * * * no one can deny that to brand the propagation of opinions dangerous to the constitution of society with social opprobrium would be a much safer measure than to punish those who act them out. If an opinion is advocated "that corn-dealers are starvers of the poor," and it is possible, by uniformly frowning upon and, if needful, excommunicating the advocates of such subversive opinions, to prevent the assemblage of that unruly mob before the corn-dealer's door altogether, how much more merciful this course would be than to let the doctrine reach that degree of influence and then punish its propounders! Mr. Mill makes reply, as we understand him, that he admits this consequence; that, strictly speaking, society has the right to guard itself against revolutionary opinions, even while only abstract; but that it wisely waives this right for the chance which always exists that by habitually listening to all abstract opinions, it may occasionally be induced to reconsider its own view, and give in its adhesion to what it at first erroneously deemed subversive doctrine. In short, society, he thinks, properly runs the risk of delaying for a while to protect itself against many really dangerous opinions which may gain ground and become practically threatening, in order that it may protect itself against the alternative and worse risk of overlooking the truth contained in some seemingly but not really dangerous opinions. This is, however, practically leaving it to the discretion of society whether in any given case it regards the practical risk or the chance of new light as the greater. The right of self-protection always exists; and if it is waived, it is only because society does not fear so much as it hopes. * * * Accordingly political and social intolerance is certainly clearly admissible,—on the theory that the only duty of society is to protect itself,—in the case of all opinions which seem to threaten, in the opinion of the majority, much more social danger than their investigation could possibly bring new light. * * *

Moreover, Mr. Mill's theory does not only leave large room for social and political intolerance, but in those cases where it does admit intolerance at all, it admits it in the highest degree. Suppose society convinced—say by bitter experience, such as that of revolutionary France—that it had far more danger to apprehend from the spread of exciting doctrine on any particular subject than enlightenment to look for from the discussion, it will be warranted in using the most effective social measures for its extinction. That is but poor "self-protection" that only half does its work. The earlier the blow is struck, the more entirely theoretic the stage in which the social heresy is extinguished, the farther it is from any actual criminal intention at the time, the better. So far from waiting till the mob is before the corn-dealer's door, according to the true principle of self-protection, society would raise a hue and cry against the social heretic when first he began to intimate that to destroy granaries of corn in order to raise the price of the remainder is a selfish and unprincipled act. Once let the teaching take the form of a popular cry,—once let selfish ends become interwoven with it,—and it might be too late. The theory of self-protection, then, will not only justify intolerance to social heresies in given cases, but in those cases will justify it at the point farthest removed from practical action; while the intellectual error, and that alone, is the danger to be feared.

* * *

We hold, then, that Mr. Mill's own theory does not permit nearly so clear a distinction between opinions and actions as is absolutely necessary for any true guarantee of social tolerance. Measure Wrong by the mere amount of tendency to imperil the admitted rights of others, and you cannot draw any satisfactory distinction between the intellectual and the practical tendencies which imperil them. Measure it, on the other hand, by a practical standard, the purpose and circumstances of the wrong-doer, and there is the broadest distinction between a theory and an instigation,—an impersonal conclusion of the intellect, and a practical recommendation which realises the whole actual significance of the injurious theory. * * *

How, then, Mr. Mill will ask, do we provide against that religious and social intolerance which, as his own essay most eloquently shows, is still so deadly a poison in English society? If we contend that the social conscience should be as free to judge and speak as the individual conscience, how are we to protest with any force against that miserable bigotry which *always* professes to speak from the impulses of a pure moral zeal, and very generally really is closely connected with the moral nature? * * * The way to convince society that it is in error is, not to deny that its conscience has any right to judge of individual conduct, but to exhibit the many great complexities of intellectual constitution which have prevented, and do prevent, men of pure life and stainless integrity from accepting these faiths; and to point out, moreover, that one of the greatest obstacles in their way is the uncharitable excommunication to which society in its pharisaism dooms them. This would be a victory over the social conscience gained by an appeal to the social conscience, and therefore, we believe, would be much more likely to be firm and permanent than one gained by merely persuading society—which it would be hard to do—that it has no concern with the individual principles of life and action, as such, at all. We always mistrust these indirect victories over either individual or social opinion. The social conscience, like the individual conscience, will not submit to be merely out-manœuvred; it takes the liberty, after all, of forming its judgments, with reference to the rights of a question, on those rights.

* * *

If Society is to be made to feel that it is to have no social judgment, no social conviction, no social likings and dislikings, on individual morals and creeds at all,—if the social mind is simply to *abstain* from all corporate acts of conviction which might carry the weak along with it, or intimidate the cowardly into base compliance,—how could we have any thing but "heresies smouldering in the narrow circle of studious persons among whom they originate"? What is it that makes opinions "blaze out far and wide," and "light up the affairs of mankind with either a true or a deceptive light," except a profound conviction on the part of the social conscience that it *is* concerned in those convictions, and *has* a real relation to them, either in the way of cordial belief or of as cordial rejection? If Mr. Mill had looked for a theory of society which, if adopted, might have the effect of prolonging so undesirable a condition of things, he could not have invented any so excellently adapted to that purpose as his own. It is the belief that society, as society, has a common life, liable to be vitally influenced by the acceptance or rejection of religious and moral faiths; it is this true belief that favours those hearty battles between conflicting sections which are so much better and healthier a sign of the times than "smouldering" orthodoxies and equally smouldering heterodoxies. If, as Mr. Mill believes, society has no such common life, it is impossible that the enunciation of truths or errors could stir up in it these elevated moods of social emotion. If common opinions are to be debarred all active expression, all signs of either approval or censure, for fear they may subdue the cowardly or silence the timid, it is impossible that the conflict between truth and error can be any thing but a weak and dropping fire carried on by individual marksmen. Mr. Mill uniformly advocates an unsocial conception of liberty which exactly corresponds to the condition of things he so eloquently condemns. * * *

JAMES FITZJAMES STEPHEN

[Mill's Fallacies] †

There is hardly anything in the whole essay which can properly be called proof as distinguished from enunciation or assertion of the general principles quoted. I think, however, that it will not be difficult to show that the principle stands in much need of proof. In order to make this clear it will be desirable in the first place to point out the meaning of the word liberty according to principles which I think are common to Mr Mill and to myself. I do not think Mr Mill would have disputed the following statement of the theory of human actions. All voluntary acts are caused by motives. All motives may be placed in one of two categories—hope and fear, pleasure and pain. Voluntary acts of which hope is the motive are said to be free. Voluntary acts of which fear is the motive are said to be done under compulsion, or omitted under restraint. A woman

† From James Fitzjames Stephen, *Liberty, Equality, Fraternity* (London, 1873), pp. 8–15, 22–23, 26–27, 43–44, 46–48, 76–79, 123, 130–31, 145–49, 153, 154, 184–85.

marries. This in every case is a voluntary action. If she regards the marriage with the ordinary feelings and acts from the ordinary motives, she is said to act freely. If she regards it as a necessity, to which she submits in order to avoid greater evil, she is said to act under compulsion and not freely.

If this is the true theory of liberty—and, though many persons would deny this, I think they would have been accepted by Mr Mill —the propositions already stated will in a condensed form amount to this: 'No one is ever justified in trying to affect any one's conduct by exciting his fears, except for the sake of self-protection;' or, making another substitution which he would also approve—'It can never promote the general happiness of mankind that the conduct of any persons should be affected by an appeal to their fears, except in the cases excepted.'

Surely these are not assertions which can be regarded as self-evident, or even as otherwise than paradoxical. What is all morality, and what are all existing religions in so far as they aim at affecting human conduct, except an appeal either to hope or fear, and to fear far more commonly and far more emphatically than to hope? Criminal legislation proper may be regarded as an engine of prohibition unimportant in comparison with morals and the forms of morality sanctioned by theology. For one act from which one person is restrained by the fear of the law of the land, many persons are restrained from innumerable acts by the fear of the disapprobation of their neighbours, which is the moral sanction; or by the fear of punishment in a future state of existence, which is the religious sanction; or by the fear of their own disapprobation, which may be called the conscientious sanction, and may be regarded as a compound case of the other two. Now, in the innumerable majority of cases, disapprobation, or the moral sanction, has nothing whatever to do with self-protection. The religious sanction is by its nature independent of it. Whatever special forms it may assume, the fundamental condition of it is a being intolerant of evil in the highest degree, and inexorably determined to punish it wherever it exists, except upon certain terms. I do not say that this doctrine is true, but I do say that no one is entitled to assume it without proof to be essentially immoral and mischievous. Mr Mill does not draw this inference, but I think his theory involves it, for I know not what can be a greater infringement of his theory of liberty, a more complete and formal contradiction to it, than the doctrine that there are a court and a judge in which, and before whom, every man must give an account of every work done in the body, whether self-regarding or not. According to Mr Mill's theory, it ought to be a good plea in the day of judgment to say 'I pleased myself and hurt nobody else.' Whether or not there will ever be a day of judgment is not the question, but upon his principles the conception of a day of judgment is fundamentally immoral. A God who punished any one at all, except for the purpose of protecting others, would, upon his principles, be a tyrant trampling on liberty.

The application of the principle in question to the moral sanction would be just as subversive of all that people commonly regard as morality. The only moral system which would comply with the principle stated by Mr Mill would be one capable of being summed up as follows: 'Let every man please himself without hurting his neighbour;' and every moral system which aimed at more than this, either to obtain benefits for society at large other than protection against injury or to do good to the persons affected, would be wrong in principle. This would condemn every existing system of morals. Positive morality is nothing but a body of principles and rules more or less vaguely expressed, and more or less left to be understood, by which certain lines of conduct are forbidden under the penalty of general disapprobation, and that quite irrespectively of self-protection. Mr Mill himself admits this to a certain extent. In the early part of his fourth chapter he says that a man grossly deficient in the qualities which conduce to his own good is 'necessarily and properly a subject of distaste, or in extreme cases even of contempt,' and he enumerates various inconveniences to which this would expose such a person. He adds, however: 'The inconveniences which are strictly inseparable from the unfavourable judgment of others are the only ones to which a person should ever be subjected for that portion of his conduct and character which concerns his own good, but which does not affect the interests of others in their relation with him.' This no doubt weakens the effect of the admission; but be this how it may, the fact still remains that morality is and must be a prohibitive system, one of the main objects of which is to impose upon every one a standard of conduct and of sentiment to which few persons would conform if it were not for the constraint thus put upon them. In nearly every instance the effects of such a system reach far beyond anything that can be described as the purposes of self-protection.

Mr Mill's system is violated not only by every system of theology which concerns itself with morals, and by every known system of positive morality, but by the constitution of human nature itself. There is hardly a habit which men in general regard as good which is not acquired by a series of more or less painful and laborious acts. The condition of human life is such that we must of necessity be restrained and compelled by circumstances in nearly every action of our lives. Why, then, is liberty, defined as Mr Mill defines it, to be regarded as so precious? What, after all, is done by the legislator or by the person who sets public opinion in motion to control conduct of which he disapproves—or, if the expression is preferred, which he dislikes—which is not done for us all at every instant of our lives by circumstances? The laws which punish murder or theft are substitutes for private vengeance, which, in the absence of law, would punish those crimes more severely, though in a less regular manner. If there were laws which punished incontinence, gluttony, or drunkenness, the same might be said of them. Mr Mill admits in so many words that there are 'inconveniences which are strictly inseparable from the unfavourable judgment of others.' What is the distinction in principle between such inconveniences and similar ones organized, defined, and inflicted upon proof that the circumstances which call for their infliction exist? This organization, definition, and procedure make all the difference between the restraints which Mr Mill would permit and the restraints to which he objects. I cannot see on what the distinction rests. I cannot understand why it must always be wrong to punish habitual drunkenness by fine, imprisonment, or deprivation of civil rights, and always be right to punish it by the infliction of those consequences which are 'strictly inseparable from the unfavourable judgment of others.' It may be said that these consequences follow, not because we think them desirable, but in the common order of nature. This answer only suggests the further question, whether nature is in this instance to be regarded as a friend or as an enemy? Every reasonable man would answer that the restraint which the fear of the disapprobation of others imposes on our conduct is the part of the constitution of nature which we could least afford to dispense with. But if this is so, why draw the line where Mr Mill draws it? Why treat the penal consequences of disapprobation as things to be minimized and restrained within the narrowest limits? What 'inconvenience,' after all, is 'strictly inseparable from the unfavourable judgment of others'? If society at large adopted fully Mr Mill's theory of liberty, it would be easy to diminish very greatly the inconveniences in question. Strenuously preach and rigorously practise the doctrine that our neighbour's private character is nothing to us, and the number of unfavourable judgments formed, and therefore the number of inconveniences inflicted by them, can be reduced as much as we please, and the province of liberty can be enlarged in a corresponding ratio. Does any reasonable man wish for this? Could any one desire gross licentiousness, monstrous extravagance, ridiculous vanity, or the like, to be unnoticed, or, being known, to inflict no inconveniences?

If, however, the restraints on immorality are the main safeguards of society against influences which might be fatal to it, why treat them as if they were bad? Why draw so strongly marked a line between social and legal penalties? Mr Mill asserts the existence of the distinction in every form of speech. He makes his meaning perfectly clear. Yet from one end of his essay to the other I find no proof and no attempt to give the proper and appropriate proof of it. His doctrine could have been proved if it had been true. It was not proved because it was not true.

* * *

Not only is an appeal to facts and experience opposed to Mr Mill's principle, but his essay contains exceptions and qualifications which are really inconsistent with it. He says that his principle 'is meant to apply to human beings only in the maturity of their faculties,' and, he adds, 'we may leave out of account those backward states of society in which the race itself may be considered in its nonage.' Despotism, he says, 'is a legitimate mode of government in dealing with barbarians, provided the end be their improvement, and the means justified by actually effecting that end. Liberty as a principle has no application to any state of things anterior to the time when mankind have become capable of being improved by free and equal discussion. Until then there is nothing for them but implicit obedience to an Akbar or a Charlemagne if they are so fortunate as to find one. But as soon as mankind have attained the capacity of being guided to their own improvement by conviction or persuasion (a period long since reached in all nations with whom we need here concern ourselves), compulsion is no longer admissible as a means to their own good, and is justifiable only for the security of others.'

It seems to me that this qualification either reduces the doctrine qualified to an empty commonplace which no one would care to dispute, or makes an incredible assertion about the state of human society. No one, I suppose, ever denied either in theory or in practice that there is a sphere within which the tastes of people of mature age ought not to be interfered with, and within which differences must be regarded as natural and inevitable—in which better or worse means that which the individual prefers or dislikes. On the other hand, no one ever suggested that it was or could be good for anyone to be compelled to do what he did not like, unless the person compelling was not only stronger but wiser than the person compelled, at all events in reference to the matter to which the compulsion applied.

* * *

A narrower interpretation would be as follows. There is a period, now generally reached all over Europe and America, at which discussion takes the place of compulsion, and in which people when they know what is good for them generally do it. When this period is reached, compulsion may be laid aside. To this I should say that no such period has as yet been reached anywhere, and that there is no prospect of its being reached anywhere within any assignable time.

Where, in the very most advanced and civilised communities, will you find any class of persons whose views or whose conduct on subjects on which they are interested are regulated even in the main by the results of free discussion? What proportion of human misconduct in any department in life is due to ignorance, and what to wickedness or weakness? Of ten thousand people who get drunk, is there one who could say with truth that he did so because he had been brought to think on full deliberation and after free discussion that it was wise to get drunk? Would not every one of the ten thousand, if he told the real truth, say in some dialect or other—'I got drunk because I was weak and a fool, because I could not resist the immediate pleasure for the sake of future and indefinite advantage'?

* * *

The great defect of Mr Mill's later writings seems to me to be that he has formed too favourable an estimate of human nature. This displays itself in the chapter ["Of Individuality, as One of the Elements of Well-Being"] by the tacit assumption which pervades every part of it that the removal of restraints usually tends to invigorate character. Surely the very opposite of this is the truth. Habitual exertion is the greatest of all invigorators of character, and restraint and coercion in one form or another is the great stimulus to exertion. If you wish to destroy originality and vigour of character, no way to do so is so sure as to put a high level of comfort easily within the reach of moderate and commonplace exertion. A life made up of danger, vicissitude, and exposure is the sort of life which produces originality and resource. A soldier or sailor on active service lives in an atmosphere of coercion by the elements, by enemies, by disease, by the discipline to which he is subjected. Is he usually a tamer and less original person than a comfortable London shopkeeper or a man with just such an income as enables him to do exactly as he likes? A young man who is educated and so kept under close and continuous discipline till he is twenty-two or twenty-three years of age will generally have a much more vigorous and more original character than one who is left entirely to his own devices at an age when his mind and his tastes are unformed. Almost every human being requires more or less coercion and restraint as astringents to give him the maximum of power which he is capable of attaining. The maximum attainable in particular cases depends upon something altogether independent of social arrangements—

namely, the nature of the human being himself who is subjected to them; and what this is or how it is to be affected are questions which no one has yet answered.

* * *

There is one more point in this curious chapter which I must notice in conclusion. Nothing can exceed Mr Mill's enthusiasm for individual greatness. The mass, he says, in all countries constitute collective mediocrity. They never think at all, and never rise above mediocrity, 'except in so far as the sovereign many have let themselves be guided and influenced (which in their best times they always have done) by the counsels and influence of a more highly gifted or instructed one or few. The initiation of all wise or noble things comes and must come from individuals; generally at first from some one individual.' The natural inference would be that these individuals are the born rulers of the world, and that the world should acknowledge and obey them as such. Mr Mill will not admit this. All that the man of genius can claim is 'freedom to point out the way. The power of compelling others into it is not only inconsistent with the freedom and development of all the rest, but corrupting to the strong man himself.' This would be perfectly true if the compulsion consisted in a simple exertion of blind force, like striking a nail with a hammer; but who ever acted so on others to any extent worth mentioning? The way in which the man of genius rules is by persuading an efficient minority to coerce an indifferent and self-indulgent majority, which is quite a different process.

The odd manner in which Mr Mill worships mere variety, and confounds the proposition that variety is good with the proposition that goodness is various, is well illustrated by the lines which follow this passage: 'Exceptional individuals . . . should be encouraged in acting differently from the mass'—in order that there may be enough of them to 'point out the way.' Eccentricity is much required in these days. Precisely because the tyranny of opinion is such as to make eccentricity a reproach, it is desirable, in order to break through that tyranny, that people should be eccentric. Eccentricity has always abounded when and where strength of character has abounded, and the amount of eccentricity in a society has generally been proportioned to the amount of genius, mental vigour, and moral courage it contained. That so few now dare to be eccentric makes the chief danger of the time.

If this advice were followed, we should have as many little oddities in manner and behaviour as we have people who wish to pass for men of genius. Eccentricity is far more often a mark of weakness than a mark of strength. Weakness wishes, as a rule, to attract attention by trifling distinctions, and strength wishes to avoid it.

Originality consists in thinking for yourself, not in thinking differently from other people.

* * *

The real question is as to social intolerance. Has a man who believes in God and a future state a moral right to disapprove of those who do not, and to try by the expression of that disapproval to deter them from publishing, and to deter others from adopting, their views? I think that he has if and in so far as his opinions are true. Mr Mill thinks otherwise.

* * *

The heretics, says Mr Mill, are grievously injured by this, and are much to be pitied, but 'the greatest harm is done to those who are not heretics, and whose whole mental development is cramped and their reason cowed by the fear of heresy. Who can compute what the world loses in the multitude of promising intellects combined with timid characters, who dare not follow out any bold, vigorous, independent train of thought lest it should land them in something which would admit of being considered irreligious or immoral?'

On this point I am utterly unable to agree with Mr Mill. It seems to me that to publish opinions upon morals, politics, and religion is an act as important as any which any man can possibly do; that to attack opinions on which the framework of society rests is a proceeding which both is and ought to be dangerous. I do not say that it ought not to be done in many cases, but it should be done sword in hand, and a man who does it has no more right to be surprised at being fiercely resisted than a soldier who attacks a breach. Mr Mill's whole charge against social intolerance is that it makes timid people afraid to express unpopular opinions. An old ballad tells how a man, losing his way on a hill-side, strayed into a chamber full of enchanted knights, each lying motionless in complete armour, with his war-horse standing motionless beside him. On a rock lay a sword and a horn, and the intruder was told that if he wanted to lead the army, he must choose between them. He chose the horn and blew a loud blast, upon which the knights and their horses vanished in a whirlwind and their visitor was blown back into common life, these words sounding after him on the wind:

> Cursed be the coward that ever he was born
> Who did not draw the sword before he blew the horn.

No man has a right to give the signal for such a battle by blowing the horn, unless he has first drawn the sword and knows how to make his hands guard his head with it. Then let him blow as loud and long as he likes, and if his tune is worth hearing he will not want followers. Till a man has carefully formed his opinions on these subjects, thought them out, assured himself of their value, and decided to take the risk of proclaiming them, the strong probability is that they are not much worth having. Speculation on government, morals, and religion is a matter of vital practical importance, and not mere food for curiosity. Curiosity, no doubt, is generally the motive which leads a man to study them; but, till he has formed opinions on them for which he is prepared to fight, there is no hardship in his being compelled by social intolerance to keep them to himself and to those who sympathise with him. It should never be forgotten that opinions have a moral side to them. The opinions of a bad and a good man, the opinions of an honest and a dishonest man, upon these subjects are very unlikely to be the same.

* * *

So far I have considered the theoretical grounds of Mr Mill's principle and its practical application to liberty of thought and discussion. I now proceed to consider its application to morals.

* * *

First, there is no principle on which the cases in which Mr Mill admits the justice of legal punishment can be distinguished from those in which he denies it. The principle is that private vices which are injurious to others may justly be punished, if the injury be specific and the persons injured distinctly assignable, but not otherwise. If the question were as to the possibility in most cases of drawing an indictment against such persons I should agree with him. Criminal law is an extremely rough engine, and must be worked with great caution; but it is one thing to point out a practical difficulty which limits the application of a principle and quite another to refute the principle itself. Mr Mill's proviso deserves attention in considering the question whether a given act should be punished by law, but he applies it to 'the moral coercion of public opinion,' as well as to legal coercion, and to this the practical difficulty which he points out does not apply. A set of young noblemen of great fortune and hereditary influence, the representatives of ancient names, the natural leaders of the society of large districts, pass their whole time and employ all their means in gross debauchery. Such people are far more injurious to society than common pickpockets, but Mr Mill says that if any one having the opportunity of making them ashamed of themselves uses it in order to coerce them into decency, he sins against liberty, unless their example does assignable harm to specific people. It might be right to say, 'You, the Duke of A, by extravagantly keeping four mistresses—to wit, B and C in London, and D and E in Paris—set an example which induced your friend F to elope with Mrs G at —— on ——, and you are a great blackguard for your pains, and all the more because you are a duke.' It could never be right to say, 'You, the

Duke of A, are scandalously immoral and ought to be made to smart for it, though the law cannot touch you.' The distinction is more likely to be overlooked than to be misunderstood.

* * *

The object of morally intolerant legislation * * * is to establish, to maintain, and to give power to that which the legislator regards as a good moral system or standard. * * * I think that this object is good if and in so far as the system so established and maintained is good. How far any particular system is good or not is a question which probably does not admit of any peremptory final decision; but I may observe that there are a considerable number of things which appear good and bad, though no doubt in different degrees, to all mankind. For the practical purpose of legislation refinements are of little importance. In any given age and nation virtue and vice have meanings which for that purpose are quite definite enough.

* * *

If this is so, the only remaining questions will be as to the efficiency of the means at the disposal of society for this purpose, and the cost of their application. Society has at its disposal two great instruments by which vice may be prevented and virtue promoted—namely, law and public opinion; and law is either criminal or civil. The use of each of these instruments is subject to certain limits and conditions, and the wisdom of attempting to make men good either by Act of Parliament or by the action of public opinion depends entirely upon the degree in which those limits and conditions are recognized and acted upon.

First, I will take the case of criminal law. What are the conditions under which and the limitations within which it can be applied with success to the object of making men better? In considering this question it must be borne in mind that criminal law is at once by far the most powerful and by far the roughest engine which society can use for any purpose. Its power is shown by the fact that it can and does render crime exceedingly difficult and dangerous. Indeed, in civilized society it absolutely prevents avowed open crime committed with the strong hand, except in cases where crime rises to the magnitude of civil war. Its roughness hardly needs illustration. It strikes so hard that it can be enforced only on the gravest occasions, and with every sort of precaution against abuse or mistake. Before an act can be treated as a crime, it ought to be capable of distinct definition and of specific proof, and it ought also to be of such a nature that it is worth while to prevent it at the risk of inflicting great damage, direct and indirect, upon those who commit it. These conditions are seldom, if ever, fulfilled by mere vices. It would obviously be impossible to indict a man for ingratitude or perfidy. Such charges are too vague for specific discussion and distinct proof on the one side, and disproof on the other. Moreover, the expense of the investigations necessary for the legal punishment of such conduct would be enormous. It would be necessary to go into an infinite number of delicate and subtle inquiries which would tear off all privacy from the lives of a large number of persons. These considerations are, I think, conclusive reasons against treating vice in general as a crime.

The excessive harshness of criminal law is also a circumstance which very greatly narrows the range of its application. It is the *ratio ultima* of the majority against persons whom its application assumes to have renounced the common bonds which connect men together. When a man is subjected to legal punishment, society appeals directly and exlusively to his fears. It renounces the attempt to work upon his affections or feelings. In other words, it puts itself into distinct, harsh, and undisguised opposition to his wishes; and the effect of this will be to make him rebel against the law. The violence of the rebellion will be measured partly by the violence of the passion the indulgence of which is forbidden, and partly by the degree to which the law can count upon an ally in the man's own conscience. A law which enters into a direct contest with a fierce imperious passion, which the person who feels it does not admit to be bad, and which is not directly injurious to others, will generally do more harm than good; and this is perhaps the principal reason why it is impossible to legislate directly against unchastity, unless it takes forms which every one regards as monstrous and horrible. The subject is not one for detailed discussion, but any one who will follow out the reflections which this hint suggests will find that they supply a striking illustration of the limits which the harshness of criminal law imposes upon its range.

If we now look at the different acts which satisfy the conditions specified, it will, I think, be found that criminal law in this country actually is applied to the suppression of vice and so to the promotion of virtue to a very considerable extent; and this I say is right.

The punishment of common crimes, the gross forms of force and fraud, is no doubt ambiguous. It may be justified on the principle of self-protection, and apart from any question as to their moral character. It is not, however, difficult to show that these acts have in fact been forbidden and subjected to punishment not only because they are dangerous to society, and so ought to be prevented, but also for the sake of gratifying the feeling of hatred—call it revenge, resentment, or what you will—which the contemplation of such conduct excites in healthily constituted minds. If this can be shown, it will follow that criminal law is in the nature of a persecution of the grosser forms of vice, and an emphatic assertion of the principle that the feeling of hatred and the desire of vengeance above-mentioned are important elements of human nature which ought in such cases to be satisfied in a regular public and legal manner.

* * *

I now pass to the manner in which civil law may and does, and as I say properly, promote virtue and prevent vice. This is a subject so wide that I prefer indicating its nature by a few illustrations to attempting to deal with it systematically. It would, however, be easy to show that nearly every branch of civil law assumes the existence of a standard of moral good and evil which the public at large have an interest in maintaining, and in many cases enforcing—a proceeding which is diametrically opposed to Mr Mill's fundamental principles.

* * *

Perhaps the most pointed of all illustrations of the moral character of civil law is to be found in the laws relating to marriage and inheritance. They all proceed upon an essentially moral theory as to the relation of the sexes. Take the case of illegitimate children. A bastard is *filius nullius*—he inherits nothing, he has no claim on his putative father. What is all this except the expression of the strongest possible determination on the part of the Legislature to recognize, maintain, and favour marriage in every possible manner as the foundation of civilized society? It has been plausibly maintained that these laws bear hardly upon bastards, punishing them for the sins of their parents. It is not necessary to my purpose to go into this, though it appears to me that the law is right. I make the remark merely for the sake of showing to what lengths the law does habitually go for the purpose of maintaining the most important of all moral principles, the principle upon which one great department of it is entirely founded. It is a case in which a good object is promoted by efficient and adequate means.

* * *

I have now said what I had to say about liberty, and I may briefly sum up the result. It is that, if the word 'liberty' has any definite sense attached to it, and if it is consistently used in that sense, it is almost impossible to make any true general assertion whatever about it, and quite impossible to regard it either as a good thing or a bad one. If, on the other hand, the word is used merely in a general popular way without attaching any distinct signification to it, it is easy to make almost any general assertion you please about it; but these assertions will be incapable of either proof or disproof as they will have no definite meaning. Thus the word is either a misleading appeal to passion, or else it embodies or rather hints at an exceedingly complicated assertion, the truth of which can be proved only by elaborate historical investigations.

WILLMOORE KENDALL

The "Open Society" and Its Fallacies†

A little over 100 years ago John Stuart Mill wrote in his essay *On Liberty* that ". . . there ought to exist the fullest liberty of professing and discussing, as a matter of ethical conviction, any doctrine, however immoral it may be considered." The sentence from which this is taken is not *obiter*: Chapter II of his book is devoted to arguments, putatively philosophical in character, which if they were sound would warrant precisely such a conclusion;[1] we have therefore every reason to assume that Mill meant by the sentence just what it says. The topic of Chapter II is the entire "communications" process in civilized society ("advanced" society, as Mill puts it);[2] and the question he raises is whether there should be limitations on that process.[3] He treats that problem as the central problem of all civilized societies, the one to which all other problems are subordinate, because of the consequences, good or ill, that a society must bring upon itself according as it adopts this or that solution to it. And he has supreme confidence in the rightness of the solution he offers. Presumably to avoid all possible misunderstanding, he provides several alternative statements of it, each of which makes his intention abundantly clear, namely, that society must be so organized as to make that solution its supreme law. "Fullest," that is, absolute freedom of thought and speech, he asserts by clear implication[4] in the entire argument of the chapter, is not to be one of several competing goods society is to foster, one that on occasion might reasonably be sacrificed, in part at least, to the preservation

---

† From *The American Political Science Review*, 54 (1960), 972–79.

1. That is approximately how Mill himself puts it: the words preceding what I have quoted are, "If the arguments of the present chapter are of any validity, . . ." The chapter is entitled "Of the Liberty of Thought and Discussion."

2. ". . . we may leave out of consideration those backward states of society in which the race itself may be considered as in its nonage." The distinction seems to turn variously on whether "mankind have become capable of being improved by free and equal discussion" and whether they "have attained the capacity of being guided to their own improvement by conviction or persuasion." On the latter point he adds, perhaps a little optimistically: ". . . a period long since reached in all nations with whom we need here concern ourselves." He refers, astonishingly, to "the present low state of the human mind," that being the

point he needs to establish the thesis there in question.

3. Who should be permitted, in the fashionable jargon of the "communications" literature, "to say what, and to whom."

4. Those who regard "absolute" as too strong a term to be deemed a synonym of "fullest" may wish to be reminded of the following passage: ". . . the appropriate region of human liberty . . . comprises . . . liberty of conscience in the most comprehensive sense: liberty of thought and feeling; *absolute* freedom of opinion and sentiment on all subjects, practical or speculative, scientific, moral, or theological. [And the] liberty of expressing and publishing opinions . . . is practically inseparable from [liberty of thought] . . ." (italics added). And: "No society . . . is completely free in which [these liberties] . . . do not exist *absolute and unqualified*" (italics added).

of other goods; *i.e.,* he refuses to recognize any competing good in the name of which it can be limited. The silencing of dissenters on behalf of a received doctrine, of an accepted idea—this is an alternative statement—is *never* justified:[5] it can only do hurt, unwarranted hurt, alike to the person silenced, to the individual or group that silences, to the doctrine or idea on behalf of which the silencing is done, and to the society in the name of which the silencers silence.[6] The quotation I started with is, then, merely the strongest, the most intransigent, of several formulations of a general prescription he makes for advanced societies. We shall do well to examine it, phrase-by-phrase, before proceeding:

"There ought to exist"—*ought,* so that the prescription is put forward on ethical grounds—"the fullest liberty"—a liberty, *i.e.,* that no one (individual, government, even society as a whole) is entitled to interfere with—"of professing and discussing"—that is, of publicly propagating—"as a matter of ethical conviction"—which, however, as any reader can quickly satisfy himself by re-examining Chapter II, is not intended to exclude other types of conviction, "intellectual" conviction for example—"any doctrine"—and "doctrine" is not intended to exclude, either, since he uses the term synonymously with "idea" and "opinion"; usually, indeed, he prefers the word "opinion"—"however immoral it may be considered"— where "immoral" also is used merely to cover what Mill considers the extreme case, the case in which, he supposes, people are least likely to refrain from silencing; and he would be equally willing, as the context shows, to write "however wrong," that is, "however incorrect," "however dangerous," "however foolish," or even "however harmful," and where "it may be considered" is recognizably shorthand for "it may be considered by anyone whomsoever."

It is fashionable, these days, in part because of a fairly recent book by the scientist-philosopher K. R. Popper,[7] to call the kind of society Mill had in mind an "open society"—by at least implied contrast with a "closed" society, that is, an "hermetically sealed" society, in which Mill's grand principle is, by definition, *not* observed. And we are told, variously, by writers whom we may call (because they so call themselves) Liberals, that we have an open society and ought to protect it against the machinations of those who

5. ". . . I deny the right of the people to exercise such coercion, either by themselves or their government. The power itself is illegitimate. The best government has no more title to it than the worst." The statement could hardly be more sweeping.
6. Not to speak of "mankind." ". . . the peculiar evil of silencing the expression of an opinion is, that it is robbing the human race; . . . those who dissent from the opinion, still more than those who hold it."
7. K. R. Popper, *The Open Society and Its Enemies* (London, 1945), 2 vols. The term "open society" is of course much older (Bergson uses a distinction between "open" and "closed" society in *Les deux sources de la morale et de la religion,* though for a quite different purpose). Popper wedded the term "open society" to Mill's ideas, and the term "closed society" to those of his *bêtes noires,* Plato especially.

would like to close it; or that we have a closed society and ought, heeding Mill's arguments, to turn it forthwith into an open society; or that democracy, freedom, progress—any or all of them—must stand or fall, according as we maintain or inaugurate or return to an open society; or that all who are opposed to the idea of the open society are authoritarians, enemies of human freedom, totalitarians. We are told all this, however, at least in its application to civilized societies in general (as opposed to the United States in particular),[8] on grounds that have not varied perceptibly since Mill set them down in the *Essay*. We are still dealing, then, with Mill's issue; and we shall think more clearly about it, I believe, if we keep it stated as much as possible in his terms—for no subsequent pleader for the open society has possessed his clarity or vigor of mind—as follows: Ought there to exist in organized society—the United States, *e.g.*—that "fullest liberty of professing and discussing" that Mill argues for? On what theoretical grounds can that liberty be defended? Is openness of the kind Mill's society would possess one of the characteristics of the *good* society? Before attempting to deal with these questions, let me pause to clarify certain aspects of his position.

I

First, Mill must not be understood as saying, over-all, something *more* extravagant than he is actually saying. He is fully aware of the necessity for laws against libel and slander, and does not deem them inconsistent with his doctrine.[9] He is aware, also, of organized society's need to protect its younger members against certain forms of expression;[1] which is to say that his "fullest liberty of professing and discussing" is to obtain only among adults. Laws prohibiting, *e.g.*, the circulation of obscene literature amongst school-children, or, *e.g.*, utterance calculated to undermine the morals (however the society chooses to define morals) of a minor, are presumably not proscribed. Nor does the doctrine outlaw sanctions against incitement to crime[2]—provided, one must hasten to add, nothing political is involved (Mill would permit punishment for incitement to, *e.g.*, tyrannicide, only if it could be shown to have resulted in an overt act). And, finally—a topic about which, as it seems to me,

8. The exception is necessary, because the American arguments are often based on the meaning of the Constitution of the United States, the First Amendment especially.

9. "Whenever, in short, there is a definite damage, or a definite risk of [definite?] damage, either to an individual or to the public, the case is taken out of the province of liberty, and placed in that of morality and law."

1. ". . . protection against themselves is confessedly due to children and persons

under age. . . ."

2. ". . . even opinions lose their immunity when the circumstances in which they are expressed are such as to constitute their expression a positive instigation to some mischievous act." To this writer's mind a curious concession, which Mill ought *not* to have made. Once it is made, a society wishing to silence this or that form of persuasive utterance has only to declare the behavior it is calculated to produce a crime, and it may silence—with Mill's blessing.

there is much confusion amongst commentators on Mill—he would permit the police to disperse a mob where a riot is clearly imminent, even if its shoutings did bear upon some political, social, or economic issue; but not, he makes abundantly clear, on grounds of any official exception to the doctrinal tendency of the shoutings. The individuals concerned would be free to resume their agitation the following morning.

This is an important point because the passage in question, dealing with the mob at the corn-merchant's house, has given Mill an undeserved reputation for having been an adherent of the clear-and-present-danger doctrine as we know it today. We may perhaps clear it up best as follows. The situations covered by the clear-and-present-danger doctrine, as applied, *e.g.*, to the Communist "threat," and by parallel doctrines in contemporary political theory,[3] are those in which Mill was *most* concerned to maintain absolute liberty of discussion—those situations, namely, in which the ideas being expressed have a tendency dangerous to the established political, social, or economic order. We must not, then, suppose his society to be one in which anarchists, or defenders of polygamy, for example, could be silenced because of the likelihood of their picking up supporters and, finally, winning the day; since for Mill the likelihood of their picking up supporters is merely a further reason for letting them speak. *All* utterance with a bearing on public policy—political, social, or economic—is to be permitted, no matter what some members of society, even the majority, even all the members save some lonely dissenter,[4] may happen to think of it. Mill must, then, also not be understood as saying something *less* extravagant than he is actually saying.

Second, what is at issue for Mill is not merely unlimited freedom of speech (as just defined) but, as he makes abundantly clear, unlimited freedom of thought as well, *and* a way of life appropriate to their maintenance. To put it otherwise: when we elevate freedom of thought and speech to the position of society's highest good, it ceases to be merely freedom of thought and speech, and becomes—with respect to a great many important matters—the society's ultimate standard of *order*.

Mill did not dwell upon the inescapable implications of this aspect of his position; it has been left to his epigones, especially in the United States, to think the position out. The open society, they

3. *E.g.*, the doctrine that enemies of liberty must not be permitted to take advantage of "civil liberties" in order to undermine and destroy them; or the doctrine that free society is entitled to interfere with free expression in order to perpetuate its own existence. Mill would certainly not have countenanced either doctrine.

4. "If all mankind were of one opinion, and only one person were of the contrary opinion, mankind would be no more justified in silencing that one person, than he, if he had the power, would be justified in silencing all mankind."

tell us repeatedly, *must* see to it that all doctrines start out equal in the market-place of ideas; for society to assign an advantaged position to these doctrines rather than those would be tantamount to suppressing those; society can, therefore, have no orthodoxy, no public truth, no standard, upon whose validity it is entitled to insist; outside its private homes, its churches, and perhaps its non-public schools, it therefore cannot indoctrinate; *all* questions are for it open questions, and must, publicly, be treated as open. If it has public schools and universities, it will be told (and with unexceptionable logic), these also must treat all questions as open—otherwise what happens to the freedom of thought and so, ultimately, to the freedom of speech of the student who might have thought differently had his teachers not treated some questions as closed? Even if in their hearts and souls all the members of the open society believe in a particular religion, or a particular church, each must nevertheless be careful in his public capacity to treat all religions and churches as equal, to treat dissent, when and as it occurs, as the peer of dogma, to treat the voodoo missionary from Cuba as on an equal plane with an Archbishop of his own church.[5] The open society's first duty (so its custodians will remind it, and if not those at home then those abroad)[6] is to freedom; and that means that it is *not* free to give public status to its beliefs, its standards, and its loyalties. Mill's disciples are completely faithful to the spirit of his thought when they insist that if we mean business about freedom, that is how it is going to have to be. The open society confers "freedom" upon its members; but it does so at the cost of its own freedom as a society.

Third, Mill denies the existence—that is to say, at any particular place and moment—not only of a public truth,[7] but of any truth whatever unless it be the truth of the denial itself. (Let us not press this last too far, however, lest it seem a mere "debater's" point; it is, of course, the Achilles' heel of all skepticisms.) Reduced to its simplest terms, the argument of the *Essay* runs as follows: whenever and wherever men disagree about a teaching, a doctrine, an opinion, an idea, we have no way of knowing which party is correct; the man (or group) who moves to silence a teaching on the ground that it is incorrect attributes to himself a kind of knowledge (Mill says an "infallibility") that no one is ever entitled to claim short of (if then) the very case where the question is sure not to arise—that is, where there is unanimity, and so no temptation to silence to begin with. When, therefore, Mill's followers demand the elevation of skepticism to the status of a national religion, and the remaking of society in that image, they are not reading into his position some-

5. Who, after all, is to say which is right?
6. As witness the sermons addressed by the New York press to the Trujillo regime.
7. Except, we must remind ourselves, the public truth that there is no public truth.

thing that is not there—for all that Mill himself, as I have intimated, preserves a discreet silence on the detailed institutional consequences of his position. They are, rather, only making specific
applications of notions that, for Mill, are the point of departure for
the entire discussion.

The *basic* position, in fine, is not that society must have no
public truth, no orthodoxy, no preferred doctrines, *because* it must
have freedom of speech; but that it must not have them *for the
same reason* that it must have freedom of speech, namely: because,
in any given situation, no supposed truth has any proper claim to
special treatment, and this in turn because it may turn out to be
incorrect—nay, *will* turn out to be at least partially incorrect, since
each competing idea is at most a partial truth. Nor is that all:
Mill's freedom of speech doctrine is not merely derivative from a
preliminary assault upon truth itself; it is *inseparable from* that
assault and cannot, I contend, be defended on any other ground. It
is incompatible with religious, or any other, belief.

Fourth, Mill is not saying that no man must be silenced because
every man has a "right" to freedom of speech. Consistent skeptic
that he is, he warns us—and from an early moment—that he dis-
claims any advantage that might accrue to his argument from an
appeal to abstract right; he is going to justify his position in terms
of "utility," in terms of "the permanent interest of a man [*sic*] as a
progressive being," whatever that may mean; and he sticks scrupulously to at least the first half of the promise throughout the *Essay*.
This raises interesting questions as to (a) what Mill could have
meant—whether indeed he means anything at all that people committed to the idea of abstract right might find intelligible—by such
words as "ethical," "immoral," etc.; as to (b) the pains Mill takes,
throughout his main argument, to reduce the question, "Should
some types of expression be prohibited in civilized society because
the ideas they express are wicked?" to the question, "Should some
types of expression be prohibited because they are intellectually
incorrect?"; and as to (c) the kind of moral fervor his followers
have poured into the propagation of his views. Everything reduces
itself for Mill to intellectual argument, where you either win or
draw or lose by the sheer appeal to reason—which, for Mill,
excludes *ex hypothesi* any appeal to revelation or authority, for that
would merely precipitate an endless discussion as to the status, from
the standpoint of reason, of revelation and authority.

The notion of a "right" to freedom of speech, a capacity on the
part of every man to say what he pleases that society must respect,
because he is *entitled* to it—of a right that men have to live in the
kind of society that Mill projects—is a later development. It occurs
in different countries for different reasons and under different auspices; but to the extent that it is intended seriously it represents a

complete break with Mill. Those who appeal to such a notion therefore have in his own shrewd example a warning that they must not
attempt to do so on his grounds;[8] and much current confusion
about the open society would be avoided if they would but take the
warning to heart. In short, if we are going to speak of a *right* to
freedom of speech, a *right* to live in an open society, we are going
to have to justify it with arguments of a different character from
Mill's, and so move the discussion onto a plane entirely different
from Mill's. We are, above all, going to have to subordinate what
we have to say to certain rules of discourse from which Mill, by his
own fiat, is happily free. For any such right is inconceivable save as
one component of a system or complex of rights, that mutually
limit and determine one another and are meaningless save as they
are deemed subject to the general proposition that we are not entitled to the exercise of *any* right unless we discharge the duties correlative to that right. Once we begin to argue from premises of that
sort we shall begin to talk sense, not nonsense, about freedom of
speech and the open society. And the essence of the sense, I hasten
to add, will be found to lie in the fact that we are no longer driving
the roots of our doctrine into the soil of skepticism, because (as I
have suggested already) once we speak of a right[9] we have already
ceased to be skeptics. And nohing is more certain than that we shall
come out with something quite different from Popper's conception
of the open society.

Fifth, Mill was fully aware (as his disciples seem not to be) both
of the novelty and of the revolutionary character of his proposal for
a society organized around the notion of freedom of speech. Just as
he deliberately cuts himself off from any appeal to the notion of
abstract right, so does he cut himself off from any appeal to tradition. Not only had no one ever before taught his doctrine concerning freedom of speech. No one had ever taught a doctrine even
remotely like his. No one, indeed, had ever discussed such a doctrine even as a matter of speculative fancy.[1] Hardly less than
Machiavelli, and more than Hobbes, Mill is in full rebellion against
both religion and philosophy, and so in full rebellion also against
the traditional society that embodies them.[2] Hardly less than
Machiavelli, he conceives himself a "new prince in a new state,"
obliged to destroy what has preceded him so that he may create
what he feels stirring within him. Hardly less than Machiavelli,
again, he is a teacher of *evil*: all truths that have preceded his are

---

8. We must distinguish here between a
"natural" or "ethical" "right" to freedom of expression and a mere constitutional right. The case for the latter could
of course be rested upon Mill's grounds,
insofar as they are valid.
9. Again, we must except the merely

constitutional right.
1. Plato, of course, contemplates a freedom of speech *situation* in Book IX of
the *Republic*; but merely to show that it
can result only in disaster.
2. *Cf.* Leo Strauss, *Thoughts on Machiavelli* (Glencoe, Ill., 1958), ch. 4, *passim.*

(as we have noted in passing above) at most partial truths, and enjoy even that status only because Mill confers it upon them. To reverse a famous phrase, Mill thinks of himself as standing not upon the shoulders of giants but of pygmies. He appeals to no earlier teacher,[3] identifies himself with nothing out of the past; and his doctrine of freedom of speech is, as I have intimated already, the unavoidable logical consequence of the denials from which his thought moves. Not, however, because it is in fact to be the public policy of the society he will found, not because it is to govern his followers' actions with respect to the freedom of thought of others, but because it is the perfect weapon—perfect because of its alleged connection with the quest for truth—to turn upon the traditional society that he must overthrow. For he who would destroy a society must first destroy the public truth it conceives itself as embodying; and Mill's doctrine of freedom of speech, to the extent that it gets itself accepted publicly, does precisely that. I do not, I repeat, believe it can be separated from the evil teaching that underlies it; and nothing could be more astonishing than the incidence of persons amongst us who because of their religious commitments must repudiate the evil teaching, yet continue to embrace the doctrine.

Sixth, Mill's most daring *démarche* in the *Essay* (and Popper's in the *Open Society and Its Enemies*) is that of confronting the reader with a series of false dilemmas: unlimited freedom of speech or all-out thought-control; the open society or the closed society; etc. I say "false" for two reasons: first, because unlimited freedom of speech and the open society are not real alternatives at all, as I hope shortly to show. And second, because the dilemmas as posed conceal the real choices available to us, which are always choices as to how-open-how-closed our society is to be, and thus not choices between two possibilities but choices among an infinite range of possibilities. Mill would have us choose between never silencing and declaring ourselves infallible, as Popper would have us believe that a society cannot be a little bit closed, any more than a woman can be a little bit pregnant. All our knowledge of politics bids us not to fall into that trap. Nobody wants all-out thought-control or the closed society; and nobody has any business pretending that somebody else wants them. For the real question is, how open can a society be and still remain open at all? Or, to put it differently, is there any surer prescription for arriving, willy nilly, in spite of ourselves, at the closed society, than is involved in current pleas for the open society?

II

That brings me to the central business of this article, which I may put as follows. Let us adjourn objections to open society doc-

3. That he had broken sharply with his father and with Bentham is, I take it, a commonplace.

trines on the ground that they are rooted in demonstrably evil
teachings. Let us also suppose, *arguendo*, that we have organized a
society in accordance with Mill's prescriptions, and for Mill's reasons. Have we then cause to suppose, as Mill thinks, that we shall
end up forwarding the interests of truth? In other words, Mill offers
us not only an exhortation but a prediction, and we wish merely to
know what would in fact happen if we did what he tells us to do.
My contention will be that, once the question is put in that way,[4]
we run up against some insuperable objections to his prescriptions
in and of themselves—objections, moreover, that remain equally
valid even if one starts out, unlike Mill, from a supposed "right,"
whether natural or constitutional, to freedom of speech. I shall
argue the objections in a logical order such that if each in turn were
overcome the remaining ones would still stand.

Mill's proposals have as one of their tacit premises a false conception of the nature of society, and are, therefore, unrealistic on their
face. They assume that society is, so to speak, a *debating club*
devoted above all to the pursuit of truth, and capable therefore of
subordinating itself—and all other considerations, goods, and goals
—to that pursuit. Otherwise, the proposals would go no further
than to urge upon society the common-sense view that the pursuit
of truth is *one* of the goods it ought to cherish (even perhaps that
one which it is most likely, in the press of other matters, to fail to
make sufficient provision for); that it will neglect this good only at
its own peril (a point that could easily be demonstrated); and that,
accordingly, it should give hard and careful thought to what kind of
provision it can make for it without disrupting unduly the pursuit
of other goods. But we know only too well that society is *not* a
debating club—all our experience of society drives the point home
—and that, even if it were one, like the UN General Assembly, say,
the chances of its adopting the pursuit of truth as its supreme good
are negligible. Societies, alike by definition and by the teaching of
history, cherish a whole series of goods—among others, their own
self-preservation, the *living* of the truth they believe themselves to
embody already, and the communication of that truth (pretty much
intact, moreover) to future generations, their religion, etc.—which
they are not only likely to value as much as or more than the pursuit of truth, but *ought* to value as much as or more than the pursuit of truth, because these are *preconditions* of the pursuit of
truth.

To put it a little differently, the proposals misconceive the strategic problem, over against organized society, of those individuals who
do value the pursuit of truth above all other things. That strategic
problem we may state as follows: *fortunate* that society that has

4. *I.e.*, as a problem for "empirical" political theory.

even a small handful—a "select minority," in Ortega y Gasset's phrase—of persons who value the pursuit of truth in the way in which Mill imagines a society valuing it. *Fortunate* that select minority in such a society, if it can prevail upon the society to provide it with the leisure and resources with which to engage in the pursuit of truth; or, failing that, at least not to stand in the way of its pursuit of truth. And *wise* that society whose decision-makers see deeply enough into things to provide that select minority—even in the context of guarantees against its abusing its privileges—the leisure and the resources it needs for the pursuit of truth. To ask more than that of society, to ask that it give that select minority freedom to treat publicly all questions as open questions, as open not only for itself in the course of its discharge of its own peculiar function but for everybody, is Utopian in the worst sense of the word; and so, certain to defeat the very purpose the asking is intended to serve. By asking for all, even assuming that all to be desirable, we imperil our chances of getting that little we might have got had we asked only for that little.

If we nevertheless waive that objection, we confront another, namely, that the proposals have as a further tacit premise a false conception of human beings, and how they act in organized society. Concretely, Mill not only assumes that speech (the professing and discussing of any doctrine, however immoral) is incapable of doing hurt in society. (He has to assume this, since he calls for non-interference with speech, while the overriding principle of the *Essay* is that society is always entitled to interfere in order to prevent hurt, whether to itself or to its individual members.) This is disturbing enough: Socrates, we recall, taught otherwise, namely, that he who teaches my neighbor evil does *me* hurt. But Mill also assumes (else again his proposal is romantic) that people can be persuaded either to *be* indifferent toward the possible tendency of what their neighbors are saying, or at least to *act* as if they were indifferent. We know nothing about people, I suggest, that warrants our regarding such an assumption, once it is brought out into the open, as valid. Thus his proposals, like all political proposals that call implicitly for the refashioning of human nature, can be enforced only through some large-scale institutional coercion. And I believe it to be this consideration, above all, that explains the failure of Mill's followers, to date, to persuade any organized society to adopt his proposals. We have no experience of unlimited freedom of speech as Mill defines it, of the open society as Popper defines it, unless, after a fashion and for a brief moment, in Weimar Germany—an experience no organized society will be eager to repeat.

Let us now turn to still another objection. I contend that such a society will become *intolerant*, one in which the pursuit of truth can only come to a halt. Whatever the private convictions of the society's individual members concerning what Plato teaches us to call the important things (that is, the things with which truth is primarily concerned), the society itself is now, by definition, dedicated to a national religion of skepticism, to the suspension of judgment as *the* exercise of judgment *par excellence*. It can, to be sure, tolerate all expression of opinion that is predicated upon its own view of truth; but what is it to do with the man who steps forward to urge an opinion, to conduct an inquiry, *not* predicated on that view? What is it to do with the man who, with every syllable of faith he utters, challenges the very foundations of skeptical society? What can it say to him except, "Sir, you cannot enter into our discussions, because you and we have no common premises from which discussion between us can be initiated?" What can it do, in a word, but silence him, and look on helplessly as within its own bosom the opinions about the important things descend into an ever greater conforming dullness? Nor—unlike traditional society, which did *not* regard all questions as open questions—need it hesitate to silence him. The proposition that all opinions are equally—and hence infinitely—valuable, said to be the unavoidable inference from the proposition that all opinions are equal, is only one—and perhaps the less likely—of two possible inferences, the other being: all opinions are equally—and hence infinitely—*without* value, so what difference does it make if one, particularly one not our own, gets suppressed?[5] This we may fairly call the central paradox of the theory of freedom of speech. In order to practice tolerance on behalf of the pursuit of truth, you have first to value and believe in not merely the pursuit of truth but Truth itself, with all its accumulated riches to date. The all-questions-are-open-questions society cannot do that; it cannot, therefore, practice tolerance towards those who disagree with it. It must persecute—and so, on its very own showing, arrest the pursuit of truth.

I next contend that such a society as Mill prescribed will descend ineluctably into ever-deepening *differences of opinion*, into progressive breakdown of those common premises upon which alone a

5. *Cf.* Bertrand de Jouvenel, *On Sovereignty* (Chicago, 1957), p. 288: "One of the strangest intellectual illusions of the nineteenth century was the idea that toleration could be ensured by moral relativism. . . . The relativist tells us that the man professing opinion A ought to respect opinion B, because his own opinion A has no more intrinsic value than B. But in that case B has no more than A. Attempts to impose either would be attempts to impose what had no intrinsic value; but also suppression of either would be suppression of what had no intrinsic value. And in that case, there is no crime . . . in the suppression of contrary opinions." On the progress in Mill from "equally valuable" to "equally and infinitely valuable," *cf.*: ". . . truth has no chance but in proportion as every side of it, every opinion which embodies any fraction of the truth, not only finds advocates, but is so advocated as to be listened to." And the presumption, he insists, is that every opinion *does* contain some fraction of the truth: ". . . it is always probable that dissentients have something worth hearing . . . and that truth would lose something by their silence."

society can conduct its affairs by discussion, and so into the abandonment of the discussion process and the arbitrament of public questions by violence and civil war. This is the phenomenon—we may call it the dispersal of opinion—to which Rousseau, our greatest modern theorist of the problem, recurred again and again in his writings.[6] The all-questions-are-open-questions society cannot endeavor to arrest it, by giving preferred status to certain opinions and, at the margin, mobilizing itself internally for their defense; for by definition it places a *premium* upon dispersion by inviting irresponsible speculation and irresponsible utterance. As time passes, moreover, the extremes of opinion will—as they did in Weimar—grow further and further apart, so that (for the reason noted above) their bearers can less and less tolerate even the thought of one another, still less one another's presence in society. And again the ultimate loser is the pursuit of truth.

Still another tacit premise of the proposals is the extraordinary notion that the discussion process, which correctly understood does indeed forward the pursuit of truth, and does indeed call for *free* discussion, is one and the same thing with Mill's unlimited freedom of speech. They rest, in consequence, upon a false conception of the discussion process. What they will produce is not truth but rather only deafening noise and demoralizing confusion. For the essence of Mill's freedom of speech is the divorce of the right to speak from the duties correlative to the right; the right to speak is a right to speak *ad nauseam*, and with impunity. It is shot through and through with the egalitarian overtones of the French Revolution, which are as different from the measured aristocratic overtones of the pursuit of truth by discussion, as understood by the tradition Mill was attacking, as philosophy is different from phosphorus.

Of the latter point we may sufficiently satisfy ourselves, it seems to me, by recalling how the discussion process works in those situations in which men who are products of the tradition organize themselves for a serious venture in the pursuit of truth—as they do in, say, a branch of scholarship, an academic *discipline*, and the community of truth-seekers corresponding to it.[7]

Such men demonstrably proceed on some such principles as these: (a) The pursuit of truth is indeed forwarded by the exchange of opinions and ideas among many; helpful suggestions do

6. See *Social Contract*, IV, i, as also *The Discourse on the Sciences and Arts*, *passim*, and Rousseau's famous letter of 1767 to the Marquis of Mirabeau. *Cf.* de Jouvenel, *op. cit.*, p. 286: "The whole of [Rousseau's] . . . large stock of political wisdom consists in contrasting the dispersion of feelings in a people morally disintegrated by the progress of the 'sciences and arts,' with the natural unity of a people in which dissociation has not occurred." As de Jouvenel notes (p. 287), Rousseau, though himself a Protestant, deplored the introduction of Protestantism into France, and on these grounds.

7. A similar point might be developed over the difference between Mill's freedom of speech and the free discussion of the traditional American town-meeting.

indeed emerge sometimes from surprising quarters; but one does not leap from these facts to the conclusion that helpful suggestions may come from just anybody. (b) The man or woman who wishes to exercise the right to be heard has a logically and temporally prior obligation to *prepare* himself for participation in the exchange, and to prepare himself in the manner defined by the community. Moreover (c), from the moment he begins to participate in the exchange, he must make manifest, by his behavior, his sense of the duty to act as if the other participants had something to teach him —the duty, in a word, to see to it that the exchange goes forward in an atmosphere of courtesy and mutual self-respect. Next (d), the entrant must so behave as to show that he understands that scholarly investigation did not begin with his appearance on the scene, that there is a strong presumption that prior investigators have not labored entirely in vain, and that the community is the custodian of —let us not sidestep the *mot juste*—an *orthodoxy*, no part of which it is going to set lightly to one side. (e) That orthodoxy must be understood as concerning first and foremost the frame of reference within which the exchange of ideas and opinions is to go forward. That frame of reference is, to be sure, subject to change, but this is a matter of meeting the arguments that led originally to its adoption, and meeting them in recognition that the ultimate decision, as to whether or not to change it, lies with the community. (f) The entrant, insofar as he wishes to challenge the orthodoxy, must expect barriers to be placed in his way, and must not be astonished if he is punished, at least in the short term, by what are fashionably called "deprivations"; he must, indeed, recognize that the barriers and the deprivations are a necessary part of the organized procedure by which truth is pursued. (g) Access to the channels of communication that represent the community's central ritual (the learned journals, that is to say) is something that the entrant wins by performing the obligation to produce a craftsmanlike piece of work. (h) The ultimate fate of the entrant who disagrees with the orthodoxy but cannot persuade the community to accept his point of view is, quite simply, isolation within or banishment from the community.

No suggestion is made that this is a complete statement of the rules as we see them operating about us in the scholarly disciplines, or that the particular forms of words employed are the happiest, or most accurate, that could be found. They do, however, seem to me to suggest the broad outlines of the paradigm of the free discussion process as it goes forward in an academic community, and to drive home its differences from the freedom of speech process as Mill defines it. Nor I think, could anything be more obvious than the answer to the question, which of the two is the more likely to forward the pursuit of truth? But this is not all. *The* point about Mill's model is that by giving equal privileges to those who are in fact opposed to or ignorant of the discussion process, it constitutes a major onslaught against Truth. The two paradigms are not only different, but incompatible.

It would not be easy, of course, to transfer the rules of the discussion process set forth here to the public forum of a society; nor is there any point in denying that the transfer would involve our openly conceding to society far greater powers, particularly as regards silencing the ill-mannered, the ignorant, the irrelevant, than it would ever enjoy under Mill's prescription. Here, however, two things must be kept in mind. First (however reluctant we may be to admit it), that society always has, and constantly exercises, the power to silence. And second, that no society is likely, within the foreseeable future, to remake itself in the image of either of the two paradigms. The question, always, is that of which of the two we accept as the ideal toward which we try to move. That is the real issue at stake between the proponents and opponents of the "open society."

MAURICE COWLING

[The Illiberalism of John Stuart Mill]†

The situation Mill feels called on to deal with—the historic mission it is his business to fulfil—is to provide a body of commanding doctrine which, by stimulating the higher intelligence of all citizens, will produce, as a consequence, not individualistic anarchy, but that sense of active participation which well-regulated societies alone are capable of providing. Mill is attempting to establish a binding philosophy, a moral, ethical and social doctrine which will both tell men what their duties are, and induce that sense of common participation, of which the great changes in European society, and the decay of old opinions, have deprived them.

* * *

At the centre of Mill's ethical teaching are to be found, involved with the principle of utility, a set of doctrines about liberty, a set of doctrines about education and a set of doctrines about the desirability of recurrent critical self-examination. None of these doctrines can be understood without reference to the others. All tend in the same direction: the content of each is the same as the content of

† From Maurice Cowling, *Mill and Liberalism* (Cambridge, 1963), pp. 12–15, 22–23, 25–26, 28–33, 41–44, 98–105.

the others. The conception he has in mind, the position to which he wishes to persuade, is the desirability of creating a society which is morally homogeneous and intellectually healthy, because most men (including the poor) not only have the opportunity to reach, but succeed in reaching, an educational level sufficient to enable them to reflect on the content of their ethical and social purposes, to replace customary deference to arbitrarily established authority by rational deference to elevated intellect, and to reach (in virtue of rational reflection) agreed, superior judgements about the character of the means by which to decide what actions are right. This is deliberate commitment to persuade to a self-conscious ethic—an outcome of the belief that only ethical or political positions which have been arrived at as a result of articulate reflection and disinterested motivation have binding authority. Mill has sufficient respect for custom to recognize that a great deal of human action must always be taken without immediate reflective questioning: he accepts the fact that, once good principles have been established as a basis for conduct, they will not need to be subjected to critical examination on every occasion. Nevertheless, above the level at which habit can judge the rationality of social convention, is a body of what Mill calls *principles* to which commitment must be given self-consciously, deliberately and after critical consideration. Each age has a principle, or set of principles, which is more fundamental than the rest: the integrity of an age (or society) is measured by the extent to which the principle is grasped, and assented to, by those who are part of it. So far as a man, or group, investigates the rationality, or truth, of a principle of action, he is acting reasonably: so far as he accepts it on trust, out of blind habit or in obedience to custom, he fails in an essential form of activity. Mill's view of history is dominated by consciousness of conflict between, on the one hand, prejudice and habit, and, on the other, the higher reasoning of the reflective mind, which succeeds, as a rational creation, in determining its motive for itself. All human history testifies to the existence of the struggle; the destiny of superior intellect in contemporary society is to carry its victories to a higher stage of accomplishment.

Mill's position, however, is not just the simple assertion of a crude, vulgar, intellectualized libertarianism. He is saying that all men have an obligation, and, once they have been educated, have the opportunity, to submit their own, and society's actions, to rational questioning. They can, in other words, and ought to, ask always for the reason for an action, or the principle an institution is supposed to embody; if the action has no reason and the institution seems to be in conflict with principle, they should abandon the one and make the other conform more closely. All men have an obligation to do this. Opinions need not be accepted because they have *been* accepted ('received' is his word) in the past: nor need they be accepted because the majority have come to accept them in the present. The individual judgement is free: a man's destiny is to exercise this aspect of his rational freedom. Truth may well be found in the judgement of an individual: an eccentric individual, defying the collective judgement of society (which may also be its collective mediocrity) may well be justified by this possibility.

Nevertheless, if it is the individual's duty (and particularly the educated individual's duty) to submit all action to scrutiny by self-conscious ethical judgement, Mill is not advocating anarchic assertion of individual freedom. The emphasis, in Mill's justification of freedom, is neither on its intrinsic goodness nor on any belief man may have in its natural rightness, but on the fact that a free individual is more likely than an unfree one to contribute to the higher cultivation. This is why he advocates recurring critical self-examination. He does not commit himself to it because it is naturally good or because it is 'natural' to man to want it. Nature is not, in Mill's view, good: all the good in the world is the result of human effort to improve Nature. If Mill comes near to regarding reflective questioning as good in itself, without regard to its consequences, he makes clear his belief that a questioning which did not produce general agreement about the desirability of the higher cultivation would have failed to be a desirable questioning. Mill can face the possibility of initial disagreement between the judgements of reflecting men because he assumes that minds which have been properly educated will ultimately agree in their view of the grounds on which individual freedom should be limited. * * * What Mill hoped for from the process of critical questioning, what he assumed to be the natural outcome of the probing for reasons, is the establishment in a healthy society (almost, indeed, as proof of the existence of a healthy society) of a body of definitive opinions whose authority is no longer in doubt because they have been reached by agreed, rational, self-evident reasoning. Mill accused Comte of being 'a morality-intoxicated man'. By this he meant that Comte, seeing that 'egoism is bound, and should be taught, always to give way to the well-understood interests of enlarged altruism' drew the erroneous conclusion that 'because the good of the human race is the ultimate standard of right and wrong . . . [therefore] the good of others is the only inducement on which we should allow ourselves to act'. Mill does not, at the superficial level, make this mistake. He is articulately hostile to 'unity' and 'systematisation', particularly when they are, in Comte's scheme, connected with the spiritual despotism of the learned. 'Why' he asks 'this universal systematising, systematising, systematising? Why is it necessary that all human life should point but to one object, and be cultivated into a system of means to a single end?': and one thinks, at this point, that Mill is as libertarian as he wishes to appear.

Yet, if one looks more closely, his reasons and expectations are scarcely less 'unified' than Comte's. He says, it is true, that 'mankind who, after all are made up of single human beings, obtain a greater sum of happiness when each pursues his own . . . than when each makes the good of the rest his only object'. Individual 'happiness' in Mill, however, means not any happiness the individual happens to desire, but the sort of elevated happiness men should (because they do?) desire. 'Mankind' would not, in Mill's view, 'obtain a greater sum of happiness' if each individual pursued an uninstructed idea of 'happiness'. When Mill uses *happiness*, he means the happiness that *rational* reflection would approve, not *any* pleasure a man *happens* to pursue. This greatly limits the range of acceptable action. When connected with the provision that happiness must be pursued 'under the rules and conditions required by the good of the rest', that 'it is incumbent on everyone to restrain the pursuit of his personal objects within the limits consistent with the essential interests of others' and that 'it is the province of ethical science to determine . . . what those limits are', it compels us to conclude that, although his ethical injunctions are not the same as Comte's, they are, in spite of the disingenuousness of the language in which they are surrounded, quite as effective in proscribing large ranges of conduct. This is not surprising: everyone who sets up as an ethical teacher condemns or excludes other sorts of ethical teaching. Mill is at liberty to criticize Comte for 'prodigiously exaggerat[ing] . . . moral restraints', and Calvinism for failing to perceive that 'between the region of duty and that of sin there is an intermediate space, the region of positive worthiness'. It is reasonable to claim, if as a utilitarian he wants to, that 'spontaneity' must be maintained if we are to approve the efforts men make to increase the good of others beyond the 'standard of altruism' which *all* have an *obligation* to reach. He is free to assert that 'sufficient gratification of the [egoistic propensities], short of excess, but up to the measure which renders the enjoyment greatest, is almost always favourable to the benevolent affections' and he may well be right to suggest that 'demanding no more . . . as a rule of conduct . . . [than that] no more should be attempted than to prevent people from doing harm to others, or omitting to do such good as they have undertaken . . . society, in any tolerable circumstances, obtains much more'.

All these things it may be legitimate to say; what is not legitimate is, in the same breath, to suppose that these injunctions are the necessary conclusions of ethical philosophy, binding on all society, or that they leave room for the belief that 'there could be more than one road to human happiness'.[1] By the side of Comte's, Mill's happiness has 'more', as he says 'than one ingredient in it': but he is saying, nevertheless, that there is *a* doctrine, one doctrine, defining the nature of happiness and the means to achieve it, and that that doctrine is binding. 'The means' involve proper disposition of the motives through critical self-examination, and sensitivity to the highest rationality humanity can reach. Happiness will not come if all men try to be saints, or if government, or public opinion, tries to make them. Theocratic government would reduce the possibility of happiness: so would a society, like the one in which Mill lived, where pressure to conform is more extensive than the pressure permitted by Mill's injunctions. Abstractly put, Mill's statements seem innocuously libertarian: when confronted with the positions they exclude, they look like the brisk resolution of an ancient difficulty.

* * *

It is in this setting and against this background that Mill's doctrine about liberty must be viewed. His detailed delimitation of the power of society (and government) in relation to the individual is made, not in view of the natural right of individuals to be free, but from regard to the consequence to the general interest of imposing limitations on the exercise of social pressure to conform. For natural rights Mill had as much dislike as Bentham. Pursuit of individual liberty for Mill is not, by itself and without regard to its consequences, a proper end of social action. Individuals must be left as free as possible from social pressure, not because they have a *right* to consideration of this sort, but because, if they are not left free, society may find it more difficult than otherwise to achieve the ends for which it exists. Individual freedom must be maximized, not because diversity of opinion is desirable in itself, but because, without diversity of opinion, men are unlikely to approach nearer to truth than they have done hitherto. What Mill means by truth is a question that requires investigation: whatever he means, it is this, and not individual liberty, which he regards as the important objective of human endeavour. The demand for liberty is not the assertion of a fundamentally binding end, but the designation of a means to the end—the end of allowing men to approach as close as possible to that highest of all pleasures which comes from mental cultivation of the closest approximation possible to knowledge of what is True. Liberty is desirable because it is only when conflict of opinion is allowed free play that all free minds are able, in unison with all others, to feel a common sense of participation in the search for the Kingdom of Truth. * * *

1. Mill, *Auguste Comte and Positivism* (Ann Arbor, Mich., 1961, and London, 1866), pp. 138–45.

Mill, then, is offering persuasion, not to a vulgarly libertarian position, but to a unitary ethic, based on a unitary noetic, which assumes neither that methods of right reasoning are various and diverse, nor that there will be ultimate divergence about its injunctions. It assumes, on the contrary, that, given liberty to reflect and freedom from pressure of mediocrity, the higher minds will use their liberty (and the lower minds, perhaps, even theirs) to play their part in establishing a disinterestedly utilitarian ethic which will have been validated by agreed philosophical procedures. The content of the ethic is a good deal less specific than is sometimes supposed: the type of moral character involved a good deal more uncertain. But of one thing there can be no doubt—in the area in which individuals should be left free to cultivate their motives, the principle of utility will cover *all* the good ends to which rational consideration should make men want to move: and the combination of liberty, utility and general culture is a Revelation-case into which is stuffed *everything* that ought, in Mill's view, to be desired by sensible men.

The political positions for which Mill is famous—delimitating the power of government and asserting the need to maintain a high degree of individual social freedom—are characteristic preoccupations of his writing at all times throughout his life. They are, however, * * * not his chief preoccupations: nor do they represent the central principle from which other positions follow. The central principle is the principle of utility put in the broad manner in which Mill puts it, and having the moral and ethical overtones with which he surrounds it. The principle may also be called the principle of liberty: but it is a sort of spiritual, moral and rational liberty more extensive than the libertarianism for which Mill's doctrine is sometimes mistaken. The doctrine is less practically libertarian in implication than is often supposed, since Mill assumes that, given as wide a freedom as possible to exercise rational choice and taking this freedom as the means, the end will be achieved, not of diversity of opinion pure and simple, but of diversity of opinion within the limits of a rationally homogeneous, agreed, social consensus about the method of judging and the right end to be approached. In considering Mill's specific political injunctions, it is necessary, therefore, to distinguish the instrumental liberties from the ultimate consensus: though, once the distinction is made, it is legitimate to examine the character of the consequences which flow from commitment to pursue the ultimate, general objective.

* * *

However, the fact that Mill claims for his doctrine the respectability of Freedom need not make us accept his rhetoric at its face value. Mill was addicted to the rhetoric of Freedom as much as to the rhetoric of Truth: but about both it is necessary to ask questions. In particular, we must ask what it is that freedom is supposed to replace, what it is that individuality is supposed to do, and what sort of individuality it is to which men are obliged to move. For, once these questions are answered, Mill's principles seem no more than preferences for one type of polity and character over another. There is nothing self-evident about his preferences: neither Truth nor variety of human accomplishment are preserves of any particular type; there is no need to credit Mill's principles with greater rationality or necessary capacity for maximizing diversity. To establish this is important. For, if it can be established that *individuality* in his writing includes less than all the ends to which men might want to move, then the principle of individuality is designed to detract from human freedom, not to maximize it.

In order to understand the nature of Mill's purpose, it is essential to avoid detailed entanglement in the principles by which relations between government, public opinion and individual action are to be regulated. Instead, we have to ask why Mill wants their respective spheres delimited. We must examine the *objective* to which the principle is directed, rather than the application of the principle itself.

*　*　*

The principle * * * leaves the impression, indeed, of being * * * definitively inquisitorial. * * * The interest of a man is not, in Mill's usage, his interest in a vulgar selfish sense: a man's interest is his interest as a progressive being—a progressive being with an obligation to be concerned for the well-being of society as a whole, and to maximize the greatest amount of happiness altogether. Often, as we have seen, there is no conflict between individual self-interest and the interest of society as a whole, but where there is, the individual's duty is to consider, not his own happiness, but the greatest amount of happiness altogether.

Now the greatest amount of happiness altogether is not maximized if men insist on following their selfish interests at the expense of general happiness: nor will it be maximized if they follow their lower, sensual natures at the expense of the higher. It will not be maximized, either, if they refuse to be educated, decline to be persuaded to the rational conclusions enjoined by their higher natures or refuse to give that deference to superiority of intellect which Mill assumes rational, educated men will always wish to give. From this it follows that, if the duty of society (or government) is to restrict individuality (when necessary) in order to maximize general utility, then individuality is likely to flourish only so long as it is connected with the higher cultivation of the sentiments. The sort of social or governmental pressure which might, therefore, be admissible on this principle is more searching than superficial attention to the principle suggests. For, if interference with individual liberty *can* be justified on the ground that interference is in the interest of others, and if the interest of others is taken to lie in producing the greatest amount of higher happiness possible, then the injunction is no less vague than before in defining the *amount* of legitimate social (or governmental) pressure, but much more specific in determining the *purpose* to which interference should be put.

Mill distinguishes, it is true, between actions which do injury to the interests of others, and those which do not; and observes that 'the inconveniences which are strictly inseparable from the unfavourable judgement of others, are the only ones to which a person should ever be subjected for that portion of his conduct and character which concerns his own good, but which does not affect the interest of others in their relations with him'. Social action is not appropriate in these cases. In cases where the interests of other people *are* affected, moral disapproval is desirable, not only of the actions themselves but of the dispositions which produce them. But 'the self-regarding faults . . . are not properly immoralities . . . They may be proofs of any amount of folly . . . but . . . the term duty to oneself; when it means anything more than prudence, means self-respect or self-development', and, along with other duties to ourselves, '[is] not socially obligatory, unless circumstances render them at the same time duties to others'. This limits the extent to which Mill will tolerate interference with individuality and might seem to make his principle more libertarian than we are suggesting. But it is necessary to ask: why is liberty to be absolute at this point? why, when no assignable damage is done to the interest of others, should a man be left free to do what he likes with himself? And Mill's answer is, not so much because diversity of individual character is desirable *in itself*, but 'because for none of [these duties to oneself] is it *for the good of mankind* that [a man] be held accountable to [his fellow creatures]', and because 'the inconvenience [which society suffers from self-regarding, self-affecting faults] is one which society can afford to bear *for the sake of the greater good of human freedom*'.

'For the sake of the greater good of human freedom', it may be objected, dismisses the view we are taking of Mill's doctrine, and it must, on the face of it, be agreed, that it does. Again, however, it is desirable to ask what *freedom* in Mill is for, and what is the *good of mankind* to which the convenience of bringing social pressure to bear is to be postponed. When the question is asked in this way, the answer will not be disappointing. For the answer is, as it always is in Mill—general social utility, the end and justification of *all* social action.

General utility for Mill means, as we know, maximization, not of *any* happiness, but of the higher happiness, the freedom of men to engage in rational pursuit of disinterestedness and truth. Maximization of the higher happiness comes when men are left free (from mediocre social pressure) to reflect on, and choose, the right action rather than the wrong one. The object of right social policy is to find the best means to achieve this end. 'The merely contingent . . . injury which a person causes to society, by conduct which neither violates any specific duty to the public, nor occasions perceptible hurt to any assignable individual except himself' *does* damage society, so far as it diminishes the stock of mental cultivation. The fact that damage *is* done, however, does not mean that society should interfere. Interference would produce consequences no less disagreeable than the consequences that flow from refusing to interfere: once the differing consequences are compared, interference must be rejected. It must be rejected because, in pursuit of 'the good of mankind' and 'for the sake of the greater good' which 'human freedom' brings, non-interference will be more conducive to utility. Where assignable damage *is* done to the interests of others, then the assignable damage outweighs the damage done by restriction of individual liberty, and punishment, or disapprobation, *has* to be imposed. But where assignable damage is not done (or, perhaps, Mill might add, cannot be measured), then men are more likely to maximize utility (despite the inconvenience) by allowing full individual liberty, than by preventing the damage a free man may do by perversely misusing his freedom.

For, even when men are free of governmental or social disapprobation, society still has means of inducing them to act rationally, disinterestedly and with a view to maximizing utility. Because the obvious, formal (and perhaps, in a way, Mill thinks, crude) agencies of public pressure are not used, it is not, therefore, to be supposed that public pressure cannot be brought to bear. Nor does Mill think that pressure ought not to be brought to bear. Pressure ought not to be contemporary society's mediocre pressure to conform to ill-conceived, unsystematic prejudice. Nevertheless,

> the existing generation is master both of the training and the entire circumstances of the generation to come; it cannot indeed make them perfectly wise and good . . . but it is perfectly well able to make the rising generation, as a whole, as good as, and a little better than, itself. If society lets any considerable number of its members grow up mere children, incapable of being acted on by rational consideration of distant motives, society has itself to blame for the consequences. Armed not only with all the powers of education, but with the ascendancy which the authority of a received opinion always exercises over the minds who are least fitted to judge for themselves . . . let not society pretend that it

needs, besides all this, the power to issue commands and enforce obedience in the personal concerns of individuals, in which, on all principles of justice and policy, the decision ought to rest with those who are to abide the consequences.

The best way of achieving a rational consensus, in other words, is to leave men as free as possible to be led into it by rational education. To maximize freedom can, in some circumstances, do damage to utility, but not as much as would be done by restricting it. When the damage done by leaving a man free is clear and assignable, then he must, regrettably, be punished: but where no assignable damage is done, then the *only* rational way to maximize utility is to leave men's minds absolutely open to the working of rational education—because it is only through rational education that unforced assent to the right means of determining the right course of action will take root.

Mill does not, in his *Applications*, emphasize these conclusions, though he believed that education should be compulsory. But Mill was attempting in *On Liberty* to protect the élite from domination by mediocrity. How he would have applied his principles in a system where the élite had triumphed, and to what extent it could have operated individualistically where a 'rational' consensus had prevailed, is another question. *On Liberty*, in the form in which it was written, so far from being an attempt to free men from the impositions of *all* doctrine, is an attempt to free them from customary, habitual, conventional doctrine. Convention, custom and the mediocrity of opinion are the enemies in Mill's mythology: the freedom he gives is given in order to subject men's prejudices to reasoning authority. *On Liberty* does not offer safeguards for *individuality*; it is designed to propagate the individuality of the elevated by protecting *them* against the mediocrity of opinion as a whole. Convention, custom, habit and public opinion are never to be trusted: all history has been a battle against them. History shows them to be oppressive: oppressions of this kind must be resisted. Once the oppressive consensus has been removed, a better one must replace it:but it would be foolish to expect an imposed consensus to achieve the objects which a rational consensus might. Mill, in fact, had grasp of an important truth—that it is no use *expecting* success from imposing a consensus by force, but that does not make him abandon the attempt to have a consensus. On the contrary: the consensus imposed by mediocrity is bad, and liberty in relation to *it* ought to be as great as possible. The means of achieving a rational consensus will not be discovered by pursuing the intuited views on which conventional opinions depend. But that does not alter the fact that the purpose in allowing men liberty, the justification of individuality, is not diversity in itself, but diversity informed by the rationally agreed education the clerisy alone can provide. Education is desir-able and self-development an obligation, because both maximize the same sort of happiness. Mill, in short, feared democracy and loved individuality, not so much because individuality would induce diver-sity, but because, by breaking up existing rigidities, it would make the world safe for 'rational' education, 'rational' thinking and the assured leadership of the 'rational clerisy'.

PATRICK DEVLIN

Morals and the Criminal Law†

The Report of the Wolfenden Committee on Homosexual Offences and Prostitution (1957) recommended, among other things, that "homosexual behavior between consenting adults in private should no longer be a crim-inal offence." The Report stressed, almost in Mill's language, "the im-portance which society and the law ought to give to individual freedom of choice and action in matters of private morality."

In the public debate that followed publication of the Report, Lord Devlin, a distinguished jurist, opposed its principles (though not all the specific recommendations) while Professors H. L. A. Hart,[1] Ronald Dworkin,[2] and Richard Wollheim[3] supported them. At the heart of the controversy was the distinction between "public" and "private" and, more broadly, the relationship between law, liberty, and morality.

A selection from Lord Devlin's argument (1958) follows. A brief state-ment by Professor Hart is included below, pp. 246–52.

The Report of the Committee on Homosexual Offences and Prostitution, generally known as the Wolfenden Report, is recog-nized to be an excellent study of two very difficult legal and social problems. But it has also a particular claim to the respect of those interested in jurisprudence; it does what law reformers so rarely do; it sets out clearly and carefully what in relation to its subjects it considers the function of the law to be. Statutory additions to the criminal law are too often made on the simple principle that 'there ought to be a law against it.' The greater part of the law relating to sexual offences is the creation of statute and it is difficult to ascer-tain any logical relationship between it and the moral ideas which most of us uphold. Adultery, fornication, and prostitution are not,

† From Patrick Devlin, *The Enforce-ment of Morals* (London, 1965), pp. 1–25.
1. "Immortality and Treason," *The Lis-tener*, 62 (July 30, 1959), 162–63; *Law, Liberty and Morality* (London, 1963); and *The Morality of the Criminal Law* (Jerusalem, 1965).
2. "Lord Devlin and the Enforcement of Morals," *Yale Law Journal*, 75 (1966), 986–1005.
3. "Crime, Sin, and Mr. Justice Devlin," *Encounter*, 13 (1959), 34–40. See also E. V. Rostow, "The Enforcement of Mor-als," *Cambridge Law Journal*, 174 (1960), 174–98, and R. E. Sartorius, "The Enforcement of Morality," *Yale Law Journal*, 81 (1972), 891–910.

as the Report points out, criminal offences: homosexuality between males is a criminal offence, but between females it is not. Incest was not an offence until it was declared so by statute only fifty years ago. Does the legislature select these offences haphazardly or are there some principles which can be used to determine what part of the moral law should be embodied in the criminal? * * * What is the connexion between crime and sin and to what extent, if at all, should the criminal law of England concern itself with the enforcement of morals and punish sin or immorality as such?

* * *

For many centuries the criminal law was much concerned with keeping the peace and little, if at all, with sexual morals. But it would be wrong to infer from that that it had no moral content or that it would ever have tolerated the idea of a man being left to judge for himself in matters of morals. The criminal law of England has from the very first concerned itself with moral principles. A simple way of testing this point is to consider the attitude which the criminal law adopts towards consent.

Subject to certain exceptions inherent in the nature of particular crimes, the criminal law has never permitted consent of the victim to be used as a defence. In rape, for example, consent negatives an essential element. But consent of the victim is no defence to a charge of murder. It is not a defence to any form of assault that the victim thought his punishment well deserved and submitted to it; to make a good defence the accused must prove that the law gave him the right to chastise and that he exercised it reasonably. Likewise, the victim may not forgive the aggressor and require the prosecution to desist; the right to enter a *nolle prosequi* belongs to the Attorney-General alone.

Now, if the law existed for the protection of the individual, there would be no reason why he should avail himself of it if he did not want it. The reason why a man may not consent to the commission of an offence against himself beforehand or forgive it afterwards is because it is an offence against society. It is not that society is physically injured; that would be impossible. Nor need any individual be shocked, corrupted, or exploited; everything may be done in private. Nor can it be explained on the practical ground that a violent man is a potential danger to others in the community who have therefore a direct interest in his apprehension and punishment as being necessary to their own protection. That would be true of a man whom the victim is prepared to forgive but not of one who gets his consent first; a murderer who acts only upon the consent, and maybe the request, of his victim is no menace to others, but he does threaten one of the great moral principles upon which society is based, that is, the sanctity of human life. There is only one explanation of what has hitherto been accepted as the basis of the criminal law and that is that there are certain standards of behaviour or moral principles which society requires to be observed; and the breach of them is an offence not merely against the person who is injured but against society as a whole.

Thus, if the criminal law were to be reformed so as to eliminate from it everything that was not designed to preserve order and decency or to protect citizens (including the protection of youth from corruption), it would overturn a fundamental principle. It would also end a number of specific crimes. Euthanasia or the killing of another at his own request, suicide, attempted suicide and suicide pacts, duelling, abortion, incest between brother and sister, are all acts which can be done in private and without offence to others and need not involve the corruption or exploitation of others. Many people think that the law on some of these subjects is in need of reform, but no one hitherto has gone so far as to suggest that they should all be left outside the criminal law as matters of private morality. They can be brought within it only as a matter of moral principle. It must be remembered also that although there is much immorality that is not punished by the law, there is none that is condoned by the law. The law will not allow its processes to be used by those engaged in immorality of any sort. For example, a house may not be let for immoral purposes; the lease is invalid and would not be enforced. But if what goes on inside there is a matter of private morality and not the law's business, why does the law inquire into it at all?

I think it is clear that the criminal law as we know it is based upon moral principle. In a number of crimes its function is simply to enforce a moral principle and nothing else. The law, both criminal and civil, claims to be able to speak about morality and immorality generally. Where does it get its authority to do this and how does it settle the moral principles which it enforces? Undoubtedly, as a matter of history, it derived both from Christian teaching. But I think that the strict logician is right when he says that the law can no longer rely on doctrines in which citizens are entitled to disbelieve. It is necessary therefore to look for some other source.

* * * I have framed three interrogatories addressed to myself to answer:

1. Has society the right to pass judgement at all on matters of morals? Ought there, in other words, to be a public morality, or are morals always a matter for private judgement?

2. If society has the right to pass judgement, has it also the right to use the weapon of the law to enforce it?

3. If so, ought it to use that weapon in all cases or only in some; and if only in some, on what principles should it distinguish?

I shall begin with the first interrogatory and consider what is meant by the right of society to pass a moral judgement, that is, a judgement about what is good and what is evil. The fact that a majority of people may disapprove of a practice does not of itself make it a matter for society as a whole. Nine men out of ten may disapprove of what the tenth man is doing and still say that it is not their business. There is a case for a collective judgement * * * only if society is affected. Without a collective judgement there can be no case at all for intervention. Let me take as an illustration the Englishman's attitude to religion as it is now and as it has been in the past. His attitude now is that a man's religion is his private affair; he may think of another man's religion that it is right or wrong, true or untrue, but not that it is good or bad. In earlier times that was not so; a man was denied the right to practise what was thought of as heresy, and heresy was thought of as destructive of society.

The language used in the * * * Wolfenden Report suggests the view that there ought not to be a collective judgement about immorality *per se*. Is this what is meant by 'private morality' and 'individual freedom of choice and action'? Some people sincerely believe that homosexuality is neither immoral nor unnatural. Is the 'freedom of choice and action' that is offered to the individual, freedom to decide for himself what is moral or immoral, society remaining neutral; or is it freedom to be immoral if he wants to be? The language of the Report may be open to question, but the conclusions at which the Committee arrive answer this question unambiguously. If society is not prepared to say that homosexuality is morally wrong, there would be no basis for a law protecting youth from 'corruption' or punishing a man for living on the 'immoral' earnings of a homosexual prostitute, as the Report recommends. This attitude the Committee make even clearer when they come to deal with prostitution. In truth, the Report takes it for granted that there is in existence a public morality which condemns homosexuality and prostitution. What the Report seems to mean by private morality might perhaps be better described as private behaviour in matters of morals.

This view—that there is such a thing as public morality—can also be justified by a *priori* argument. What makes a society of any sort is community of ideas, not only political ideas but also ideas about the way its members should behave and govern their lives; these latter ideas are its morals. Every society has a moral structure as well as a political one: or rather, since that might suggest two independent systems, I should say that the structure of every society is made up both of politics and morals. Take, for example, the institution of marriage. Whether a man should be allowed to take more than one wife is something about which every society has to make up its mind one way or the other. In England we believe in the Christian idea of marriage and therefore adopt monogamy as a moral principle. Consequently the Christian institution of marriage has become the basis of family life and so part of the structure of our society. It is there not because it is Christian. It has got there because it is Christian, but it remains there because it is built into the house in which we live and could not be removed without bringing it down. The great majority of those who live in this country accept it because it is the Christian idea of marriage and for them the only true one. But a non-Christian is bound by it, not because it is part of Christianity but because, rightly or wrongly, it has been adopted by the society in which he lives. * * *

We see this more clearly if we think of ideas or institutions that are purely political. Society cannot tolerate rebellion; it will not allow argument about the rightness of the cause. Historians a century later may say that the rebels were right and the Government was wrong and a percipient and conscientious subject of the State may think so at the time. But it is not a matter which can be left to individual judgement.

The institution of marriage is a good example for my purpose because it bridges the division, if there is one, between politics and morals. Marriage is part of the structure of our society and it is also the basis of a moral code which condemns fornication and adultery. The institution of marriage would be gravely threatened if individual judgements were permitted about the morality of adultery; on these points there must be a public morality. But public morality is not to be confined to those moral principles which support institutions such as marriage. People do not think of monogamy as something which has to be supported because our society has chosen to organize itself upon it; they think of it as something that is good in itself and offering a good way of life and that it is for that reason that our society has adopted it. I return to the statement that I have already made, that society means a community of ideas; without shared ideas on politics, morals, and ethics no society can exist. Each one of us has ideas about what is good and what is evil; they cannot be kept private from the society in which we live. If men and women try to create a society in which there is no fundamental agreement about good and evil they will fail; if, having based it on common agreement, the agreement goes, the society will disintegrate. For society is not something that is kept together physically; it is held by the invisible bonds of common thought. If the bonds were too far relaxed the members would drift apart. A common morality is part of the bondage. The bondage is part of the price of society; and mankind, which needs society, must pay its price.

* * *

The answer to the first question determines the way in which the second should be approached and may indeed very nearly dictate the answer to the second question. If society has no right to make judgements on morals, the law must find some special justification for entering the field of morality: if homosexuality and prostitution are not in themselves wrong, then the onus is very clearly on the lawgiver who wants to frame a law against certain aspects of them to justify the exceptional treatment. But if society has the right to make a judgement and has it on the basis that a recognized morality is as necessary to society as, say, a recognized government, then society may use the law to preserve morality in the same way as it uses it to safeguard anything else that is essential to its existence. If therefore the first proposition is securely established with all its implications, society has a prima facie right to legislate against immorality as such.

The Wolfenden Report, notwithstanding that it seems to admit the right of society to condemn homosexuality and prostitution as immoral, requires special circumstances to be shown to justify the intervention of the law. I think that this is wrong in principle and that any attempt to approach my second interrogatory on these lines is bound to break down. I think that the attempt by the Committee does break down and that this is shown by the fact that it has to define or describe its special circumstances so widely that they can be supported only if it is accepted that the law *is* concerned with immorality as such.

The widest of the special circumstances are described as the provision of 'sufficient safeguards against exploitation and corruption of others, particularly those who are specially vulnerable because they are young, weak in body or mind, inexperienced, or in a state of special physical, official or economic dependence.' The corruption of youth is a well-recognized ground for intervention by the State and for the purpose of any legislation the young can easily be defined. But if similar protection were to be extended to every other citizen, there would be no limit to the reach of the law. The 'corruption and exploitation of others' is so wide that it could be used to cover any sort of immorality which involves, as most do, the co-operation of another person. Even if the phrase is taken as limited to the categories that are particularized as 'specially vulnerable', it is so elastic as to be practically no restriction. This is not merely a matter of words. For if the words used are stretched almost beyond breaking-point, they still are not wide enough to cover the recommendations which the Committee make about prostitution.

Prostitution is not in itself illegal and the Committee do not think that it ought to be made so. If prostitution is private immorality and not the law's business, what concern has the law with the ponce or brothel-keeper or the householder who permits habitual prostitution? The Report recommends that the laws which make these activities criminal offences should be maintained or strengthened and brings them (so far as it goes into principle; with regard to brothels it says simply that the law rightly frowns on them) under the head of exploitation. There may be cases of exploitation in this trade, as there are or used to be in many others, but in general a ponce exploits a prostitute no more than an impresario exploits an actress. The Report finds that 'the great majority of prostitutes are women whose psychological makeup is such that they choose this life because they find in it a style of living which is to them easier, freer and more profitable than would be provided by any other occupation. . . . In the main the association between prostitute and ponce is voluntary and operates to mutual advantage.' The Committee would agree that this could not be called exploitation in the ordinary sense. They say: 'It is in our view an over-simplification to think that those who live on the earnings of prostitution are exploiting the prostitute as such. What they are really exploiting is the whole complex of the relationship between prostitute and customer; they are, in effect, exploiting the human weaknesses which cause the customer to seek the prostitute and the prostitute to meet the demand.'

All sexual immorality involves the exploitation of human weaknesses. The prostitute exploits the lust of her customers and the customer the moral weakness of the prostitute. If the exploitation of human weaknesses is considered to create a special circumstance, there is virtually no field of morality which can be defined in such a way as to exclude the law.

I think, therefore, that it is not possible to set theoretical limits to the power of the State to legislate against immorality. It is not possible to settle in advance exceptions to the general rule or to define inflexibly areas of morality into which the law is in no circumstances to be allowed to enter. Society is entitled by means of its laws to protect itself from dangers, whether from within or without. Here again I think that the political parallel is legitimate. The law of treason is directed against aiding the king's enemies and against sedition from within. The justification for this is that established government is necessary for the existence of society and therefore its safety against violent overthrow must be secured. But an established morality is as necessary as good government to the welfare of society. Societies disintegrate from within more frequently than they are broken up by external pressures. There is disintegration when no common morality is observed and history shows that the loosening of moral bonds is often the first stage of disintegration, so that society is justified in taking the same steps to preserve its moral code as it does to preserve its government and other essential institutions.[4] The suppression of vice is as much the law's business as the suppression of subversive activities; it is no more possible to define a sphere of private morality than it is to define one of private subversive activity. It is wrong to talk of private morality or of the law not being concerned with immorality as such or to try to set rigid bounds to the part which the law may play in the suppression of vice. There are no theoretical limits to the power of the State to legislate against treason and sedition, and likewise I think there can be no theoretical limits to legislation against immorality. You may argue that if a man's sins affect only himself it cannot be the concern of society. If he chooses to get drunk every night in the privacy of his own home, is any one except himself the worse for it? But suppose a quarter or a half of the pop-

4. It is somewhere about this point in the argument that Professor Hart in *Law, Liberty and Morality* discerns a proposition which he describes as central to my thought. He states the proposition and his objection to it as follows (p. 51). 'He appears to move from the acceptable proposition that *some* shared morality is essential to the existence of any society [this I take to be the proposition on p. 12] to the unacceptable proposition that a society is identical with its morality as that is at any given moment of its history so that a change in its morality is tantamount to the destruction of a society. The former proposition might be even accepted as a necessary rather than an empirical truth depending on a quite plausible definition of society as a body of men who hold certain moral views in common. But the latter proposition is absurd. Taken strictly, it would prevent us saying that the morality of a given society had changed, and would compel us instead to say that one society had disappeared and another one taken its place. But it is only on this absurd criterion of what it is for the same society to continue to exist that it could be asserted without evidence that any deviation from a society's shared morality threatens its existence.' In conclusion (p. 82) Professor Hart condemns the whole thesis in the lecture as based on 'a confused definition of what a society is.'

I do not assert that *any* deviation from a society's shared morality threatens its existence any more than I assert that *any* subversive activity threatens its existence. I assert that they are both activities which are capable in their nature of threatening the existence of society so that neither can be put beyond the law.

For the rest, the objection appears to me to be all a matter of words. I would venture to assert, for example, that you cannot have a game without rules and

that if there were no rules there would be no game. If I am asked whether that means that the game is 'identical' with the rules, I would be willing for the question to be answered either way in the belief that the answer would lead to nowhere. If I am asked whether a change in the rules means that one game has disappeared and another has taken its place, I would reply probably not, but that it would depend on the extent of the change.

Likewise I should venture to assert that there cannot be a contract without terms. Does this mean that an 'amended' contract is a 'new' contract in the eyes of the law? I once listened to an argument by an ingenious counsel that a contract, because of the substitution of one clause for another, had 'ceased to have effect' within the meaning of a statutory provision. The judge did not accept the argument; but if most of the fundamental terms had changed, I daresay he would have done.

The proposition that I make in the text is that if (as I understand Professor Hart to agree, at any rate for the purposes of the argument) you cannot have a society without morality, the law can be used to enforce morality as something that is essential to a society. I cannot see why this proposition (whether it is right or wrong) should mean that morality can never be changed without the destruction of society. If morality is changed, the law can be changed. Professor Hart refers (p. 72) to the proposition as "the use of legal punishment to freeze into immobility the morality dominant at a particular time in a society's existence.' One might as well say that the inclusion of a penal section into a statute prohibiting certain acts freezes the whole statute into immobility and prevents the prohibitions from ever being modified.

ulation got drunk every night, what sort of society would it be? You cannot set a theoretical limit to the number of people who can get drunk before society is entitled to legislate against drunkenness. The same may be said of gambling. * * *

In what circumstances the State should exercise its power is the third of the interrogatories I have framed. But before I get to it I must raise a point which might have been brought up in any one of the three. How are the moral judgements of society to be ascertained? By leaving it until now, I can ask it in the more limited form that is now sufficient for my purpose. How is the law-maker to ascertain the moral judgements of society? It is surely not enough that they should be reached by the opinion of the majority; it would be too much to require the individual assent of every citizen. English law has evolved and regularly uses a standard which does not depend on the counting of heads. It is that of the reasonable man. He is not to be confused with the rational man. He is not expected to reason about anything and his judgement may be largely a matter of feeling. It is the viewpoint of the man in the street—or to use an archaism familiar to all lawyers—the man in the Clapham omnibus. He might also be called the right-minded man. For my purpose I should like to call him the man in the jury box, for the moral judgement of society must be something about which any twelve men or women drawn at random might after discussion be expected to be unanimous. * * *

Immorality then, for the purpose of the law, is what every right-minded person is presumed to consider to be immoral. Any immorality is capable of affecting society injuriously and in effect to a greater or lesser extent it usually does; this is what gives the law its *locus standi*. It cannot be shut out. But—and this brings me to the third question—the individual has a *locus standi* too; he cannot be expected to surrender to the judgement of society the whole conduct of his life. It is the old and familiar question of striking a balance between the rights and interests of society and those of the individual. This is something which the law is constantly doing in matters large and small. To take a very down-to-earth example, let me consider the right of the individual whose house adjoins the highway to have access to it; that means in these days the right to have vehicles stationary in the highway, sometimes for a considerable time if there is a lot of loading or unloading. There are many cases in which the courts have had to balance the private right of access against the public right to use the highway without obstruction. It cannot be done by carving up the highway into public and private areas. It is done by recognizing that each have rights over the whole; that if each were to exercise their rights to the full, they would come into conflict; and therefore that the rights of each must be curtailed so as to ensure as far as possible that the essential needs of each are safeguarded.

I do not think that one can talk sensibly of a public and private morality any more than one can of a public or private highway. Morality is a sphere in which there is a public interest and a private interest, often in conflict, and the problem is to reconcile the two. This does not mean that it is impossible to put forward any general statements about how in our society the balance ought to be struck. Such statements cannot of their nature be rigid or precise; they would not be designed to circumscribe the operation of the law-making power but to guide those who have to apply it. * **

I believe that most people would agree upon the chief of these elastic principles. There must be toleration of the maximum individual freedom that is consistent with the integrity of society. * * * It is not confined to thought and speech; it extends to action, as is shown by the recognition of the right to conscientious objection in war-time; this example shows also that conscience will be respected even in times of national danger. The principle appears to me to be peculiarly appropriate to all questions of morals. Nothing should be punished by the law that does not lie beyond the limits of toleration. It is not nearly enough to say that a majority dislike a practice; there must be a real feeling of reprobation. Those who are dissatisfied with the present law on homosexuality often say that the opponents of reform are swayed simply by disgust. If that were so it would be wrong, but I do not think one can ignore disgust if it is deeply felt and not manufactured. Its presence is a good indication that the bounds of toleration are being reached. Not everything is to be tolerated. No society can do without intolerance, indignation, and disgust; they are the forces behind the moral law, and indeed it can be argued that if they or something like them are not present, the feelings of society cannot be weighty enough to deprive the individual of freedom of choice. I suppose that there is hardly anyone nowadays who would not be disgusted by the thought of deliberate cruelty to animals. No one proposes to relegate that or any other form of sadism to the realm of private morality or to allow it to be practised in public or in private. It would be possible no doubt to point out that until a comparatively short while ago nobody thought very much of cruelty to animals and also that pity and kindliness and the unwillingness to inflict pain are virtues more generally esteemed now than they have ever been in the past. But matters of this sort are not determined by rational argument. Every moral judgement, unless it claims a divine source, is simply a eling that no right-minded man could behave in any other way without admitting that he was doing wrong. It is the power of a common sense and not the power of reason that is behind the judgements of society. But before a society can put a practice beyond the limits of tolerance there must be a deliberate judgement that the practice is injurious to society. There is, for example, a general abhorrence of homosexuality. We should ask ourselves in the first instance whether, looking at it calmly and dispassionately, we regard it as a vice so abominable that its mere presence is an offence. If that is the genuine feeling of the society in which we live, I do not see how society can be denied the right to eradicate it. Our feeling may not be so intense as that. We may feel about it that, if confined, it is tolerable, but that if it spread it might be gravely injurious; it is in this way that most societies look upon fornication, seeing it as a natural weakness which must be kept within bounds but which cannot be rooted out. It becomes then a question of balance, the danger to society in one scale and the extent of the restriction in the other. * * *

The limits of tolerance shift. * * * I suppose that moral standards do not shift; so far as they come from divine revelation they do not, and I am willing to assume that the moral judgements made by a society always remain good for that society. But the extent to which society will tolerate—I mean tolerate, not approve—departures from moral standards varies from generation to generation. * * * Laws, especially those which are based on morals, are less easily moved. It follows as another good working principle that in any new matter of morals the law should be slow to act. By the next generation the swell of indignation may have abated and the law be left without the strong backing which it needs. But it is then difficult to alter the law without giving the impression that moral judgement is being weakened. This is now one of the factors that is strongly militating against any alteration to the law on homosexuality.

A third elastic principle must be advanced more tentatively. It is that as far as possible privacy should be respected. * * * The police have no more right to trespass than the ordinary citizen has; there is no general right of search; to this extent an Englishman's home is still his castle. * * *

This indicates a general sentiment that the right to privacy is something to be put in the balance against the enforcement of the law. Ought the same sort of consideration to play any part in the formation of the law? Clearly only in a very limited number of cases. When the help of the law is invoked by an injured citizen, privacy must be irrelevant; the individual cannot ask that his right to privacy should be measured against injury criminally done to another. But when all who are involved in the deed are consenting parties and the injury is done to morals, the public interest in the moral order can be balanced against the claims of privacy. The restriction on police powers of investigation goes further than the affording of a parallel; it means that the detection of crime committed in private and when there is no complaint is bound to be rather haphazard and this is an additional reason for moderation. These considerations do not justify the exclusion of all private immorality from the scope of the law. I think that, as I have already suggested, the test of 'private behaviour' should be substituted for 'private morality' and the influence of the factor should be reduced from that of a definite limitation to that of a matter to be taken into account. Since the gravity of the crime is also a proper consideration, a distinction might well be made in the case of homosexuality between the lesser acts of indecency and the full offence, which on the principles of the Wolfenden Report it would be illogical to do.

The last and the biggest thing to be remembered is that the law is concerned with the minimum and not with the maximum; there is much in the Sermon on the Mount that would be out of place in the Ten Commandments. We all recognize the gap between the moral law and the law of the land. No man is worth much who regulates his conduct with the sole object of escaping punishment, and every worthy society sets for its members standards which are above those of the law. We recognize the existence of such higher standards when we use expressions such as 'moral obligation' and 'morally bound.' * * *

It can only be because this point is so obvious that it is so frequently ignored. Discussion among law-makers, both professional and amateur, is too often limited to what is right or wrong and good or bad for society. There is a failure to keep separate the two questions I have earlier posed—the question of society's right to pass a moral judgement and the question of whether the arm of the law should be used to enforce the judgement. The criminal law is not a statement of how people ought to behave; it is a statement of what will happen to them if they do not behave; good citizens are not expected to come within reach of it or to set their sights by it, and every enactment should be framed accordingly.

The arm of the law is an instrument to be used by society, and the decision about what particular cases it should be used in is essentially a practical one. Since it is an instrument, it is wise before deciding to use it to have regard to the tools with which it can be fitted and to the machinery which operates it. Its tools are fines, imprisonment, or lesser forms of supervision (such as Borstal and probation) and—not to be ignored—the degradation that often follows upon the publication of the crime. Are any of these suited to the job of dealing with sexual immorality? The fact that there is so much immorality which has never been brought within the law shows that there can be no general rule. It is a matter for decision in each case; but in the case of homosexuality the Wolfenden Report rightly has regard to the views of those who are experienced in dealing with this sort of crime and to those of the clergy who are the natural guardians of public morals.

* * *

This then is how I believe my third interrogatory should be answered—not by the formation of hard and fast rules, but by a judgement in each case taking into account the sort of factors I have been mentioning. The line that divides the criminal law from the moral is not determinable by the application of any clear-cut principle. It is like a line that divides land and sea, a coastline of irregularities and indentations. There are gaps and promontories, such as adultery and fornication, which the law has for centuries left substantially untouched. Adultery of the sort that breaks up marriage seems to me to be just as harmful to the social fabric as homosexuality or bigamy. The only ground for putting it outside the criminal law is that a law which made it a crime would be too difficult to enforce; it is too generally regarded as a human weakness not suitably punished by imprisonment. All that the law can do with fornication is to act against its worst manifestations; there is a general abhorrence of the commercialization of vice, and that sentiment gives strength to the law against brothels and immoral earnings. There is no logic to be found in this. The boundary between the criminal law and the moral law is fixed by balancing in the case of each particular crime the pros and cons of legal enforcement in accordance with the sort of considerations I have been outlining. The fact that adultery, fornication, and lesbianism are untouched by the criminal law does not prove that homosexuality ought not to be touched. The error of jurisprudence in the Wolfenden Report is caused by the search for some single principle to explain the division between crime and sin. The Report finds it in the principle that the criminal law exists for the protection of individuals; on this principle fornication in private between consenting adults is outside the law and thus it becomes logically indefensible to bring homosexuality between consenting adults in private within it. But the true principle is that the law exists for the protection of society. It does not discharge its function by protecting the individual from injury, annoyance, corruption, and exploitation; the law must protect also the institutions and the community of ideas, political and moral, without which people cannot live together. Society cannot ignore the morality of the individual any more than it can his loyalty; it flourishes on both and without either it dies.

* * *

I return now to the main thread of my argument and summarize it. Society cannot live without morals. Its morals are those standards of conduct which the reasonable man approves. A rational man, who is also a good man, may have other standards. If he has no standards at all he is not a good man and need not be further considered. If he has standards, they may be very different; he may, for example, not disapprove of homosexuality or abortion. In that case he will not share in the common morality; but that should not make him deny that it is a social necessity. A rebel may be rational in thinking that he is right but he is irrational if he thinks that society can leave him free to rebel.

A man who concedes that morality is necessary to society must support the use of those instruments without which morality cannot be maintained. The two instruments are those of teaching, which is doctrine, and of enforcement, which is the law. If morals could be taught simply on the basis that they are necessary to society, there would be no social need for religion; it could be left as a purely personal affair. But morality cannot be taught in that way. Loyalty is not taught in that way either. No society has yet solved the problem of how to teach morality without religion. So the law must base itself on Christian morals and to the limit of its ability enforce them, not simply because they are the morals of most of us, nor simply because they are the morals which are taught by the established Church—on these points the law recognizes the right to dissent—but for the compelling reason that without the help of Christian teaching the law will fail.

The Case for Mill

ALBERT WILLIAM LEVI

The Value of Freedom: Mill's Liberty (1859–1959) †

I

Exactly a hundred years ago John Stuart Mill published his *On Liberty*. It had been projected as early as four years before when Mill was in Rome in the middle of January 1855, and it is just possible that the first draft was written under the heavy winter Italian sun in Naples and Palermo in the months following. Published at a moment of extreme reaction in the course of Western political history, it is sometimes easy to forget just how contrary was its message to the spirit of the times. Napoleon III was dictator of France. Serfdom still flourished in Russia and slavery in the United States. Most of the Balkans lay under the tyranny of Turkish rule, and in that very Italy in which the treatise was conceived the prisons were filled with men who called themselves partisans of freedom. And yet, so much of the liberal spirit of England in the wake of the first Reform Bill worked in Mill that he thought the political tyranny of autocratic despots had given way to a certain progress in human affairs when political power must henceforth "emanate from the periodical choice of the ruled." It expresses precisely one of those over-optimistic traits which must have made the work a slight anachronism in his time but perfectly at home in our own. Mill's belief that the problem of freedom was one of social tyranny rather than political despotism is a conviction which we a hundred years later may well share, but it is hardly a valid conclusion from an observation of the age in which he lived.

Perhaps it is just this timelessness, this passion for the abstract which Mill owes to Benthamism, which makes the *On Liberty* a statement of liberal principle so radical and at the same time so fundamental that it surely ranks with *The Social Contract* and *The Communist Manifesto* as a source for the political and social theory of the Western world. At any rate, it has had a checkered and by no means unambiguous history; and, so marked have been the admirations and antagonisms which it has aroused, that these atti-

† From *Ethics*, 70 (1959), 37–46.

tudes which it has provoked are perhaps an excellent diagnostic instrument concerning the political climate of the times. In 1861 it was translated into Russian and became a thorn in the flesh of the Czar's secret police; but fifteen years later another slav, Peter Kara-georgevitch, later to become King of Serbia, painstakingly translated it himself into his native tongue. Moreover, prior to the second World War at precisely the moment when Harold Laski and the intellectual leaders of the British Labor Party were appealing to it as a sacred text of political principle, the Japanese Emperor Hiro-hito, deeming it a potent source of the contagious disease of *kiken-shiso* (dangerous thoughts), banished it from the public domain. Source of moral principle, or of contagion, or perhaps both, I shall ask three questions about it in this paper: (1) What is the essence of Mill's position? (2) How in this work does he relate the concepts of freedom and of value? (3) Viewing it now in this centenary of its publication, can one rightly maintain that the main structure of Mill's argument still holds against the economic, political, and philosophical changes of a hundred years?

II

The avowed intention of *On Liberty* is to examine the nature and limits of the power which society can legitimately exercise over the individual, and the reasonable conclusion to which it comes is that the sole end for which this power may rightfully be exercised is the protection of society. But as the argument proceeds, Mill finds it necessary to introduce two subordinate pleas which together really constitute the affirmative core of the entire essay: the first is for complete liberty of thought and discussion within the political order; the second is for the free development of individuality however and wherever it may need to flower. The two pleas seem at first sight to belong to different realms of discourse, for the chief restrictions against the absolute freedom of the intellect in its thought and expression ordinarily come from the political prerogatives of church and state whereas the chief impediment to that free experiment with different modes of life (which both springs from, and is productive of, different forms of character and temperament) is the more informal tyranny of social pressure and the strangling conformity which it seeks to impose. But the political and the social are not finally realms which are so easily separated. The tyranny of the majority may express itself either in the formal structure of legal enactment or in the more subtle social pressures by which society has learned to exercise its mandates. Collective opinion may seek to interfere with individual independence both through civil penalties and through social ostracism and disdain, and that liberty of conscience which in the individual is the source of open and public expressions of opinion is at the same time the motivating power framing the pattern of taste and the structure of the individual life plan. Mill knew well that the same mode of perception which had dictated his much-criticized relations with Mrs. Taylor was also at the root of his equally suspect opinions concerning socialism, the emanicapation of women, and British foreign policy. Belief and conduct form one seamless fabric, and the essence of the focal self may show itself in behavior which may be alternatively (and probably in either case artifically) classified as social or political. It appears therefore that political and social freedom are but two sub-classes of a single value universal; if they stand or fall, they must stand or fall together.

Is it the case, then, that this value universal is to be asserted absolutely and without qualification? Attention to Mill's argument shows that this is not the case; all assertions about liberty are to be qualified by reference to two further principles: the principle of rationality and the principle of social utility. The first indicates the area in which all libertarian prescriptions are to be applied; the second is the very justification of the value of liberty itself. Everything which Mill says about liberty is meant to apply to human beings in the maturity of their faculties; for children, primitives, mental defectives, barbarians—all those, in short, incapable of being improved by rational discussion—it has no meaning. And to say, as Mill does, that "liberty, as a principle has no application to any state of things anterior to the time when mankind have become capable of being improved by free and equal discussion," is to provide a clue to the theory of the civil liberties which, I shall argue, was dearest to Mill's heart, although it could not be explicitly stated because of the old Benthamian lumber never finally cleared away. For Mill's ultimate justification of the civil liberties is that principle of utility which he regarded as the final appeal on all ethical questions. Civil liberties promote the welfare of even that society which attempts blindly to suppress them: they are instrumental in the achievement of the greatest happiness for the greatest number. Thus, curiously enough, even the value of freedom as a prerequisite for the attainment of truth is a relative matter. Mill's passionate partisanship for freedom of thought and discussion, his recognition that truth is one of the fruits of rationality and that the intellect must be free to come to such conclusions as it must, does not explicitly transcend the utilitarian argument. He is, of course, always on the side of the true opinion, but in the name of consistency he must insist that even the truth of an opinion is one of the ingredients in its utility. Thus, in a certain sense there is an implicit conflict between the principle of rationality and the principle of utility which are Mill's guideposts in the application of the libertarian principle.

There is, indeed, a paradox here, and it appears even in Mill's own language. For when he says, "I regard utility as the ultimate appeal on all ethical questions; but it must be utility in the largest sense *grounded on the permanent interests of man as a progressive being*," already pleasure as an end has been qualified by the requirements of the qualitatively human, of growth, and of process. But the essence of the difficulty springs, I think, from the incongruity between Mill's deep-seated sympathy for the purely individual in experience and the highly socialized form of the moral utilitarianism which he had inherited from Bentham. The classical mode of the justification of individual liberty is the doctrine of natural rights. Guaranteed by God, or inherent in the order of Nature, these rights are absolute, inalienable, and self-evident. But Mill specifically abandons a natural rights theory of the civil liberties in favor of the doctrine that they are a public utility. ("It is proper to state that I forgo any advantage which could be derived to my argument from the idea of abstract right, as a thing independent of utility.") And in so doing, in suggesting that the values of freedom are primarily social values, he opens the way for society itself to be the judge of freedom's social utility. But if the judgment of the social value of freedom is left to that type of democratic choice in which the authority resides in a majority of those whose interests are at stake (and it is difficult to interpret Mill's intention in any other way), then just this (ironically enough) is to invite that very tyranny of the majority against which the essay *On Liberty* was specifically directed.

The solution of the paradox is a theory congruent with Mill's basic ideas although not stated explicitly in *On Liberty*, and it would press him further away from the unsympathetic rigor of Benthamism toward the more fluid doctrine of the Idealists or of Dewey. It would be neither a "natural rights" nor a "public utility" but a *self-realizational* theory of the civil liberties. The natural rights doctrine hinges upon a theological foundation which cannot be proved to the satisfaction of a secular age. The social utility doctrine plays into the hands of a possible tyranny of the majority and gives insufficient attention to the absoluteness of liberty as an individual requirement. But the proponent of a self-realizational theory might argue in the following way. Those same selves which deliberate about the disposition of their personal lives also must deliberate about questions of social policy. And just as there must be freedom of self-determination for the inner life, so there must be freedom for public discussion and deliberation about outward acts. Selves are largely formed and continually remade in the process of interacting with their fellows, and the very formation of responsible selves *requires* that they speak freely, respond to the words of others, develop the latent powers of their reason by testing the alternatives before them. For however the self is a social emergent, growing out of a prior social environment, *selfhood is axiologically prior to society*, and society must respect individuality in its own nature as the source of all values. In a certain sense Mill recognized this. "The worth of a State," he said, "in the long run is the worth of the individuals composing it." But he did not explicitly state that even beyond its social utility, the freedom of thought and discussion is *the very condition of the making of persons*. It is, I think, implied in the concept of "utility in the largest sense, grounded on the permanent interests of man as a progressive being"; and if Mill had elaborated it, such a statement would have passed beyond both a Lockean theory of nautral rights and a Benthamian theory of social utility. And it would have been a return to Aristotle. For it would have insisted that freedom is at once a natural right and an absolute requirement but one which stems from *the natural fact* that only through its enjoyment can the potentiality of the human animal be actualized, and that only through its exercise can man attain the perfection of his rational and his moral powers.

III

It seems clear that Mill's Benthamism commits him to a defense of freedom of thought and discussion which finds these to be primarily an instrument in the formation of the public mind and therefore shifts their justification from the self-determination of the individual to the self-determination of society. Interference with public discussion in an attempt to safeguard sacred institutions from attack is intrinsically an illegitimate power, and even when public opinion is itself at one with coercive government in this attempt, it cannot be vindicated. And this because opinion is not merely the possession of its owner, but a public property instrumental in either affording access to a new truth or providing for the revivication of an old. The censorship of individual opinion is therefore in Mill's conception not a private injury but a public damage. It inhibits the corrigibility of social error, and it puts an end to that faith in social experimentalism which holds that mistakes within the realm of social policy can be rectified by experience and exposed within the arena of open public discussion. That "steady habit of correcting and completing . . . opinion" is the only guarantee of success in the perfecting of public as it is in the perfecting of private judgment. This is the culminating insight of chapter ii of *On Liberty*.

But it is also clear that Mill's heart lies with the free development of individuality which is itself the condition of all that we understand by society, civilization, and culture, and that in this sympathy is to be found the real clue to the relation between "freedom" and "value" in his system. And this is precisely the burden of chapter iii, "Of Individuality as One of the Elements of Well-Being." The relation of Mill's treatment of the liberty of thought and discussion in chapter ii to his passionate defense of individuality in chapter iii is problematic. On the surface it is a distinction between the inward domain of consciousness and the outward domain of individual self-expression, between the freedom to form new opinions and the freedom to carry them out in one's life, between the need to discover new truths and the need to commence new practices, and perhaps in the orderly outline of the work in Mill's mind this was the original intention. But as one compares the treatment of the two themes in the final draft, it becomes ever more difficult to preserve this specific distinction; and indeed, by a subtle shift of emphasis, the social reference of the two topics becomes almost precisely reversed. In the first place, as Mill himself observes, it is difficult to distinguish sharply between the formation of opinion and its expression or publication. Therefore, in a certain sense freedom of speech is as much a concern of the inner life as is freedom of thought. But even more, the inner freedom of thought is treated from the standpoint of a Benthamite doctrine of utility while the arguments for individuality (though not without Benthamite implications) are couched in intrinsic or absolutist terms. This therefore looks very much like the paradox of an "external" defense of an inner freedom followed by an "internal" defense of an outer freedom. It is certainly true that both defenses are based upon Mill's native sympathy for pluralism—upon the belief that diversity itself is a good and not an evil, that it is "useful" that there should be not only differences of opinion, but also varieties of character and differences in actual experiment with alternative modes of life, and that both of these forms of pluralism are, in effect, a public utility. But in the chapter on individuality this form of proof is minimized and subordinated to that very type of Aristotelian argument or of self-realizational theory which, as I have pointed out, the chapter on freedom of thought and discussion so explicitly lacks. It is the "proper condition of a human being arrived at the maturity of his faculties to use and interpret experience in his own way." And, "The human faculties of perception, judgment, discriminative feeling, mental activity, and even moral preference are exercised only in making a choice." And, "He who chooses his plan for himself employs all his faculties." And finally the famous: "Human nature is not a machine to be built after a model, and set to do exactly the work prescribed for it, but a tree, which requires to grow and develop itself on all sides, according to the tendency of the inward forces which make it a living thing."

The argument is distinctly and unmistakably Aristotelian. The external inducement to such acts as are not congruent with our feelings and our character renders us passive and not energetic. He who exercises deliberate decision employs all those faculties which are specifically human: observation; reasoning and judgment; purposive choice; and, once the choice is made, the firmness of will and self-control to hold fast to the decision. It might be a digest of the relevant portions of the *Nicomachean Ethics.*

Once the self-realizational principle is established, it is possible to turn the argument toward its implementation in a world which constitutes a threat to independence and strength of character. Once it has become clear that "among the works of man which human life is rightly employed in perfecting and beautifying, the first in importance surely is man himself," Mill can state the case against a society which has finally gotten the better of individuality, which exercises over the individual life a hostile and dreaded censorship, which has established as the most respectable of social positions that of those who give unquestioning allegiance to the cult of conformity.

The last half of chapter iii of *On Liberty* is perhaps the most rewarding and the most miraculous to a contemporary audience newly sensitized to the dangers of other-direction and seeing before its very eyes that hatred of peculiarity of taste and eccentricity of conduct which *On Liberty* pointed out in 1859. When Mill goes on, as he clearly does, to recommend examples of non-conformity and eccentricity for their own sakes, it is a great temptation to applaud his courage without at the same time paying marked attention to his aim. But the aim is of the essence of the prescription: it is to combat all of those modern influences which are hostile to pure individuality and to score against that despotism of custom which is a perpetual threat to the self-determination of the independent self.

It is perhaps only if one looks at the outward form of the argument that one can say that for Mill freedom is to be justified by its utility. For clearly, its inner kernel is that freedom is itself the precondition for the achievement of all value. Thus a position which on superficial inspection seems to make freedom subordinate to value, upon closer examination makes value subordinate to freedom. In the end this is no paradox. Considerations of both freedom and value are referable to the individual self; and for any self, values are its substantive achievement as freedom is its procedural requirement. Therefore the question of rank is morally irrelevant; freedom and value are mutually implicative. If perceptual objects are for Mill "a permanent possibility of sensations," then valuational objects are for him a permanent possibility of satisfactions, and these values (affective-volitional meanings, as they are) can only be maximized when the individual is free to express his own nature, to construct the pattern of his life, to use and interpret experience in his own way.

It is perhaps finally possible to explain the paradox of the relation between Mill's utilitarian defense of freedom of thought and discussion and his absolute insistence upon the value of individuality in this way. A distinction which begins as one between an inner and an outer realm, between the formation of opinion and the pursuance of a line of conduct hinges in the last analysis upon the form of emphasis employed. In the chapter on thought and discussion this emphasis is upon the pressures which are outwardly and coercively directed upon the formation of opinion. In the chapter on individuality the emphasis lies in the exhortation to the self to maintain itself as a self. The emphases are competely and mutually implicative, for freedom has at least two dimensions or two conditions: external permissiveness and the authentic power of self-directive decision. Chapter ii of *On Liberty* explores the first; chapter iii is primarily devoted to the second. And yet, lurking underneath and thickening the plot of emphasis is another force at work. It is the eternal strife of systems coming to a head in Mill's own personal philosophical development, and it infects *On Liberty* with its utilitarian defense of the civil liberties as it infects the *Utilitarianism* with its qualitative distinction among the pleasures. Both of these great works unfold with an undercurrent of confusion and inconsistency, and it is, I think, because of the quaint circumstance that Mill is at once a Benthamite by ruthless education and an Aristotelian by persuasion and natural election. Much of his most fruitful work is the consequence of this tension, and it would be a task both Procrustean and unrewarding to force the polarities into a format of exact logic. Therefore of the ethical development expressed in the essay *On Liberty* (as of that in the *Utilitarianism*) I think we may rightly say that it is a passionate and embattled Mill breaking from the vestigial wrappings of Benthamite doctrine toward the explicit standpoint of an Aristotelian moral philosophy.

IV

"What then is the rightful limit to the sovereignty of the individual over himself? Where does the authority of society begin? How mucy of human life should be assigned to individuality, and how much to society?" This is the set of questions with which the fourth section begins, and it emphasizes once again that the central argument of the essay *On Liberty* hinges upon the strategic distinction between that part of individual conduct which has consequences for the welfare of others and which is, hence, amenable to the rightful regulation of society, and that part which, comprising the inward domain of consciousness (and including conscience, thought, feeling, opinion, and sentiment in all matters scientific, moral, or theological) is the appropriate region for the most absolute human freedom. But what kind of questions, indeed, are these that Mill is asking? On the surface it would appear that they are questions of legal jurisdiction to be settled by supplying a *factual proposition*. What is individual is simply that which does not injure the interests of another. What is socially relevant is "any part of a person's conduct [which] affects prejudicially the interests of others." In practice it may not always be easy to make the distinction (and Mill both admits the difficulty and in his treatment of "applications" strives heroically to overcome it); but once the distinction *is* made and any individual instance classified, the moral imperative follows automatically. At this level the distinction between the individual and society is a *sociological distinction*, and the problem of freedom is transformed into a problem of applied sociology. Is this all that Mill is saying? I do not think so.

The boundary between the individual and society is not merely the demarcation of a sociological territory; it is meant also to fix a limit within the domain of values, to inclose also the geography of the spirit. For I do not think it can be doubted that to the more pedestrian sociological distinction between the individual and society Mill adds a dimension of moral idealism. His approving reference to Lord Stanley is revealing, for it shows the form of the moral distinction which has been influential in the formation of his thinking. "All matters relating to thought, opinion, conscience appear to me to be without the sphere of legislation; all pertaining to social act, habit, relation to be within it. . . ." But the first are just the "inward domain of consciousness" which Mill has recognized in his introductory remarks and which, as contrasted with political interaction and social functioning, has a privileged status in the realm of values. This seems to imply that the genuine problem of freedom is meaningful only if we separate the "outer" realm of property relations, power relations, and socially consequential conduct from the sensitiveness and intelligence which constitute the activities of the spirit. The desires of men, their acquisitiveness, their ambition, their social strivings have a right to be treated with *social justice* (and hence are fit objects for political regulation and social control); but only those qualities of moral perception and intellectual capability which go into the formation of attitudes and beliefs have a right to the completest, the most uncontrolled *liberty*. Justice (as Mill was to show in the *Utilitarianism*) is a social virtue, for since it deals with the externals of community behavior, it bears always a determinate relation not merely to the moral norm of equality but to the political facts of legality. Liberty in a sense transcends the realm of the social altogether, although it stands to it almost as the moral a priori stands to the moral facts which it is used to justify and explain. It is like the profound difference expressed in the Bill of Rights of our own Constitution, for while Article I states that "Congress *shall make no law* respecting the establishment of religion, or prohibiting the free exercise thereof; or abridging the freedom of speech, or of the press . . .," Article V states on the contrary that "no person . . . shall be deprived of life, liberty, or property *without due process of law.* . . ." It is the same angle of vision which Mill has appropriated from Lord Stanley for it too presupposes that "all matters relating to thought, opinion, conscience" are "without the sphere of legislation" while "all pertaining to social act, habit, relation" are "within it."

The understanding of Mill's argument in the essay *On Liberty* lies in an appreciation of his dualistic mode of perception, in the distinction between the individual and society at the sociological level, and in the distinction between man's inwardness and his outwardness at the moral level. And surely some of the difficulties and the ambiguities which his critics have pointed out are due to a tendency on Mill's own part to obscure the differences between these two modes of analysis. The fact is, I think, that Mill not infrequently uses the language of social psychology to advance the claims of his moral idealism, and that this practice, so prevalent in chapter iv of the essay, is the precise analogue of using the formal statement of the social utility argument to advance the claims of the civil liberties actually held on self-realizational grounds which we have already encountered in chapter ii.

Be that as it may, Mill's two distinctions, intimately related as they are in his work, have been the target of two lines of powerful criticism, each springing from an essentially monistic point of view. Bosanquet in *The Philosophical Theory of the State* and in the name of his own brand of absolute idealism has challenged Mill's distinction between the inwardness and the outwardness of the moral nature. Dewey in *The Public and Its Problems* and in the name of his own brand of pragmatism has challenged Mill's distinction between the individual and society. But since neither Bosanquet nor Dewey has been at pains to distinguish explicitly the sociological from the moral elements in Mill's argument, the point of the two criticisms is much the same.

It is not possible to reproduce Bosanquet's criticisms in detail, but he notes that for Mill the central life of the individual is something to be carefully fenced off against the impact of hostile social forces, and he finds it unthinkable that individuality, genius, fullness of life, and completeness of development should not be evoked by the play of relations in society, but should rather lie (as he thinks Mill thought it did) in an inner self to be cherished by inclosure and made impervious to those external influences which might damage or corrupt. This denial of Mill's claim concerning the inwardness of the moral nature leads Bosanquet to the further assertion that Mill's demarcation between the individual and the social cannot strictly be maintained. His brief and somewhat inadequate examination of Mill's "applications" in the fields of punishment for irreligion or immorality, the restrictions upon trade, and the institution of marriage are used to further this contention. The heart of Bosanquet's argument is that Mill's discrimination between justified and unjustified social interference in the life of the individual as based upon the supposed distinction between "self" and "others" simply will not hold up; and, true to his monistic presuppositions, he finds Mill's mistakes in social philosophy as illustrated in *On Liberty* to be in the class of those errors "characteristic of all conceptions which proceed by assigning different areas to the several factors of an inseparable whole."

Dewey too denies the antithesis between the individual and the social, but, unlike Bosanquet, it is not in the name of an organicism founded upon an idealistic logic or a wholistic aesthetics but in the name of a more adequate social psychology. In his opinion too there can be no isolated and independent individual, but the reasons for this lie ultimately in a genetic account of individual selfhood. Selves are formed in the process of social interaction, they have their genesis in role-taking and linguistic communication, they gain their identity by their identification with primary social institutions. This account has two implications. In the first place, since there are strictly organic conditions which lead men to social relations, no social theory based upon abstractions (such as "individuals" who have "rights" by "nature") can ever be adequate. In the second place, since the relation of individual-society is always mediated by such intervening associations as family, church, professional group, etc., if Dewey had simply maintained that "some primary groupings had claims which the state could not legitimately encroach upon . . . then the celebrated modern antithesis of the Individual and Society and the problem of their reconciliation would not have arisen. The problem would have taken the form of defining the relationship which non-political groups bear to political union." Dewey does not deny that there are social problems of freedom, but his whole point of view is implicit denial of the terms in which Mill sets the problem.

V

Can the criticisms of Bosanquet and Dewey be sustained? Each has a certain implicit proposal for terminological reform, and perhaps even an alternative format in which to set the issues, and surely this is valuable for the development of social philosophy; but in the end Mill's arguments, I think, are not seriously compromised. Perhaps the best proof of this is that finally both Bosanquet and Dewey are forced to reformulate Mill's distinctions in their own terms. Bosanquet may find uncongenial Mill's distinction between "self" and "other," but he is ultimately forced by the very logic of his own position to admit that "individual mind" is the focal point of the world as experienced, and so in his own formulation the distinction reappears as that between "the individual mind" and "the mind of society." Dewey may find uncongenial Mill's distinction between the Individual and Society, but common sense suggests to him that some human acts have consequences for others, while other human acts affect only the individual immediately concerned, and so in his own work the distinction reappears as that between two forms of social transactions, the public and the private.

We are confronted here with four levels of analysis. The dichotomy of individual-social implies the standpoint of social psychology. The dichotomy of inner-outer implies the standpoint of moral idealism. The dichotomy of individual mind-social mind implies the standpoint of idealistic metaphysics. And the dichotomy of private-public implies the standpoint of political control. Mill, as we have noticed, uses both the first two, and as I have also pointed out, it is at least understandable that some of the difficulties which his critics have had are due to his inconvenient habit of using a sociological distinction to illuminate a moral claim. On the other hand, it is quite interesting to see Bosanquet transform the problem into one of metaphysics, and it is distinctly valuable to have Dewey turn our attention to the more specific issues of political control.

But whether we address the issue at the level of social psychology, ethics, metaphysics, or political control, Mill is surely right: *at some central core of individuality a line of strict demarcation must be drawn,* and it must be maintained with all the resources of political or philosophical power. We may see the problem (as David Riesman has formulated it in the sociological language of our time) as that of maintaining the inner life of the individual against the pressures toward conformity of a large urbanized society. We may see it (in terms which T.V. Smith has learned from the songs of Emily Dickinson) as the protest of the purest privacy against the claim of the solidest institutionalism. Or we may see it (in the wise admonitions of Zachariah Chaffee or Alexander Meiklejohn) as the claim of the civil liberties to absolute respect against the counterclaim of the political state. But "the drawing of the line"—difficult as it may be in practice—is an absolute necessity. It is Mill's peculiar virtue that in the essay *On Liberty* he has stated the problem with a freshness and a moral passion (and also perhaps with a many-sidedness productive of confusion) which is classic, and that he has dramatized "the line of demarcation" in a fashion which attempts to do justice not only to our sociological good sense but also to our ethical intuitions. From him perhaps even more than from Kant or from Jefferson we have become aware that *in the drawing of the line* is the expression of our moral nature because it is our most profound assertion of the *value* of freedom.

DAVID SPITZ

Freedom and Individuality: Mill's *Liberty* in Retrospect†

I

It is a truism that much of the confusion in political theory is less the work of political theorists than of their commentators. Ranking high in the list of intellectual victims in this regard, John Stuart Mill is still being belabored today for errors he did not commit, assumptions he did not make, conclusions he did not draw, and confusions he did not originate. This is not to suggest the presence of an ingrained fallibility or ill will in his critics; they have scored frequently, and with telling effect. Yet today, after a century of such criticism, most of it converging on his essay *On Liberty*, his work remains more of a formidable testimony to the spirit of rational liberalism than most of his critics are willing to concede.

* * *

II

Let us consider, first, certain criticisms of, or approaches to, Mill's essay that I believe to be fundamentally irrelevant or misleading.

1. *That Mill's ideas are tainted by their source.* It is sometimes asserted that the proper way to understand Mill's essay is in historical, even biographical, terms. In these terms, Mill's argument for religious toleration is explained by saying that, as a freethinker in religion, he personally resented and resisted the pressures of the established Church; his much beleaguered association with Harriet Taylor is cited to account for Mill's attack on conformity in matters of taste and morals; and, similarly, the older Mill's tyrannizing of his son is said to be responsible for Mill's argument in defense of the liberty of the individual to develop freely.[1]

---

† From Carl J. Friedrich, ed., *Liberty* (New York, 1962), pp. 176–226.
1. All three of these points were advanced by Professor Currin V. Shields in a paper read at the annual meeting of the American Political Science Association, Washington, D.C., September 11, 1959; as also in his introduction to the Library of Liberal Arts edition of Mill's *On Liberty* (New York, 1956), pp. xx–xxi.

I confess that I find such an approach devoid of merit. The day may well come when meddlers in clinical research will relate—and judge accordingly—passages in *On Liberty* to the accidental burning in Mill's father's house of the first volume of Carlyle's manuscript on the French Revolution, or to Mill's morbid thoughts of suicide as a young man, or to the fact that he was once arrested and imprisoned for distributing birth control literature in the slums of London,[2] or to the startling but absurd "hypothesis" already ventured by Plamenatz that Mill's *On Liberty* was "written by a sick man in his premature old age."[3] There is no need to multiply examples, for they would all turn out to be instances of the genetic fallacy that perennially bedevils discussions of this kind when critics are either unable or unwilling to come to grips with an argument on its own merit.

2. *That Mill's ethics are other than what his critics would like them to be.* On a more sophisticated level, a good many critics have raised loud objection to Mill's essay largely because its ethical assumptions derive from a qualified utilitarianism. This, they have argued, deprives him of any effective case for many of his crucial distinctions, all of which require grounding in absolute moral principle. Because of this alleged "poverty of Mill's ethical end," one critic writes, he cannot really tell us which of many diverse ways of life is truly best, which human behavior is good and which bad, which interests are permanent and which transitory, and so on. In short, he has no way of *really* vindicating his moral distinctions and judgments.[4]

Now, for those who both believe in a deity and "know" what its teachings are, or who are committed to a doctrine of natural right that yields them what they regard as an equally infallible insight into the true nature of things, or who profess to have an intuitive grasp of the human condition that enables them authoritatively to distinguish between right and wrong conduct, Mill's failure to provide an absolutistic ethic grounded on their own particular principle may indeed seem sufficient reason to reject his argument *in toto.* But criticism of this kind misses the very heart of Mill's argument. He wrote his essay not because he lacked an ethical standard—for the principle of utility (and I am not here concerned to argue the rightness or wrongness of this principle), however uncertain and inadequate a moral principle it may appear to be to nonutilitarians, *is* an ethical standard—but because he denied that any man or group of men could ever possess the type of absolute knowledge

---

2. For an account of this incident, which goes unmentioned in Mill's *Autobiography,* see Bertrand and Patricia Russell, *The Amberley Papers* (New York, 1937), 2:247–49.

3. John Plamenatz, *The English Utili-* *tarians* (Oxford, 1949), p. 123.

4. Theodore B. Fleming, Jr., "John Stuart Mill's Essay 'On Liberty': A Critical Analysis" (unpublished doctoral dissertation, Yale University, 1957), p. 70 and *passim.*

which would entitle them to suppress ethical standards other than their own. If Mill had thought that he himself possessed this knowledge, or that the keys of truth had by some mysterious alchemy been delivered into his custody, his own case for individual liberty would have been pointless. Not that anyone who professes to be guided by an absolute ethical principle will necessarily try to compel others to live according to its dictates, merely that he is not generally eager to secure for others a liberty to depart from the "right" prescriptions. But Mill valued liberty and diversity precisely because he rejected the possibility of such an absolutistic conception of morality.

3. *That Mill is an extremist in his position.* Mill is frequently taken to task for pushing his argument to absurd extremes. But it turns out in all too many cases that it is the critic who, by failing to note Mill's qualifications or by stretching the plain meaning of his words, makes more of Mill's argument than Mill himself intended.

Thus we find critics representing, or, more strictly, misrepresenting, Mill's concern for individuality and his distaste for the idea of men being governed solely by custom, to mean that Mill had no use for any customs whatever and regarded individuality as the only legitimate value, which would in effect make him out to be a utopian or ultranihilist.[5] But this is not only irrelevant to, it is completely at odds with, Mill's fundamental thoughts on these subjects. This is readily seen if we only look, for example, at the title of the third chapter of the essay *On Liberty*, where Mill speaks "Of Individuality, as *One* of the Elements of Well-Being" (my italics); or at the statement early in his introductory chapter that "some rules of conduct . . . must be imposed . . . ," or at his repeated insistence that individuality should assert itself only "in things which do not primarily concern others."

In a similar farfetched vein, and because Mill included strength of character as one of the essential elements of individuality, it has been argued that Mill is oblivious to qualities in man other than his strength—in the literal sense of "strong characters" who are good simply because they are strong. Hence, Mill would be compelled, according to one critic at least, to endorse a character like Al Capone.[6] And this is said of the same Mill who not only listed strength of character as but *one* of the essential elements of individuality, who not only in his *Utilitarianism* explicitly professed his own fidelity to the Golden Rule, but who also uttered the famous sentence: "It really is of importance, not only what men do, but also what manner of men they are that do it."

Finally, but only because I would not belabor this point, we find

5. See, for example, Gertrude Himmelfarb, *Lord Acton: A Study in Con-* *science and Politics* (Chicago, 1952), p. 75.
6. Fleming, *op. cit.*, p. 68.

critics treating Mill's argument for diversity as if it were a plea for any and all kinds of diversity, including even pathological abnormality, and as though Mill were utterly unconcerned with how much diversity a society can afford. That this is a ludicrous interpretation of Mill is revealed when these very critics triumphantly (as they think) quote Mill against himself as saying: "There is not a more accurate test of the progress of civilization than the progress of the power of co-operation."[7] And what, one might ask, is the point of Mill's entire essay, and in particular of the questions set forth at the beginning of Chapter IV, if it is not only to admit the claims of authority but also to ask what are the rightful or legitimate, as distinct from the illegitimate, exercises of that authority? It is curious, indeed, that this attempt of Mill's critics to turn Mill against himself destroys their own interpretation of Mill, not Mill's position.

4. *That mass tyranny is a myth that happened to suit Mill's partiality for aristocracy.* Many of Mill's critics charge him with an elitist or aristocratic bias; they see him as an apologist for elite minorities against the sweep of democratic majorities, or of what he called the "despotism of a collective mediocrity." They indict him, too, for entertaining what they hold to be a grand illusion, namely, that individuality is in fact being smothered by the pressures of conformity, that we are in danger—to use Tocqueville's phrase—of a tyranny of the majority. The critics insist that there was no such tyranny either then or since: not in the England of Mill's day,[8] not in the America of Tocqueville's day,[9] nor in the America of our own time.[1] His entire essay, therefore, they conclude, is directed against an imaginary evil.

That there is a grain of truth in this line of criticism is undeniable. It is true that Mill displayed a considerable bias in favor of intellectually eminent men; he respected men of superior mental gifts and attainments; he valued genius. It is true, also, that a society capable of producing a Herbert Spencer, a Thomas Carlyle, and a John Stuart Mill is clearly not a society in which *all* individuality is stifled or one in which *all* intellectual superiority goes unrecognized and unrewarded. The very fact, indeed, that men like Mill were free to protest that men were not free, or were in danger of losing their freedom, testifies to what may be called the "openness" of that society. It is true, further, that the social despotism that Mill feared was a pressure of conformity known to every society and every age;

7. Mill, *Dissertations and Discussions* (Boston and New York, 1864–75), 1:191.
8. See the citations in J. C. Rees, *Mill and His Early Critics* (Leicester, England, 1956), pp. 9–14, 56.
9. See, for example, the comments of Jared Sparks in H. B. Adams, *Jared Sparks and Alexis de Tocqueville* (Baltimore, 1898), pp. 43–44.
1. So, for example, Louis Hartz, *The Liberal Tradition in America* (New York, 1958), especially pp. 128–34.

it could not, consequently, be attributed simply to the coming of democracy, or to the England of his own time. The problem is not whether such pressure exists, for it always does; the question turns rather, on what forms and degrees of intensity that pressure takes. If it remains no more than censure, the individual subjected to it may well find that he can, nonetheless, go his way. But if that social disapproval is translated into law, or into economic sanctions or physical violence, any or all of which would make it impossible or extraordinarily difficult for him to persist in his heterodoxy, then tyranny enters. It is not the mere existence of an antagonistic public sentiment but the actual exercise of a legal or economic or physical power to enforce that sentiment so as to deprive an individual of his legitimate rights that constitutes oppression.[2]

All this, I think, can properly be said against Mill. Yet it is not enough to dispose of Mill's essential position on these matters. The elements of truth that still remain in Mill's argument far outweigh these misconceptions. It is surely insufficient merely to point to Mill's high regard for intellectual eminence and his concomitant distaste for tyranny by the majority, however this tyranny may be conceived (and I shall argue in a moment that there is a sense in which it is properly conceived by Mill), and conclude from this that Mill is concocting here no more than an aristocratic fable. One would have to show, in addition, that with respect to these matters Mill was both fundamentally wrong and fundamentally at odds with the principle of democracy. And this, I am convinced, cannot be shown. On the contrary, three things at least can and must be said in defense of Mill.

(*a*) To respect and to seek to foster the emergence of intellectual eminence is in no sense inconsistent with democracy. What democracy requires is equality of opportunity; it does not stipulate equality of talent or intelligence or reward. Indeed, to insist upon equality of opportunity is to ask for no more than the first condition for the discovery of true inequality of talent. Only one who emerges first in a fair race can legitimately be termed the winner; and democracy seeks not to stack the cards against the best but to assure him that the race will be run fairly.

What would convert this regard for intellectual eminence into an apologia for aristocracy would be the imputation that such superiority of knowledge and understanding is the peculiar and exclusive attribute of a particular social class or elite, and the insistence, following from this, that such a class or elite is alone entitled to rule. But—and this is crucial—this imputation and insistence can

2. I have argued this point in greater detail in my *Democracy and the Challenge* of *Power* (New York, 1958), chap. 5.

nowhere be found in Mill. To the contrary, he repeatedly and consistently affirms, as did his father before him, that aristocratic rule,
with all its deleterious effects on the character of rulers and ruled
alike, is the principal barrier to good government. He invariably
argues, therefore, that those who govern must, before everything
else, be held constitutionally accountable to the ruled. "The honor
and glory of the average man," Mill writes, "is that . . . he can
respond internally to wise and noble things, and be led to them
with his eyes open." But there is never the suggestion in Mill that
if the average man does not voluntarily follow the initiative of intellectually eminent men, he must be compelled to do so. Everything
that Mill ever wrote, pre-eminently in *On Liberty* and its superb
companion volume *Representative Government*, is a flat denial of
this aristocratic principle.

It is true that Mill was equally concerned not to have "the opinions of masses of merely average men" dominate and stifle the
"individuality of those who stand on the higher eminences of
thought." In this respect Mill was indeed opposed to the intolerance of tradition-bound majorities. But here, too, three things
need to be said: first, this plea for the right of difference, or even
eccentricity, applied to those matters that did not *primarily* affect
the interests of others—that is, it applied to the self-regarding
rather than to the other-regarding sphere of human conduct;[3] second, although Mill "dreaded the ignorance and especially the selfishness and brutality of the mass," he anticipated a time when men
would no longer need to dread these things; he held it, rather, as a
"merely provisional" view warranted only "so long as education
continues to be so wretchedly imperfect";[4] and third, Mill was
also, and just as strongly, opposed to the intolerance of and con-
sequent tyranny by bureaucrats and officials. Nor was he what one
critic has called him—an apologist for intellectual snobs.[5] He
pleaded instead, and for a clearly defined area, only the cause of
those who are different and who, though despised and rejected, often become the movers and makers of the world.

Unless, then, diversity of character and the possession of superior
brains are to be deemed an intrinsic affront to democracy, I think
the allegation that Mill was an elitist and an aristocrat is
unfounded.

---

3. It is to be noted, for example, that
Mill carefully distinguishes "questions of
social morality," where he thinks the
public, or the overruling majority, is
likely to be right more often than not—
because there it is asked to judge of its
own interests—from "questions of self-
regarding conduct," where he thinks the
public, considering only its own preference, is likely to be wrong. *On Liberty*,
chap. 4.
4. Mill, *Autobiography* (New York,
1924), pp. 162–64.
5. The phrase is Professor Shields';
see p. 203, note 1, above.

(*b*) Notwithstanding what I said earlier in criticism of Mill's idea of the tyranny of the majority, I want to argue now that there is a very real sense in which Mill was correct in his apprehension of this danger. I do not see in what other terms we are to account for the treatment of American Indians and Negroes by the dominant white majority; or of Jews by Christians; or of Mormons by gentiles; or—but need one canvass the full depth of human experience to make the point?

What all this suggests is that in the world we inhabit, as in the world of John Stuart Mill, there is always a pressure on men to conform. This pressure is manifested in various ways—from statutes that disallow socially disapproved acts, to acts of violence and the imposition of economic sanctions by private groups in an effort to prevent men from pursuing legitimate goals, to acts of social discrimination, including ostracism and disdain. This pressure is also called by various names—from conformity to adjustment to "togetherness." But whatever the technique or the label employed, this essential fact remains: that what every society esteems, and seeks to produce, is the tranquilized, and tranquilizing, man. What is valued is harmony, congeniality; what is expected is a due measure of diffidence, even perhaps of obsequiousness; what is achieved, or at least intended, is the anonymous, not the autonomous, man. And it was to oppose this pressure and this result, this very real "tyranny" of majority opinion that stifles the mind and banishes creative or merely dissident ideas, that Mill entered his plea for diversity and freedom and individuality.

(*c*) It remains to be added that Mill's opposition to unbridled majority rule, far from being antidemocratic, is of the very essence of democracy (though I am aware that at this point majoritarian theorists of democracy will doubtless disagree with me). But surely I need not here labor the point that one of the essential conditions of a democratic state, as democracy is commonly understood in the Western world, is the free play of conflicting opinions, the right of men freely to disagree and to organize with others in the more effective pursuit of their diverse values. What Mill sought was a principle that would enable men in a democratic state to recognize and respect the line between the legitimate power of the majority and the rights of dissident minorities. Whatever his success or failure in drawing that line—and of this, more later—to term his effort at drawing it a mark of aristocratic bias is to strain all credulity.

5. *That Mill retracted his argument in his later work.* For lack of space I omit here one of the more inexplicable of the many fallacious arguments leveled against *On Liberty*—namely, the contention that although Mill urged that the state *require* an education

for every child, he did not favor state support for education and would not permit the state to *provide* it[6]—and turn instead to what shall here be the last of the irrelevant or misleading criticisms of Mill's essay. This is the attempt to play Mill against himself by confronting the doctrines of *On Liberty* with those of his allegedly later and maturer work, the posthumously published essay *On Social Freedom.*[7]

But even if *On Social Freedom* had been written by Mill, it does not necessarily follow that it is more convincing as a criticism of *On Liberty* than any other book critical of *On Liberty* would be; for it might well be that the Mill of *On Liberty* can be shown to have been wiser than the Mill of *On Social Freedom.*[8] I am persuaded by the evidences and argument of J. C. Rees,[9] however, that Mill did not write *On Social Freedom*; hence, it is unnecessary to undertake such an examination.

Finally, a brief digression on the most mindless of all irrelevancies! Some, but happily not all, of Mill's critics think they can refute Mill by quoting, sometimes at length, from an opposing political philosopher or critic of Mill. Bernard Bosanquet[1] and James Fitzjames Stephen are perennial favorites of those invited to sit in judgment—Bosanquet on the ideas of freedom and individuality, Stephen on these and just about everything else in, or allegedly in, Mill's essay. Now, clearly, to quote Bosanquet or Stephen or anyone else proves only that Bosanquet or Stephen or that Someone Else said what he said, not that he was right or that he proved his case against Mill. Occasionally, however, one encounters the argument that Mill must surely be in the wrong, for the overwhelming bulk of the literature on his essay is adversely critical. But so crudely

6. The passage concerning education on which this misconception of Mill is based is to be found in *On Liberty*, chap. 5, p. 161. It is easy to show, however, that throughout his life Mill was a consistent defender and advocate of the principle that the state has an obligation not merely to require but also *to provide in some measure* for the education of its children. This demonstration I must leave for a later occasion. Here it may be enough to call attention to but two of many facts that do not square with the impression of his critics: one, that Herbert Spencer, who was no stranger to Mill, castigated Mill precisely for his defense of, rather than opposition to, government intervention in education (see Spencer's *Social Statics* [New York, 1873], p. 367 ff.); the other, that Mill explicitly committed himself to this position in earlier works—for example, his *Principles of Political Economy*—where he said: "Education . . . is one of those things which it is admissible in principle that a government should provide for the people. The case is one to which the reasons of the noninterference principle do not necessarily or universally extend," (*Principles of Political Economy*, 7th ed., Ashley, ed. [Clifton, N. J., 1909], Book 5, chap. 11, pp. 953–54.)

7. Published in two installments in the first volume of the *Oxford and Cambridge Review* (June and Michaelmas Term, 1907), with authorship imputed to Mill. The first (and larger) portion was republished as a separate volume by the Columbia University Press in 1941, with an introduction by Dorothy Fosdick, and with authorship again imputed to Mill.

8. For an ingenious (but, to this writer, unconvincing) argument to the contrary, see James P. Scanlan, "J. S. Mill and the Definition of Freedom," *Ethics*, 68 (1958), 194–206, especially 201–6.

9. Rees, *Mill and His Early Critics*, pp. 38–54, 61–63.

1. *The Philosophical Theory of the State*, 4th ed. (London, 1923), especially chap. 3, sec. 3.

quantitative an approach ignores the quality both of the respective critics and of their arguments, and is thus unworthy of attention.

III

We come now to those criticisms of Mill's essay that deserve a more respectful hearing, even if they do not always carry conviction. But before scrutinizing them, it might be well to emphasize at the outset two important considerations frequently ignored by his critics. One of these is the simple fact that Mill, model of lucidity though he was, could occasionally slip into an inept phrasing of his ideas.[2] Where such is the case, many a critic has had an easy time of it by rendering Mill's argument in its most vulnerable terms. But Mill, as any other writer of his stature, should be given the benefit of literary doubt; if such a rendering seems egregiously out of line with his obvious intent, there is a prima facie case for challenging its pertinence—particularly where it is possible to construe his argument in terms more in keeping with his general outlook and level of intellectual sophistication.

The second consideration is that even where critics have scored a telling case against this or that element of Mill's essay, they have frequently vitiated their own argument by driving it to extremes. An essay such as Mill's is, in the nature of the case, bound to limp here and there—to do less than full justice to all the pertinent facts, to overlook some and overweigh others, and even to go astray in some of its conclusions. But even when Mill can be shown to founder on some particular point, his critics, too often mistaking the part for the whole, have been curiously myopic about the truly important elements of insight in his argument.

Both of these points will be detailed in the course of our examination of the major criticisms of *On Liberty*. Briefly stated, these criticisms come to the following:

1. *That Mill, in defending freedom of expression, is caught between the conflicting claims of abstract right and utilitarianism.* In raising this objection, Mill's critics are fond of laboring the point that his commitment to the doctrine of abstract or natural right, as he had learned it from Coleridge and Aristotle, cannot be squared with his devotion, however qualified, to the tenets of utilitarianism, as expounded by Jeremy Bentham and his own father.[3] Mill, so the critics urge, argues that there is a sphere of self-regarding conduct which society must respect under any and all circumstances, from

---

2. For an analysis of certain deficiencies in Mill's style that make for troublesome constructions, see, for example, Alexander Bain, *John Stuart Mill* (London, 1882), pp. 174–83.

3. The essays by Mill that have given greatest credence to this twofold yet seemingly disparate commitment are those on Bentham and Coleridge, reprinted in his *Dissertations and Discussions*, 1:355–417, and 2:5–78. For the substitution of Aristotle for Coleridge, see Albert W. Levi, "The Value of Freedom: Mill's Liberty (1859–1959)," *Ethics*, 70 (1959), 43.

which it follows—to Mill's critics at least—that Mill presumably recognizes inviolable or natural rights that inhere in the individual by virtue of his humanity. But if this is so, how, they ask, could Mill reject, as he expressly did, "any advantage which could be derived to my argument from the idea of abstract right as a thing independent of utility"?

The bearing of this criticism becomes particularly apparent when the critics come to grips with two of Mill's central propositions: on the one hand, his insistence on defending freedom of expression, along with freedom of thought itself, as though it were something in the nature of an absolute and, therefore, inviolable right; and, on the other hand, his recognition, no less emphatic, that society has a right to interfere with an individual's conduct for the sake of its own preservation, a right which comes into play whenever the individual's conduct is bound to affect adversely the interests of others. Plainly, these two propositions cancel each other out; for if, as Mill concedes, *all* expression is by its nature other-regarding, it cannot be defended as an absolute and inviolable right of the individual. Indeed, Mill himself is forced to admit that under certain circumstances—e.g., where unrestrained expression is likely to produce harmful effects—society can properly take steps to curb freedom of expression.[4] But if this is so, the critics continue, what Mill is really defending is not the absolute right of the individual to speak his mind freely, but his right to do so only when, and to the extent that, he does not transgress society's claim to protect itself from harm. The principle at stake, then, becomes one of relative, not absolute, right, or, to put it in terms of practical policy, one of establishing the line at which freedom of expression should be limited. What appeared to be a reliance on the doctrine of abstract right turns out to be merely an application of utilitarian criteria. To be sure, it is still possible to salvage from Mill's argument a defense of the right to freedom of expression on absolute grounds by regarding it, as he does on occasion, to be a form of self-regarding conduct in the sense that it is indispensable to and "practically inseparable from" freedom of thought. But here too the critics think they have the advantage of the argument, for they can then presumably show that in that case it is impaled on the second horn of the contradiction: if freedom of expression is a form of self-regarding conduct, no conceivable ground remains, least of all on Mill's own terms, for political or social action to curb freedom of expression in the interests of collective self-protection.

---

4. Some critics have gone so far as to make a *reductio ad absurdum* out of this concession by Mill. Thus Christian Bay, *The Structure of Freedom* (Stanford, 1958), p. 127, argues that once a breach is made with regard to freedom of expression in general, the principal victim is bound to be freedom of expression on political issues. In the same vein, some of the "new conservatives" would even have us believe that in this respect Mill was, of all things, a totalitarian *malgré lui!*

It is difficult to deny that arguments such as these have a surface plausibility of a kind. Taking the wording of a portion of Mill's essay at its face value, but disregarding all else that he wrote, one can find enough to construct the outlines of the dilemma of which the critics make so much. But if Mill's work as a whole is taken into account, it becomes quite improbable that he was ever an adherent of a natural rights approach to the problems of political life. And if this is true, all criticism on this score becomes quite pointless.

Consider, first, what it is that Mill actually says. He affirms as "the appropriate region of human liberty . . . liberty of conscience in the most comprehensive sense, liberty of thought and feeling; *absolute* freedom of opinion and sentiment on all subjects, practical or speculative, scientific, moral, or theological" (my italics). Then, after conceding that "the liberty of expressing and publishing opinions may seem to fall under a different principle, since it belongs to that part of the conduct of an individual which concerns other people," he nevertheless seeks to bring it within the protection of the same principle by contending that freedom of expression, "being almost of as much importance as the liberty of thought itself and resting in great part on the same reasons, is practically inseparable from it."

Mill's critics take this to mean that he in effect regards and would treat freedom of expression on a par with freedom of thought. But this is decidedly not the case, as a careful reading of the passage in question will readily bear out. Mill does not say that freedom of expression is of the same importance as freedom of thought; he says it is *almost* as important. He does not rest its defense on the same reasons; he would defend it *in great part* on the same reasons. He does not say that freedom of expression is identical to or inseparable from freedom of thought; he says only that it is *practically* inseparable from it. Any interpretation of Mill's teaching that ignores these nuances of qualification and distinction does less than justice to its meaning, and this becomes all the more certain when we consider the context in which this portion of Mill's argument occurs. For, as it happens, the very same paragraph which specifies the various liberties necessary to man is also the paragraph which cautions, in unmistakable terms, that they are to be exercised only so long as they do not involve harm to others.

All of which leads to the inescapable conclusion that Mill did not regard freedom of expression as an absolute or natural right, as something which may not be curbed under any circumstances. His argument must rather be read to mean that freedom of expression constitutes a right of the highest priority, a right which can be justi-fied per se, whereas the right of government or of society to curb freedom of expression is a subordinate one conditioned on the first.

When, for example, Mill argues at another point in his essay that actions are never to be accorded the same freedom as opinions, and that "even opinions lose their immunity when the circumstances in which they are expressed are such as to constitute their expression a positive instigation to some mischievous act," his qualification would apply *a fortiori* to the alleged absolute right of freedom of expression whenever a dire emergency requires that it be curbed. His argument is thus to be understood as a guide to practical conduct, as a statement of policy which clings to complete freedom of speech as a valid general rule for "normal" periods and which sanctions restraint for exceptional or emergency situations only. So understood, the argument is not subject to the dilemma discerned by Mill's critics; for such a dilemma presupposes that the two principles—that of freedom of expression and that of self-protection—are on a par with each other, thus making it impossible to distinguish an order of priority between them.

Where the critics have gone astray has been in their failure to take account of the relative and conditional quality of the principles advocated by Mill, however much he may seem to have phrased them in absolute terms for polemical purposes. They formulate the problem as though Mill had assigned equal weights to the principle of freedom of expression for the individual and that of society's right to survival, or self-protection; from their formulation, it would seem to follow that the two cannot be reconciled in principle. But this, I think, is entirely to misread Mill's intent and argument: the first principle, that of freedom of expression, is indeed first; the second, that of society's right to protect itself from harm, is but a qualification, a subordinate principle of limitation. And, as Mill had occasion to write elsewhere, it would indeed be "a strange notion that the acknowledgment of a first principle is inconsistent with the admission of secondary ones."[5] Stated this way—that anyone should be free to say what he likes, provided only that, in doing so, he does not endanger the existence of the group or do harm to others—the problem is not one of reconciling principles at all, but of judging the wisdom of any proposed measure to curb freedom of expression in terms of the relative order of the principle and its qualification. This does not, to be sure, offer a foolproof guarantee against misjudging the relative urgencies of the moment, against suppressing a speech or a book, for example, on the ground that it endangers society or harms others when it does not actually do so; but then, no set of principles, however stated, is immune to this possible abuse.

It turns out, then, that the choice for Mill never devolved on the

5. *Utilitarianism*, Everyman ed. (London and New York, 1910), chap. 2, p. 22; and see further chap. 5, p. 59.

insoluble problem of deciding between the conflicting, yet equal, claims of natural or abstract right and utility but, rather, on the eminently utilitarian problem of weighing the relative merits of a prior and a subordinate principle, of qualifying the primary principle of freedom of expression by the practical requirements of the principle of self-protection. I conclude, therefore, that Mill did not in fact abandon his utilitarianism for a principle of abstract right, even if his particular brand of utilitarianism was not in all respects that of Bentham.[6]

2. *That Mill poses a false dichotomy between self-regarding and other-regarding acts.* I think it can properly be said that Mill's attempt to distinguish two types of human conduct, the personal and the social—or what he calls self-regarding and other-regarding acts—entails a number of theoretical and practical difficulties. But here, as elsewhere, critics go much too far when they deny that there is any merit at all in Mill's distinction. Freedom for the individual, they argue, would be little more than a triviality if the distinction had any merit; but since, in their view, it has none, we are left with nothing but a theoretically unsound argument that does not admit of any clear-cut application in practice. Let us consider these points in turn.

(*a*) When Mill, to take the first line of criticism, singles out the self-regarding type of human conduct as being beyond the jurisdiction of society or the state on the ground that it affects the interests of no one but the agent himself, is he not positing a distinction that is essentially sterile? So, for example, argues Sabine when he objects that "an act that affects no one but a single person probably will not affect him very much."[7] In one sense this is perhaps true, as Mill himself conceded when he observed that "whatever affects himself may affect others through himself." But it does not follow that the distinction is without some vital bearing on the issue; unquestionably, there is a considerable range of conduct, including even deviant conduct, which has at best but an indirect or remote effect on others and which, for that reason, can be construed as *primarily* self-regarding. Consider such well-known cases of idiosyncratic behavior as Vincent van Gogh's mutilation of his own body, or Toulouse-Lautrec's dissipation in drink, or Modigliani's addiction to drugs. Should these be called forms of self-regarding behavior, and, if so, are they indeed trivial, as so many of Mill's critics would insist? To say that they are other-regarding would beg the entire question by implying that these idiosyncrasies did in fact affect the

6. If any doubt remains on this score, one need only advert to Mill's rejection of the notion of essences (e.g., as in his *System of Logic*, Book 1, chap. 6, sec. 3) as proof that he did not subscribe to any species of natural right doctrine.

7. George H. Sabine, *A History of Political Theory*, rev. ed. (New York, 1950), p. 711.

interests of others adversely, which they demonstrably did not. One could go even further to argue that in many, if not all, such cases conduct of this kind is indeed self-regarding in the most compelling personal sense if it can be related to the creative gifts of the artist. In that event, freedom to indulge in such conduct is anything but trivial, and the same would apply to far more numerous cases of "normal" personal behavior.

To be sure, the distinction between these and other forms of conduct which have obvious social consequences is frequently blurred. In many cases, however, human actions can be, and are, in fact, sorted out one way or the other, and anyone presuming to say that conduct is trivial merely because it is self-regarding betrays a lack of psychological insight into what it is that constitutes the unique concerns of an individual. To him, in fact, it may be his own "private" life and nothing else—or, as Mill would have put it, his self-regarding conduct—that is the very axis of his claim to personality. And it is no less vital a concern of any society which prizes freedom if we but recall the consequences that have always followed whenever the notion of private conduct was not recognized. The theory and practice of modern totalitarianism speak eloquently on this score.

(b) Having convinced themselves that Mill's argument is vitiated by a protean theoretical distinction, critics find it easy to conclude that it is inherently incapable of practical application. Mill puts forward, as the "very simple" yet absolutely governing principle of his essay,

> . . . that the sole end for which mankind are warranted, individually or collectively, in interfering with the liberty of action of any of their number is self-protection. That the only purpose for which power can be rightfully exercised over any member of a civilized community, against his will, is to prevent harm to others.

This, of course, is hardly a novel notion. It was said by Rousseau and by others before him; and as Mill's contemporary critics were quick to point out, it constitutes one of the most stale commonplaces in political philosophy. For it still leaves open the questions: What is the meaning of "harm"? Is it *moral* harm or *physical* harm, or both? Moreover, who is to tell, and by what criteria, whether a particular action does or does not cause harm to other people? Is a "village atheist" flaunting his fishing pole on a Sunday morning an offender by Mill's standard? How, by the same standard, is one to judge the practice of birth control, or of polygamy, and the like? The fact of the matter is, as Harold Laski and others have argued, "that we can have no information as to the social relevance of any act until we consider its consequences."[8] But since not all

8. H. J. Laski, *Authority in the Modern State* (New Haven, 1919), p. 55.

consequence can be anticipated, there is no way of knowing whether an action is self-regarding or other-regarding until those consequences have in fact occurred; which means that we may not be able to tell whether an action does or does not concern or bring harm to others until well after that action has taken place. Thus, Mill' distinction (it is said) is not a guide to practical conduct at all; at best, it can be employed only as a standard for judging an act *post factum*.

But this is only the beginning of the difficulties that Mill's critics have with his argument. Mill, they insist, makes a damaging concession when he seeks to limit the scope of self-regarding conduct to those matters that do not *primarily* concern or affect the interests of others, and introduces the notion of a "distinct and assignable obligation." Who, they object, is to say what *primarily* concerns others? If society can interfere with a man for purposes of self-protection, does it not follow that its right to interfere is limited only by its own judgment of its interests and of those matters that are of primary concern to it? Where, then, does self-regarding conduct begin, and what liberties can the individual claim save those that are given to him by society? Further, to bring in the notion of a distinct and assignable obligation only raises the questions: What is an obligation? Which obligations are assignable? And who is to assign them?

If, for example, we take Mill's illustration of drunkenness—that no person should be punished simply for being drunk, but a soldier drunk on duty should be punished—we see the difficulty, if not the impossibility, of applying Mill's principle. All drunkenness clearly involves the risk that some damage might be done; hence, on Mill's own showing, society always has a right to interfere. If it does not, it is presumably because such interference is considered unnecessary or undesirable in the particular instance, not because society lacks the right to do so.

And to the extent that Mill's argument entails the concept of obligation, it is well to remember that obligation is inescapably social in all its ramifications. Whether defined as a moral norm or as a legal prescription, obligation always refers to social rights and duties. It is not the act but the situation in which the act occurs that gives the act its meaning. And an obligation drawn to fit the situation is always social.

These criticisms seem to me largely unexceptionable. Yet their total impact is not quite as paralyzing to Mill's argument as many a critic would have us believe.[9] What robs this line of criticism of

9. In fact, Mill himself was fully aware of many of these difficulties. In his *System of Logic*, Book 6, chap. 9, sec. 2–3, he noted the impossibility of isolating any single phenomenon and denied that human actions, for example, are unrelated to or unaffected by other phenomena. In his correspondence, moreover, he repeatedly stressed the importance of unforeseen or, as he termed them, "unobvious" consequences, and called attention to the difficulty of attempting to draw a line in practical affairs on the basis of a general principle. See *The Letters of John Stuart Mill*, Elliot, ed. (London, 1910), 2:9, 95, 185.

much of its force is the qualification, already noted, that the two principles expounded in Mill's work are not coequal but ranked in the order of their urgency. Suppose we grant, for example, that *all* conduct, down to one's deciding what one should eat for dinner, can have social consequences. Does it follow as a matter of principle that *all* conduct ought to be made equally subject to punitive or regulatory action by society or the state? Clearly, we are dealing here with distinctions of degree that cannot be subsumed under general principles but that cannot be disregarded in practice without depriving an individual of all human rights and freedoms. Therefore, when Mill speaks of matters that do not *primarily* concern or adversely affect the interests of others, he is on clearly reasonable ground; for surely one's religion and his sexual practices, his choice of friends and occupation and place of residence, his freedom to decide between reading a book or attending an athletic event, and the like, are not *always* matters of concern to others. All that Mill is arguing here is that so long as one's actions do not injure the legitimate interests of other people, or do not have a deleterious effect on society's welfare, they ought not to be interfered with by society. Thus, for Mill, the self-regarding becomes the primary principle: each man, if he is to realize his potentialities as a man, must be free to do those things that *primarily* concern him and do not adversely affect the interests of others;[1] to that end, the individual needs an area of freedom within which he should be unrestrained from doing those things that are by common-sense standards personal. Where harm is done, the subordinate or other-regarding principle enters to protect society.

Admittedly, this rendering of the problem, valid though I think it is, does not altogether save Mill's formula. It is true, of course, that no general principle can state the conditions of its application in all cases, but Mill's principle is peculiarly liable to this difficulty. It does tell us that it is improper to impose social or legal restraints simply because we may dislike the other man's actions. It suggests, further, that when there is any doubt as to whether an action is self-regarding or other-regarding, the benefit of the doubt should be reserved for the self-regarding side when making the distinction. A principle of measure and appropriateness is thus built into this kind of utilitarian reasoning that should not be depreciated or ignored. Nevertheless, Mill's distinction cannot be maintained in

---

1. In an article which appeared too late for consideration here, Professor Rees contends that Mill's critics are wrong in their indictment of Mill on this point because they fail to note the significance of the terms Mill employs in drawing his distinction between self-regarding and other-regarding acts. There is an important difference, Rees holds, between saying that an action merely affects or concerns another person and saying that it affects his *interests*. See "A Re-Reading of Mill on Liberty," *Political Studies*, 8 (1960), 113–29. Unfortunately, this point deserves lengthier consideration than it is possible to give in this article.

its pristine form, for, because so many human actions are of the mixed type, Mill would have been on sounder ground had he contented himself with pointing out that they embody varying degrees of social implication. He could then have argued that it is not the act but the situation in which the act occurs that is crucial, from which it follows that, depending on circumstances, certain acts should be treated *as if* they were private. When society stands to gain by permitting men to act freely, their conduct should be treated accordingly.

It may be useful, perhaps, to add one final note. Too much, I think, has been made of Mill's deficiency in drawing this distinction between self-regarding and other-regarding acts. Even if we concede the validity of *all* the criticisms that have been leveled against his treatment, I do not think—as I shall argue later—that the larger thesis Mill was concerned to defend is thereby destroyed. For if men are to make any claim to liberty at all, it can only be because in some sense they value the right of an individual to act differently from his fellows, to be in some respects a *unique* person. And the fulfillment of such a value, it is clear, can only come about in a society that recognizes, however vaguely and ambiguously, the importance of privacy. But this brings us, in part, to the next major criticism of Mill's essay.

3. *That Mill's conception of individuality amounts to a plea for social irresponsibility.* One major line of attack on Mill has not been a direct challenge to the more immediate political element in his thinking but rather an attempt to point out what are considered to be serious flaws in his sociology and psychology. To be specific, many critics have argued (*a*) that Mill's idea of individuality is altogether ambiguous and unclear—so much so that in one writer's view Mill is identified as "the prophet of individualism . . . the prophet of an empty liberty and an abstract individual,"[2] whereas to another writer the reverse is true, Mill's thoughts being said to move "always on a grand scale, embracing the universal, allowing the individual to slip from notice";[3] (*b*) that what is at fault is not Mill's *definition* of individuality but rather "his psychological and sociological conception of the *conditions* necessary to the development of

2. Ernest Barker, *Political Thought in England, 1848 to 1914,* 2d ed. (London, 1928), pp. 7, 10; and cf. the bizarre statement by Crane Brinton, *Ideas and Men* (New York, 1950), pp. 432–33, who, by tearing Mill's words out of all meaningful context, would have us believe that "parts of Mill's writings sound today like the writing of a conservative defender of old-fashioned individualism against the New Deal." Brinton's statement is all the more incomprehensible in

view of what Mill says in his *Socialism* (Chicago, 1879) and, even more pointedly, in his *Principles of Political Economy,* Book 2, chap. 1, sec. 3, where he goes so far as to assert that if he had to choose, he would prefer communism with all its evils to the society of his day.
3. Georg Brandes, *Creative Spirits of the Nineteenth Century* (London, 1924), p. 200.

individuality,"[4] or, more severely, that Mill's attempt to emphasize the importance of the individual to the utmost leads him to forget that there is no such thing as individuality without society;[5] and (c) that Mill's effort to relate individuality to a utilitarian ethics "grounded on the permanent interests of man [or a man] as a progressive being"[6] succeeds only in leading him into additional difficulties.

In dealing with these criticisms, it may be useful to consider them at two levels of discourse. I shall ask first, and *in seriatim*, whether and to what extent these interpretations of Mill's doctrine are valid. It will then remain to consider whether their total effect, if valid, would in fact seriously undermine the main burden of Mill's argument.

(*a*) Consciousness of individuality is a relatively recent phenomenon in human history. Historically, man has been a social animal in the ultraexistential sense. It was only with the Renaissance that the individual and his needs began to move closer to the center of human thought, and Mill was thus in line with a post-medieval tradition which he carried forward when he stressed not merely the reality but the unique importance of the individual. In doing this, he did not mean to imply that the individual was something altogether apart from and unrelated to the society in which he lived and of which he was a product; his point was merely that each individual is a unique constellation of personal qualities significantly different from those of his fellow men—qualities which must be prized and encouraged for their creative potentialities.[7]

From this standpoint, most of the criticisms that are based on an extreme reading of Mill's teaching are, to put it mildly, confusing or wrong. On the one hand, there are those who take this concern with individuality to mean that Mill was a defender of social and economic individualism in the narrower sense, which clearly was not

4. R. A. Nisbet, *The Quest for Community* (New York, 1953), p. 228.
5. So, for example, L. W. Lancaster, *Masters of Political Thought, III: Hegel to Dewey* (Boston, 1959), p. 132, alleges that Mill talks "as if the individual and society were two distinct things. . . . [But] surely, society and the state cannot exist apart from the individual persons composing them. . . . it does not seem possible to put the 'individual' and 'society' into different categories, regarding the former as the only reality and the latter as purely imaginary."
6. Fleming calls attention to the fact that the original editions of Mill's essay, both in England and in the United States, speak of "man," but that the later People's edition, which is also the text of the Everyman's edition, renders

this as "a man." Since I have not seen the drafts of Mill's original manuscript, I do not know whether the insertion of the article "a," which gives the text a different connotation, was intended by Mill or was merely the result of a printer's error, as seems more likely in view of Mill's stated refusal ever to revise this work. It would be pointless, therefore, to discuss the bearing of this on the problem stated in the text.
7. It does not argue against Mill's values here to say, as does Isaiah Berlin, for example (*Two Concepts of Liberty* [Oxford, 1958], pp. 40ff.), that most men are content merely to be recognized as individuals by others without aspiring to anything more. Mill could have rightly insisted that one is a precondition of the other.

the case; and on the other hand, oddly enough, Mill has also been taken to task by others for losing sight of the individual in a system of abstract and universal truths. Both views can be shown to be utterly without ground. Nevertheless, Mill cannot be absolved from some share of responsibility for confusion on this score; he never tired of emphasizing the crucial importance of individuality of thought and character, but he failed to make clear just what he meant by "individuality." Sometimes he seemed to equate individuality with difference alone, as when he argued for the development of the individual in his richest diversity, thus implying that mere difference in itself is a virtue. At other times, however, he pleaded for the value of originality. Originality, as Mill emphasized in his essay "On Genius," need not be identified with the discovery of new truth; it is enough if the individual discovers truths by himself even if they are truths already known to and accepted by others. Originality, in other words, is a process of discovery, not an attribute of that which is discovered; from which it would seem to follow that originality, though incontestably one of Mill's hallmarks of individuality, need not include eccentricity of conduct or difference of values. Thinking for himself, the original mind might well arrive in fact at conclusions altogether consistent with those current in his society and thus turn out to be a conformist after all. It cannot be argued that conformity on such terms negates the claim to individuality, for as long as a decision is arrived at through autonomous thought, it meets Mill's notion of originality. How, then, one may ask—and this, of course, is what troubles the critics—can Mill continue to identify individuality with difference or self-gratification or eccentricity per se?

The answer, I would suggest, is that Mill's plea for diversity must not be read in psychological terms as an argument for eccentricity in itself. It must rather be understood as a plea for a system of social arrangements which would allow each individual maximum freedom to develop his own bent. Mill viewed the human being as an organism—not as a "machine" or a "sheep" but as "a tree, which requires to grow and develop itself on all sides, according to the tendency of the inward forces which make it a living thing." We do not, therefore, enhance what is best in men by grinding down their unique or individual characteristics into a dead uniformity, but rather by cultivating them. This is why Mill was led to assert that a person's "own mode of laying out his existence is the best, not because it is the best in itself, but because it is his own mode." And this, too, is why, however we define it, individuality cannot be understood save in such terms as incorporate the elements of spontaneity, diversity, and the latitude of choice provided by freedom of expression and mutual criticism.

(b) Surely it is a misreading of Mill to interpret him as believing that the individual is the only reality and that society is purely imaginary. In fact, it is only by recognizing that the reverse is the more true, that it was Mill's very clear awareness of the reality of society and of its pressures upon the individual, that we can understand why Mill was led to write *On Liberty* at all. The one element of plausibility in this criticism of Mill, I think, is the contention that Mill's argument, at least as he develops it in this essay, does not give *sufficient* attention to the fact that the process of individualization is itself a social process, and that, from this standpoint, however much an individual may be at odds with society in a given situation, his individuality—and the very fact that it clashes with the demands of his society—is itself the result of a socializing process. In this sense, individuality is not intrinsically in opposition to sociality but emerges from it. Individualization and socialization, that is to say, always work together to produce a single human entity, even one in rebellion against the accepted norms of his society. He becomes an individual, a total and unique human being, only in and through society, only as a social product. In every aspect of his being, he remains, therefore, a social being at the same time that he is an autonomous and self-legislating person.

I do not mean to overstate this point, for we have ample evidence to show that the processes of modern society, with its increased technology and specialization, its increased alienation of man from himself, from the instruments and products of his labor, and from his human associations, have led to a fragmentation of the individual so serious as to have brought the concepts of alienation and anomy into common currency. Nevertheless, it is perhaps true that Mill's idea of the social and pyschological conditions requisite for the formation of individuality focuses in such an extreme way on the one aspect—the innate qualities—of an integral whole as to split it off from itself and thereby divest it of much of its meaning.

Here again, however, a word of caution must be entered. The fact that one becomes an individual only in and through a social process has little to do with, or at least does not eliminate the problem raised by, the claims of a given society upon a given individual in a concrete situation. We do not normally argue, for example, that because an individual is the child of his parents, and could not have become what he is without the benefit of his parentage, that he has no claims whatever *against* them should they attempt to mold him completely in their image. By the same token, we cannot ignore the claims of individuality when these run counter to social pressures.

(c) One of the lesser joys afforded teachers of logic and moral philosophy is the opportunity to display what they take to be Mill's fallacious argument uniting, or attempting to unite, Bentham's greatest happiness principle as a standard of social good with the desire for one's own greatest pleasure as the individual's only motive. That Mill went on to qualify his hedonism by asserting that pleasures can be graded as superior or inferior in moral quality put him—or so the critics argue—in still further logical difficulty; for then, as Sabine triumphantly notes, he was "in the indefensible logical position of demanding a standard for the measurement of a standard, which is a contradiction in terms, and also reduced his utilitarianism to complete indefiniteness."[8]

If these criticisms are valid, then Mill's further attempt in *On Liberty* to relate his values of freedom and diversity and individuality to the *"permanent* interests of man as a *progressive* being" (my italics), would only compound his difficulties. For what are the permanent, as distinct from the transitory, interests of man, and who is to determine them? What is meant by a progressive as distinct from a nonprogressive being, and who is to establish the criteria for this distinction? Finally, is it necessarily true that the permanent interests of man, however these may be conceived, are in fact furthered only by the self-regarding decisions of individuals and never by the acts of society? Surely compulsory vaccination and compulsory education, not to speak of distasteful tax laws and traffic regulations, may well conduce to the permanent interests of man even though there might be some who are foolish enough to dispute this. Whose judgment, then, shall prevail—the individual's or society's? If Mill's self-protection principle is permitted re-entry here, society's right to control and direct the individual in such matters is beyond disclaimer. Freedom of individuality, of tastes and pursuits, may at times, then, be required to give way to Mill's principle that society has a right to protect itself from harm.

These and similar criticisms are not altogether without validity. They lose much of their force, however, if we recall that Mill's argument, on one possible interpretation, may be taken as a defense of individuality not simply in terms of rationalistic hedonism but also on the ground that individual character has intrinsic value. Like Kant's, Mill's commitment is not really to happiness—as Bentham, for example, conceived this term—but to respect for the moral personality; "he believed," as his ablest biographer put it, "in individuality and self-development as ends in themselves and as the only means to the end of human welfare."[9] For happiness, as Mill was later to argue in his *Autobiography,* eludes men when they seek it as a direct or immediate aim; it is rather a by-product that comes to men in the course of their other activities.

8. Sabine, *op. cit.,* pp. 707–8.
9. Michael St. John Packe, *The Life of* *John Stuart Mill* (New York, 1954), p. 490.

However—to move now to the second level of our discussion—suppose we grant the general validity of these and similar criticisms of Mill's idea of individuality. Does it follow that they effectively undermine Mill's main argument? Do they, for example, demonstrably show that Mill's plea for individuality constitutes nothing less than an argument for social irresponsibility? I think not, and much of what I have already said by way of rejoinder or qualification to some of the specific criticisms in this context also tend to corroborate this judgment. Here I would only add that Mill, understanding as he did the need for social control and political stability, nevertheless pleaded for a society that would give maximum freedom to man to grow according to his own nature and desires because he anticipated that the net income of such an arrangement would be a more harmonious and happier society than one based on the contrary principle. Not all men, to be sure, share this anticipation; and there are others who do what they can to render its achievement impossible. But unless we value a static society inhabited by men of a like mold, we need to develop, even more than we presently have, those diversities of character and temperament that are the indispensable prerequisites of social improvement. To this end, individuality—with all the ambiguities that may attach to its definition—must be furthered rather than denied. Indeed, it is the mark of a civilized man (and of a mature society) that he recognizes and respects the inescapable fact that such ambiguities are inherent in a concept such as individuality; for he knows that to define individuality in a precise and final way is only to destroy it.

4. *That Mill misconceives the nature, and hence the proper limits, of freedom.* Mill's critics assert that Mill is at times confused and imprecise as to the nature and limits of freedom. They argue, among other things, that (*a*) he seems to conceive of liberty primarily, if not solely, in a negative sense, as the absence of restraints; most commonly, therefore, he views law and liberty, or social authority and liberty, as opposing forces, when, in fact, the critics argue, law and liberty always constitute two related aspects of a single whole; that (*b*) Mill speaks of liberty fairly consistently as the freedom of a man to do with himself as he desires; yet, the critics contend, a number of his illustrations can be cited to show that when he speaks of man's freedom to do as he desires, what he really has in mind is only man's freedom to do as he *ought* to desire; or else these illustrations can be taken as an indication that Mill has no clear understanding of precisely what he means when he speaks of man's desires; and that (*c*) Mill does not, in *On Liberty* at least, give sufficient attention to economic and organizational threats to liberty, or even, for that matter, to legal or political infringements on liberty. Let us consider these several points in turn.

(*a*) For Mill, as for Hobbes, liberty is the absence of restraints; it follows that any interference by society, whether through law or through its moral code, constitutes an invasion of liberty. And so, like Hobbes, Mill is compelled by his own premise to reason that law and liberty necessarily stand in an inverse relationship to each other: the more law, or social authority, the less freedom—and vice versa. It would also seem to follow from this understanding of liberty that only a despot, entirely unfettered by either law or moral rules, can truly be said to possess complete freedom of action. But Mill also argues, in one of his early articles, that measures of political and social reform are not to be rejected merely because they are contrary to liberty; to oppose them for that reason alone, he said, merely "leads to confusion of ideas."[1] This, his critics are quick to point out, testifies to a fundamental confusion in Mill's thinking, a confusion that can only be removed by revising what they regard as his erroneous idea of freedom. He is confused, or at least inconsistent, to the extent that in his earlier essay he recognized freedom as a qualified rather than an absolute social value, whereas in *On Liberty* he affirmed a contrary and extreme view that "all restraint, *qua* restraint, is an evil." Only by redefining his notion of liberty, the critics argue, could Mill have escaped this inconsistency and made political sense.

There is, I believe, a legitimate criticism to be made of Mill's position here, but it happens to be the reverse of that put forward by his critics. They think Mill was wrong in defining freedom as he did in *On Liberty* but right in thinking that political and social measures are not to be condemned even when they run counter to the clear implications of his definition. I would contend, somewhat to the contrary, that Mill is correct in his definition but wrong in some of his inferences with respect to its bearing on the role of law.

As a matter of sheer definition and nothing more, Mill is on unimpeachable ground when he argues that law, being a form of restraint, is necessarily an invasion of liberty. Clearly, to the man who is hindered by the law from doing what he wants to do, there is a denial of freedom. In this purely formal sense of the term, then, I do not see what objection can be taken to Mill's definition or to the implication he drew from it that law and liberty consequently stand in an inverse relationship to each other.

What is at fault here is not the consistency of the argument from definition but Mill's failure to do full justice to the nature and effect of law as such, and, most of all, his neglect of the fact that law may, in a particular situation, operate as a restraint on a restraint: by restraining some, it may give others a degree of free-

1. Mill, "Periodical Literature–Edinburgh Review," *Westminster Review*, 1 (1824), 509.

dom they would not otherwise possess. So too with social authority. An employer may impose restraints on his employee, but a labor union which restrains the employer may free the employee from those restraints, or from some of them; as the law in turn by restraining certain practices on the part of the union may free the employee from restraints the union might otherwise impose on him. Freedom, that is to say, is not a fixed whole like an apple pie, into which the law cuts, and with each cut takes a piece away. Freedom in the real world is meaningful only when it is reduced to a complex system of individual liberties and concomitant restraints, each restraint operating to limit an action that someone else might take to deny a particular liberty to another person. The question then is not one of law versus liberty, or social authority versus liberty, but rather one involving a multitude of decisions as to *who* shall enjoy *which* liberties, under *what* circumstances and for *what* purposes, and *which* specific restraints, consequently, need to be imposed to make such enjoyment possible. To say, as Mill does, that "all restraint, *qua* restraint, is an evil," is in these terms misleading, and prevents Mill from emphasizing what he well understands: that a legal restraint may, in a given situation, become the indispensable condition for the exercise of a social freedom.

(*b*) In the history of political thought, two conceptions of liberty have long been opposed to each other. These are the liberty to do as one wants versus the liberty to do as one should. In general, Mill commits himself to the first of these conceptions of liberty. In various ways throughout his essay he repeats the principle, set forth in his introductory chapter, that with respect to self-regarding conduct society cannot rightfully interfere with the freedom of any man:

> His own good, either physical or moral, is not a sufficient warrant. He cannot rightfully be compelled to do or forbear because it will be better for him to do so, because it will make him happier, because, in the opinions of others, to do so would be wise or even right. These are good reasons for remonstrating with him, or reasoning with him, or persuading him, or entreating him, but not for compelling him or visiting him with any evil in case he do otherwise. To justify that, the conduct from which it is desired to deter him must be calculated to produce evil to someone else. . . . Over himself, over his own body and mind, the individual is sovereign.

All this seems clear and straightforward enough until Mill seeks to illustrate the application of his principle. He offers, by way of example, the case of a man about to cross an unsafe bridge, and tells us that, if the bridge is known to be unsafe and there is no time to warn the man of his danger, it is proper for a public officer or any one else to seize that man and turn him back, "without any real infringement of his liberty; for liberty consists in doing what one desires, and he does not desire to fall into the river." It is true that Mill distinguishes here between the certainty of this mischief as against its danger and would limit such interference only to those cases where there is absolute certainty of the consequences which would follow if the individual decided to cross the bridge. Clearly, however, this is a secondary matter of application which does not affect the main principle for which Mill is arguing. Lest this example be taken as a single departure from an otherwise steadfast principle, Mill offers still a second illustration to the same effect—namely, that no man has a right to sell himself into slavery:

> His voluntary choice is evidence that what he so chooses is desirable, or at least endurable, to him, and his good is on the whole best provided for by allowing him to take his own means of pursuing it. But by selling himself for a slave, he abdicates his liberty; he foregoes any future use of it beyond that single act. He therefore defeats, in his own case, the very purpose which is the justification of allowing him to dispose of himself. . . . The principle of freedom cannot require that he should be free not to be free. It is not freedom to be allowed to alienate his freedom.

These illustrations have furnished critics of Mill with an argument that he was guilty of a basic intellectual ambiguity when he defined liberty as he did. One line of such criticism can of course be found in representatives of the English idealist school—notably in Bosanquet. They insist that when Mill spoke of "desire" in each of the two illustrations, the term "desire" could only mean man's real or ultimate will as distinct from his actual or momentary will. Otherwise, they contend, Mill's defense of any legal or social action taken in either case would clearly make no sense of his major premise that liberty consists in the absence of all restraint on that which a man desires for himself. Is not such action, the critics ask, an interference with a man for his own good, *both* physical and moral? If this is so, does this not imply, as Bosanquet, for example, insisted, "that it may be right, according to the principle of liberty, to restrain a man, for reasons affecting him alone, from doing what at the moment he proposes to do"? Are we not then "entitled to argue from the essential nature of freedom to what freedom really demands, as opposed to what the man momentarily seems to wish"?[2] So Bosanquet, and so, too, various idealist critics of Mill.

Other critics of Mill who are not committed to the idealist distinction between man's real and his actual will also find Mill's examples confusing, though for other reasons. Ritchie, for example, argues that if we are to take Mill's illustrations as guidelines for the application of his principles, "there is almost no limit to the

2. Bosanquet, *op. cit.*, pp. 64–65.

amount of interference or restraint which would be justified."[3] An interesting variant of Ritchie's argument can be found, more recently, in Lancaster, who raises the following objection:

> There are many things which people really do not desire to do, but few of them are as clear as the one suggested. The circumstances surrounding most human choices in a modern society are so numerous and complicated that the individual can scarcely be expected readily to know which one is best for him—i.e., which one he "really" desires. In view of the fact that these complicated situations are the typical ones, Mill's principle is of little or no help.
>
> Even more to the point, and more damaging to the end which Mill obviously had in view, is the fact that his reasoning in the example that he gives may easily be used to justify the most extreme interference with individual liberty. Thus, a religious enthusiast might decide by similar reasoning that, since the heretic really wishes his own salvation, he must be prevented from holding beliefs which, in the opinion of the enthusiast, make salvation impossible. Any individual choice could be interfered with on similar grounds, since those with power to do so can always argue that they are as sure of the result which they would prevent as the man in Mill's example is sure that the bridge is safe.[4]

In brief, whether they hail from the idealist tradition or prefer a more empirical approach, the critics agree that these examples, as well as others that Mill offers in the same vein, defeat the very principle that he was anxious to establish; for his examples suggest, if they suggest anything at all, that Mill would defend legal or social interference with a man for reasons that affect him alone, so as to prevent him from doing what at the moment he proposes to do. To the idealist, such as Bosanquet, this is "in germ the doctrine of the 'real' will, and a conception analogous to that of Rousseau when he speaks of a man 'being forced to be free' ";[5] to others, it means merely that Mill denied in his examples what he affirmed in his statement of principle.

It must be conceded, I think, that there is a sense in which much of this criticism is both pertinent and valid. Mill's choice of language is unfortunate; for when he admits that interference with a man seeking to cross an unsafe bridge is an infringement but not a "real" infringement of his liberty, he gives his argument a turn which would seem to identify it with the arguments of the idealist philosophers. Moreover, by failing to anticipate through his examples the whole range of choices open to men, and what their exercise implies for his political principles, he left uncertain, and per-

3. D. G. Ritchie, *The Principles of State Interference* (London, 1891), p. 86.

4. Lancaster, *op. cit.*, p. 134.

5. Bosanquet, *op. cit.*, p. 65.

haps rendered unconvincing, the relevance and applicability of those principles to actual social problems.

But here again, it must be insisted, the critics display their habitual itch to overextend themselves; they carry their criticisms to extremes which would nullify any type of political theory, their own included. For what they demand, in effect, is nothing less than a set of political recipes, a set of specific instructions for this or that particular problem. And this, of course, cannot be supplied. Mill, like any other political philosopher, is writing a book of political principles, not a catalogue of *do's* and *don'ts*. As such, his book cannot anticipate all contingencies, nor can his examples do more than *illustrate* his meaning. Consider, for example, what is involved in his argument granting society, or the state, the right to prevent a man from selling himself into slavery. Is Mill saying anything more here than that, on any sane reading of human history, we are entitled to make certain assumptions about human nature, specifically in this case that no man *wants* to be a slave, that no human being —unless he is a child, or momentarily delirious, or so agitated as to be unable to govern his actions by reflective thought—would *voluntarily* sell himself into slavery? If, therefore, a man were actually to express a willingness to contract himself into slavery, it could only be because the circumstances which surround him are such as to "force" him into this action; seeing no feasible alternative, he finds himself compelled to become a slave. What Mill sought to protect was man's *permanent* freedom of voluntary choice, a freedom which is irretrievably taken from him by the one act of selling himself into slavery; for, says Mill, he is then "in a position which has no longer the presumption in its favor that would be afforded by his voluntarily remaining in [a state of freedom]."

If it is correct to assume that slavery is contrary to man's actual desires, and that society or the state may therefore properly interfere with an individual's momentary willingness to sell himself into slavery, how much more correct is it to assume that no rational man desires to commit suicide, and to infer from this that it is right for society or the state to prevent a man from committing suicide? In the absence of information to the contrary, are we not entitled to assume that he is being forced to take this drastic step only by the pressure of momentary circumstances?

This reading of Mill, of course, does not altogether confute Bosanquet's insistence that in all this Mill is really adverting to the essential nature of human freedom and human will, building not on what an actual man says he wants but on what a rational man would really want. However, it seems to me to go a long way toward reconciling Mill's own definition of freedom with the requirements of human survival—at least as Mill understands those requirements.

And since there is no political theory that does not rest on *some* assumptions, whether stated or unstated, about the nature of man and of the human condition, Mill's argument is no more subject to criticism in this respect than is any other political theory. Moreover, the idealist objection here is quite beside the point. As an empiricist, Mill did not have to make a distinction between a real and an actual will to vindicate his principle; it was enough for his purpose to recognize that man is a bundle of conflicting desires and to distinguish between those which are grounded permanently in man's make-up and those which may sway him from time to time; it does not speak against this empirical approach to say that man's desires fall into some kind of hierarchical order.

Similar considerations apply to Lancaster's critique of Mill on this point. Where the range and complexity of alternatives open to an individual are so bewildering that he cannot make a well-defined choice one way or the other, where the situation is so blurred and the conflict of choices so great as to leave the individual thoroughly confused and unable to decide, then the state, regardless of how it acts, cannot be said to be interfering with him in any sense which violates Mill's teaching; for whether it pushes him in one direction or the other, it does not violate his desires. Moreover, although such ambiguities of choice unquestionably bedevil much of human life, they do not govern all of it; and when Lancaster argues that the individual cannot be expected to know which of the many and complex choices open to him is "best," it does not follow that he cannot decide which of them he actually wants. He chooses what he desires, as a hungry man confronted with an enticing array of foods at a *smörgosbord* chooses, however falteringly, what he desires; and to say, with the idealist philosophers, that he does not choose what he "really" desires, or even, with a gastronomical empiricist, what is "best" for him, is in no sense to prove that he is unable to exercise effective choice of some kind.

(c) One of the most glaring faults for which Mill's essay can properly be taken to task is its curious failure to deal with what was then, and remains now, one of the greatest sources of danger to individual freedom—the power of social and economic organizations. One need not subscribe to Harold Laski's extreme view that ". . . it is upon the issue of property that the whole problem of liberty hinges today, as it has always done in the past,"[6] to recognize that individual liberties have not always found their maximum security under the hegemony of near-dynastic economic empires like the Ford and Du Pont and Rockefeller enterprises, or within the near-

6. H. J. Laski, *Liberty in the Modern State*, rev. ed. (New York, 1949), p. 15. But compare Mill's statement in 1871 that "the land question and the relation between labour and capital are the points on which the whole of politics will shortly turn." *Letters*, 2:311.

feudal world of the modern corporations, or in the petty domains of lesser landlords and businessmen. Certainly, Mill himself was fully aware of this problem in certain of his other writings.[7] Yet, oddly enough, he gives all too little attention to this vital aspect of his problem in *On Liberty*, contenting himself with but a few short pasages on free trade and on the limits of governmental interference with economic activity.

Similarly, in what is perhaps one of his more startling sins of omission, Mill fails here, though not in other writings, to explore the role of organization as a countervailing power. If individual liberties are threatened, as they are, by great economic and social organizations; or if power has passed, as Mill believes it has, "more and more from individuals, and small knots of individuals, to masses [so] that the importance of the masses become constantly greater, [and] that of individuals less," until we have arrived at the point where "the individual is lost and becomes impotent in the crowd"; it may well be that individual liberties and the recovery of individuality can effectively be secured only through "greater and more perfect combination among individuals." No single individual, that is to say, can hope successfully to resist the tides and tendencies of public opinion or of the great organizations. But if individuals were to band together in the common pursuit of their common interests, they might through such combination significantly influence the course of events. That "such a spirit of combination is most of all wanted among the intellectual classes and professions," was, for Mill, a ludicrous spectacle and lamentable in its consequences.[8] What is crucial for us, however, is the fact that although Mill elsewhere appreciated the importance of voluntary association as a means of protecting the individual from economic exploitation and intellectual subjection, he did not incorporate this insight into his discussion here.

It is curious, finally, that whereas Mill in *On Liberty* did appreciate and dwell upon the evils of bureaucracy, he did not somehow realize that the translation of social prejudice into law, and into actions taken by police and administrative officials, might well constitute a more important threat to liberty than would mere manifestations of social disapproval and disesteem. I think Russell has unnecessarily overstated a good point when he argues that in our day the police constitute the most serious danger to liberty "in most civilized countries";[9] for, although it cannot be denied that even in the Western democracies the police are guilty of many crimes of

7. For example, *Principles of Political Economy*, Book 4, chap. 7, and Book 5.
8. See his essay on Civilization in *Dissertations and Discussions*, vol. 1, espe- cially pp. 189–218; the quotations are on pp. 189, 214, 215.
9. Bertrand Russell, *Portraits from Memory* (London, 1956), p. 127.

omission and commission, there is a considerable distance to be traveled before one can equate the malpractices of some police officers or police systems with "the police," or to hold that the police are, in fact, more the invaders than they are the defenders of freedom, or more of a menace to individual liberties than are the great economic and religious power organizations or the bands of self-appointed vigilantes who harass racial and religious minority groups and political nonconformists. Nevertheless, the petty tyrannies of the police, as of bureaucrats and political office holders generally, constitute a major and continuing affront to the democratic idea of free men in a free society. More than this, the laws enacted in response to the demands of powerful interest groups demonstrate only too well that liberty is endangered not so much by man's capacity to dislike other men as by his capacity to injure them.

Still, it should be borne in mind, in extenuation of Mill, that On Liberty is an essay, not a treatise, and as such need not, and could not, cope with all contingencies or possibilities. In so far as such criticisms focus on Mill's omissions, they do not argue against his larger thesis; they merely indicate further avenues of exploration and application to extend the scope of his thesis to what Mill called man's other-regarding conduct.

IV

If what I have said thus far is at all justified, the numerous criticisms leveled against Mill's essay, whether taken singly or in combination, neither destroy nor seriously impair the validity of its central argument, however much they may qualify it in some respects. This, to say the least, is a far cry from the intemperate judgment of the more extreme of Mill's critics who dismiss his essay as a good illustration of how a book in political theory ought not to be written or, worse still, as the product of a sentimental moralist venting his personal prejudices and idiosyncrasies, and doing so in a rhetoric which bemuses only literary connoisseurs or those already committed to his views.[1] As against these and other dim judgments of Mill's performance, I would argue that Lord Morley was far closer to a just appraisal of its qualities when he said of On Liberty that "The little volume belongs to the rare books that after hostile criticism has done its best are still found to have somehow added a cubit to man's stature."[2]

What, then, are the positive contributions of On Liberty that still make it a landmark in the history of political thought? If these came to nothing more than establishing the essential impregnability of Mill's major principles to the assaults considered heretofore, they would constitute enough of a formidable claim to that distinction.

1. As alleged, for example, by H. M. Roelofs, The Tension of Citizenship (New York, 1957), p. 182.

2. John Morley, Recollections (New York, 1917), 1:61.

But the essay, I would urge, has other claims to our critical esteem as well. Of these, it may be enough here to mention only two.

1. *Mill reformulated the problem of freedom so as to give it contemporary relevance and application.* The issue that Mill raised with regard to the problem of freedom was in many respects a different one, and certainly more important in its implications, from that generally allowed him, or even from what he himself considered to be the central question of his essay. That issue, simply put, is whether, and how, conflicting interests can be reconciled in a modern democratic state without victimizing the individual either in his relations to the institutions of government or in his personal claims against the pressures of mass sentiment.

To appreciate the essential modernity of this question, one has only to recall that, with the qualified exception of Tocqueville, political thinkers before Mill had explored almost every other major aspect of political freedom without seriously coming to grips with the second—and, in Mill's judgment, the more significant—dimension of that problem, namely, that of respecting the requirements of individuality as against the demands of a controlling majority opinion.

To take a diametrically opposed conception of freedom, when the Greeks talked of liberty, they had in mind, primarily, the liberty of a whole people, of the *polis* or community-state, as against the tyrant or foreign oppressor. Liberty to them was the liberty of a commonwealth. The people were thought of as a homogeneous unit —a body of men who shared the same values and pursued a common way of life and who consequently sought their fulfillment as men not in the relative privacy of their homes or of their fulfillment as men not in the relative privacy of their homes or of their "self-regarding" activities, as Mill would have put it, but in the life of the *polis* itself. To be a man was pre-eminently to be a social or political animal. Hence the classical conception of liberty did not recognize, much less focus on, the right of an individual (or group) to do as he (or it) might choose; it built instead on the right of the people as a whole to follow their own ways. This is why Greek thinkers could identify the community with the state and liberty with a particular way of life.[3] This is why Socrates could properly be charged with a crime for teaching disrespect of the gods, and why Socrates in turn, in the *Republic*, could urge that all those who did not conform to the common ways and teach the "right" things should be sent into exile.

Even Hobbes and Locke, though they broke in important

3. Cf. Fustel de Coulanges, *The Ancient City*, trans. Small, 4th ed. (Boston, 1882), Book 3, chap. 17; but see *contra* A. H. M. Jones, *Athenian Democracy* (Oxford, 1957), chap. 3, especially pp. 43–45, and E. A. Havelock, *The Liberal Temper in Greek Politics* (New Haven, 1957), especially the Introduction and chap. 13.

respects from the classical tradition, bypassed the problem of mass tyranny in complete silence. To Hobbes, the problem of liberty was one involving the relations between the individual and his "alien" government; and because Hobbes feared the possible consequences of an individual's unrestrained actions, liberty to him was largely a matter of how far the law lets people alone. To Locke, who viewed the problem from the standpoint of the relations between the individual and his "own" government, and who feared the possible consequences of actions taken by a government separated from the people, liberty was primarily conceived of as the right to cherish one's own property and to have one's own government. Moreover, Locke—like Milton before him—excluded a portion of the community, e.g., Catholics, atheists, and other blasphemers, from the protection of civil society. For all three, further, the people were still seen as a relatively homogeneous entity; consequently the problem of freedom still turned, as with the classical political philosophers, on the relations between the people and the government. To be sure, the authors of the American Constitution, and later of *The Federalist*, introduced an innovation when they made greater allowance for a truth stated but not developed by Aristotle—that a political society rests in some respects on a heterogeneous and divided people—and when they squarely confronted the possibility of a majority using the leverage of government to tyrannize; but they, too, limited themselves to the relations between the individual or the group and the government. It remained for Tocqueville, in his celebrated *Democracy in America*, to point out that the problem goes beyond the mere relationship between the individual and government to embrace all other relations which may affect the freedom of the individual. But whereas Tocqueville saw and brilliantly expounded this new dimension of the problem of liberty, he confined himself largely to a description of its actual operation and effects, and of its tendencies and potential dangers, although he was not unaware of certain forces that might mitigate the gravity of conformist pressures. And yet, for all his perspicacity, he did not ask the question Mill was later to raise: What is the principle or principles that a democratic society *ought* to observe so as to make it possible for diverse groups and conflicting creeds to function within a livable framework of government? What is more, Mill went beyond Milton and Locke to extend the scope of freedom to include all men and not merely those who have, broadly speaking, the "right" faith. The holders of power, he cautioned, are not always identical with those over whom it is exercised, so that "self-government" is "not the government of each by himself, but of each by all the rest." Hence it follows that individual liberty might well be endangered even by a government chosen by and responsible to the people, or by the people themselves acting directly.

It is true of course, as I noted earlier, that Mill neglected to consider in any detail the nature and implications of political interferences with individual freedom and, hence, did not see that in a democracy some political interference may actually curb acts of private interference with individual freedom, and thus serve to enhance, rather than to curtail, some freedoms for some men; but this neglect is to be accounted for by Mill's belief that such political invasions were more a potential than an actual danger, more a threat to the future than to the society of his own day:

> The majority have not yet learned to feel the power of the government their power, or its opinions their opinions. When they do so, individual liberty will probably be as much exposed to invasion from the government as it already is from public opinion.

Believing as he did, then, that the immediate threat to individuality derived not from the mandates of law but from the pressures of public sentiment, Mill sought throughout his life, and increasingly in his later years, to emphasize his conviction that intellectual stagnation was the real ultimate threat to democracy. It is not surprising, therefore, to find in his essay strong and repeated expressions of concern for the nonlegal restraints that seemed to him, as to Tocqueville, to vitiate or endanger individual and group liberties—restraints imposed by physical violence, economic sanctions, and most of all by the play of public sentiment or, as he and Tocqueville called it, the tyranny of the majority. I think Mill's case would have been stronger had he seen that it is not so much the play of public sentiment as the actual exercise of coercive power to enforce that sentiment that constitutes tyranny. But who in contemporary America can seriously deny that Mill was eminently correct in his terrible account of the blights of conformity?[4]

> The danger which threatens human nature [wrote Mill] is not the excess, but the deficiency, of personal impulses and preferences. . . . In our times, from the highest class of society down to the lowest, everyone lives as under the eye of a hostile and dreaded censorship. Not only in what concerns others, but in what concerns only themselves, the individual or the family do not ask themselves, what do I prefer? or, what would suit my character and disposition? or, what would allow the best and highest in me to have fair play and enable it to grow and thrive? They ask themselves, what is suitable to my position? what is usually done by persons of my station and pecuniary circumstances? or (worse still) what is usually done by persons of a sta-

---

4. In what must surely be one of the more remarkable utterances in political literature, Crane Brinton *does* deny this, saying of *On Liberty* that "it is not a prescient book. . . . Neither Mill's hopes nor his forebodings are quite pertinent today." *English Political Thought in the Nineteenth Century* (London, 1933), p. 98.

tion and circumstances superior to mine? I do not mean that they choose what is customary in preference to what suits their own inclination. It does not occur to them to have any inclination except for what is customary. Thus the mind itself is bowed to the yoke: even in what people do for pleasure, conformity is the first thing thought of; they like in crowds; they exercise choice only among things commonly done; peculiarity of taste, eccentricity of conduct are shunned equally with crimes, until by dint of not following their own nature they have no nature to follow: their human capacities are withered and starved; they become incapable of any strong wishes or native pleasures, and are generally without either opinions or feelings of home growth, or properly their own. Now is this, or is it not, the desirable condition of human nature?

In this, as in so many things, Mill closely anticipated what later writers have seized upon and exploited as a fundamental insight. For in his discussion of conformity, Mill accurately and concisely set forth the theme and central hypothesis of David Riesman's recent and popular book *The Lonely Crowd*—from the expression in Mill's *Liberty* that "At present individuals are lost in the crowd," to the basic distinction that Riesman draws between inner-directed and other- or tradition-directed men.[5] What, after all, is Mill decrying in the lengthy passage I have quoted if not the emergence into undue prominence of the other-directed individual? What is he pleading if not the cause of the inner-directed man? And to the extent that Mill in the middle of the nineteenth century was able to see a tendency that has since become a central characteristic of our own society, he can hardly be dismissed as a man without relevance and vision. I suppose that some of Mill's detractors would quickly remind us that in this respect Mill has but aligned himself with his usual lost cause; but I hardly think this historical judgment impairs the validity of his argument. On the contrary, I think it makes his plea only the more urgent.

What is important in Mill, then, is that he did understand and systematically treat the hitherto neglected problem of the relations between individuals and groups within a single political and social system, seeking in the process not merely to describe what men actually did but *to discover and prescribe a principle* by which they might test the propriety or impropriety of both governmental and social interferences with individual behavior. In this respect his essay, for all its shortcomings, represents a major advance in the literature of political thought.

2. *Mill propounded the essential elements of the liberal case for freedom of expression.* "Many things," said the Greek sophist Protagoras, "hinder certainty—the obscurity of the matter and the

5. Compare with David Riesman, *The Lonely Crowd* (New Haven, 1950), espe- cially pp. 166, 266, 300–302, 304.

shortness of man's life." Because Mill respected this judgment, claiming no final certainty for himself and refusing to concede it in others, he put the case for freedom of expression on different, and broader, grounds than Milton had done before him. He urged it not only on behalf of truth itself, though he insisted that freedom of opinion and expression is a necessary condition for the discovery of truth, but also for the sake of the individual and of society. He recognized full well, as MacIver expressed it, that "the right of the majority is not the rightness of the majority";[6] and he understood, to quote Morley again, that "repression, whether by public opinion or in any other way, may be the means of untold waste of gifts that might have conferred on mankind unspeakable benefits."[7] Hence Mill insisted that man must be free to think, to choose, and to learn from his own mistakes both for the sake of truth and for his capacity to mature as a self-directed being. To do so does not mean that men need *reject* all received doctrines as untrue, merely that they be free to *test* such doctrines by all the resources of reason.[8] And this was what Mill reaffirmed in *On Liberty*, with the added emphasis that it was indispensable to any society if it is to avert stagnation. What is more, a society faces precisely the same choice between progress and stagnation when it is confronted by the challenge of new ideas; for here, too, it is only by man's free exercise of reason that truth can be distinguished from falsehood.

All of which is enough to indicate how ludicrous some of Mill's critics make themselves when they go off on an epistemological deep end to argue that Mill is here denying the possibility of attaining truth or, worse still, to indulge themselves in the grand *non sequitur* that, for Mill, the test of truth is nothing more than its historical success in winning acceptance in the free competition of the market. The confusion here between the epistemological problem and Mill's concern with the social conditions making for, or discouraging, the exercise of reason is too obvious to need elaboration. Nor, save for the thought processes of Dostoevsky's Grand Inquisitor, is it possible to say, with one of Mill's critics, that the unrestricted competition of ideas should be discouraged for fear that falsehood might then prevail over truth and thus destroy the moral basis of society.[9] One who feels himself sufficiently omniscient to urge that what is needed is "a firm official stand for what is known as right, true, and good,"[1] can well dismiss Mill's case with-

6. R. M. MacIver, *The Modern State* (London, 1926), p. 456.
7. *Critical Miscellanies* (London, 1904–8), 3:47.
8. See Mill's early speech on the Church (1829), reprinted in the World's Classics edition of his *Autobiography*, Laski, ed. (London, 1924), p. 322; also his *Spirit of the Age*, Hayek, ed. (Chicago, 1942), p. 14.

9. Thus Gerhart Niemeyer, "A Reappraisal of the Doctrine of Free Speech," *Thought*, 25 (1950), 251–74, especially pp. 257, 271–72. See in the same vein Walter Berns, *Freedom, Virtue, and the First Amendment* (Baton Rouge, La., 1957); but see *contra* my paper "Freedom, Virtue, and the New Scholasticism," *Commentary*, 28 (1959), 313–21.
1. Niemeyer, *op. cit.*, p. 273.

out further ado; but for those of us who lack such self-assurance, there is no evading the choice as Mill sees it. What disturbs critics of this stripe, I suspect, is not that Mill was opposed to truth but that, as an admirer of Mill once put it, Mill wished men "not to take authority for truth but truth for authority."[2]

It was anything but a spirit of jest, therefore, that inspired Mill to urge that, in the absence of an opposing idea, it might be well to contrive one. A contemporary reviewer of Mill's essay—sharing, one might add, the phobias of the aforementioned critics—reacted to this proposal with horror:

> Toleration of devil's advocates is a different thing from institution of them. Would Mr. Mill conceive it to be advantageous to the formation of his maid-servant's enlightened opinion upon the excellence of chastity, that she should be invited to spend her Sunday afternoon in earnest controversy upon the matter with a profligate dragoon from Kensington barracks . . . ?[3]

To which Mill's rejoinder, needless to say, would have been distinctly in the affirmative—except that, as a prudent man, he would also have insisted on the proviso that the afternoon be restricted to "earnest controversy." Indeed, he might have added that, in expressing horror at the prospect of an afternoon so spent, the critic himself betrayed a lack of firm conviction about "the excellence of chastity." And the same, *mutatis mutandis,* may be said today of those who denounce Mill's argument "in the name of a higher morality."[4]

What is fundamental to Mill's whole approach, of course, is the altogether salutary reminder that we are not infallible creatures; that truth cannot be attained in any complete and final sense; that what we take to be truth must therefore be held tentatively and undogmatically; and that we must always be prepared, as rational men, to subject the beliefs we hold to be true to the test of new data and new experiences. This reflection, if I understand Mill correctly, is his essential case for liberalism; and it is still very much the case a century later, made all the more compelling by the cumulative pressures which society today exerts upon the individual.

C. L. TEN

Mill on Self-Regarding Actions†

In the essay *On Liberty*, Mill put forward his famous principle that society may only interfere with those actions of an individual

2. G. J. Holyoake, *Bygones Worth Remembering* (London, 1905), 1:279.
3. Quoted in Rees, *Mill and His Early Critics*, p. 33.
4. Niemeyer, *op. cit.*, p. 273.
† From *Philosophy*, 43 (1968), 29–37.

which concern others and not with actions which merely concern himself. The validity of this principle depends on there being a distinction between self-regarding and other-regarding actions. But the concept of self-regarding actions has been severely criticised on the ground that all actions affect others in some way and are therefore other-regarding. The notion of self-regarding actions appears to be completely discredited. Very recently, however, there has been some dissatisfaction with the traditional debunking of Mill on this score. Two serious and important attempts to reinterpret the principle were made by Mr J. C. Rees in an article entitled 'A Re-Reading of Mill on Liberty',[1] and by Mr Alan Ryan in two brief but extremely useful contributions.[2] My aim is to discuss these reinterpretations of Mill, and on the basis of this, build up what I think is the correct account of Mill's notion of self-regarding actions.

I

After lucidly documenting the traditional interpretation of Mill's notion of self-regarding actions, Mr J. C. Rees proceeds to show why this interpretation is mistaken and to give his own version of Mill's doctrine. According to the traditional interpretation, self-regarding actions are actions which affect only the agent and have no effect on others. Against this Mr Rees argues that self-regarding actions are those actions which do not affect the *interests* of others. His case for this reinterpretation is based on the following claims: (a) that there is an important difference between just 'affecting others' and 'affecting the interests of others', and that at crucial stages when he is stating his principle Mill brings in the word 'interests'; and (b) that Mill could not be thinking of 'effects' when he put forward his principle for he freely admitted that self-regarding actions affected others.

With respect to (a) it is of course true that Mill often used the word 'interests' in stating his case for liberty, but what is not readily conceded is that Mill saw any distinction between 'interests' and 'effects' in the way that Mr Rees does. Mr Rees writes: '. . . [Interests] depend for their existence on social recognition and are closely connected with prevailing standards about the sort of behaviour a man can legitimately expect from others. A claim that something should be recognised as an interest is one we should require to be supported by reasons and one capable of being made the subject of discussion. On the other hand I could be very seriously affected by the action of another person merely because I had an extraordinarily sensitive nature and no claim to have others respect these tender spots would be recognised as amounting to an interest. How one is affected by a theatrical performance depends partly on one's tastes, but the interests of a businessman would be affected by a tax

1. *Political Studies*, 8 (1960), 113–29.
2. 'Mr McCloskey on Mill's Liberalism', *Philosophical Quarterly*, 14 (1964), 253–60, and 'John Stuart Mill's Art of Living', *The Listener* (October 21, 1965), pp. 620–22.

on business property no matter what his tastes or susceptibilities; just as the interests of a university are affected by a scheme to establish a research institute in the same area (in a common subject of course) whether the university authorities welcome the idea or not.' However, in *Utilitarianism* Mill explicitly stated what he meant by 'interests': '. . . laws and social arrangements should place the happiness, or (as speaking practically it may be called) the interest, of every individual, as nearly as possible in harmony with the interest of the whole; . . .' 'Interest' then is for him synonymous with 'happiness'. This being the case, Mr Rees's attempt to drive a wedge between 'affecting others' and 'affecting the interests of others' fails. For the latter expression turns out to mean no more than 'affecting the happiness of others' and does not now appear to differ in any important sense from merely 'affecting others'. The fact that Mill seems to use these two expressions, together with other expressions like 'conduct which concerns only himself', without distinguishing between them should then present no real difficulty. Whenever such expressions are used, they all refer to actions which do not affect the happiness of others. Mill assumed that whatever 'affects' others or 'concerns others' will only do so through its influence on their happiness. There is no need to accept Mr Rees's suggestion that '. . . the ambiguity of the word "concerns" is responsible for concealing a coherent theory based on "interests" rather than "effects". . . .'. Mr Rees's distinction between 'interests' and 'effects' is not one which Mill subscribed to, and any problem arising therefrom would be non-existent for him.

But we are still left with Mr Rees's second argument. If Mill did not distinguish between interests and effects, was he not guilty of a blatant contradiction in admitting that self-regarding actions affected others? I do not think so. Mill's principle did not necessarily depend on there being an area of human actions which had absolutely no effect on others. Self-regarding actions were for him actions which did not *directly* affect others. This is quite clear from a passage which Mr Rees himself draws attention to as presenting some difficulties for his reinterpretation of Mill: 'But there is a sphere of action in which society, as distinguished from the individual, has, if any, only an *indirect interest*; comprehending all that portion of a person's life and conduct which affects only himself, or if it also affects others, only with their free, voluntary, and undeceived consent and participation. *When I say only himself, I mean directly, and in the first instance*; for whatever affects himself, may affect others through himself; . . .'. All the evidence which Mr Rees presents to show that Mill was aware that self-regarding actions could affect others can be explained in the light of this passage. Mill merely meant that these self-regarding actions affected others *indirectly*, even if sometimes seriously. Mill's admissions can be accounted for in terms of a distinction which he clearly made between direct and indirect interests or direct and indirect effects, and need not depend on an alleged distinction which Mr Rees attributes to him between interests and effects.

According to Mill an action indirectly affects others or, what amounts to the same thing, the interests of others, if it affects their happiness simply because they dislike it, or find it repugnant or immoral. Soon after stating his principle, he picked out three areas of self-regarding actions in which individual liberty should prevail. The difference between other-regarding and self-regarding actions in the area of 'tastes and pursuits' is expressed in terms of actions which 'harm' our fellow creatures on the one hand, and actions which do not harm them 'even though they should think our conduct foolish, perverse or wrong' on the other. Again, before he put forward his own principle he considered certain attitudes which he thought had worked against the cause of freedom. He criticised those who 'have occupied themselves rather in inquiring what things society ought to like or dislike, than in questioning whether their likings or dislikings should be a law to individuals'. His principle was meant to oppose such attitudes. He was clearly aware that self-regarding actions could be disliked by others or regarded with abhorrence by them.

Sometimes these feelings of abhorrence and dislike can be intense and genuine. I think that when Mill spoke of self-regarding actions 'seriously affecting' others, he had such cases in mind. He deplored a state of affairs in which punishment and severe social pressures were brought to bear on actions which merely aroused society's intense dislike and repugnance. Thus he pointed out that, 'wherever the sentiment of the majority is still genuine and intense, it is found to have abated little of its claim to be obeyed'. We have such a situation if a society, consisting of a majority of Muslims, prohibited the eating of pork. Mill pointed out that the practice is 'really revolting' to such a people who 'also sincerely think that it is forbidden and abhorred by the Deity'. He said that the only tenable ground we could have for condemning such a prohibition would be that 'with the personal tastes and self-regarding concerns of individuals the public has no business to interfere'. In other words, only by adopting the principle he put forward in the essay could we have a reason for ruling out the appeal to the majority's genuine feelings of repugnance and revulsion as a ground for interfering with individual liberty. Mill's essay *On Liberty* was a protest against the appeal, which he felt was so often made, to such feelings of the majority as relevant and good reasons for restricting the actions of individuals. According to him they are in themselves never relevant or good reasons for interference. If the only reason that can be given for wishing to restrict an individual's freedom is an appeal to such feelings, then that individual's action is a self-regarding one. If, however, the action violates 'a distinct and assignable obligation' then an additional factor appears which takes it out of the self-regarding class. But even so Mill insisted that we should give the proper reason for interference: 'If, for example, a man, through intemperance or extravagance, becomes unable to pay his debts, or having undertaken the moral reponsibility of a family, becomes from some cause incapable of supporting or educating them, he is deservedly reprobated, and might be justly punished; but it is for the breach of duty to his family or creditors, not for the extravagance'. He wanted to revise the framework within which questions about individual liberty and society's right of interference are raised and answered. He tried to do this by limiting the type of reasons that could legitimately be given for interference with liberty. There are certain reasons, like the majority's feelings of repugnance, which by themselves are irrelevant and should not be given as a basis for restricting the freedom of the individual.

II

But what has the notion of self-regarding actions to do with utilitarianism? Mill said that his case for liberty was based on an appeal to 'utility in the largest sense, grounded on the permanent interests of a man as a progressive being'. What does he mean by this? I do not think that we can fully understand the nature of his defence of individual liberty unless we find an answer to this.

Mr Ryan has argued that *On Liberty* is not inconsistent with utilitarianism, but on the contrary it is the working out of the consequences of a utilitarian doctrine which runs through many of Mill's writings. Mill distinguished between law and morality on the one hand, and prudence and aesthetics on the other. The area of law and morality is other-regarding and only in this area can sanctions or punishment be applied. Law and morality differ only in the type of sanction that is used. The sanction behind morality is that of public opinion or social disapproval. To say that an action is wrong or immoral is to say that it must be stopped by society at least through the pressure of public opinion. Mill's famous principle may, according to Mr Ryan, be regarded as a limitation of morality to the other-regarding sphere. Self-regarding actions do not belong to the area of morality and we cannot therefore apply sanctions to them.

I find all this extremely valuable and Mr Ryan has presented his case with great cogency. But he takes for granted that a utilitarian morality is other-regarding, and hence an action can only be said to be immoral when it harms persons other than the agent. The notion of 'harm to others' is, however, a complex one, and Mill interpreted it in a way that is radically different from Bentham. *On Liberty* may be a utilitarian tract, but if it is, there is still a world of difference between Mill's utilitarianism and Bentham's. Mill's essay may indeed be fruitfully regarded as a rebellion against Benthamite utilitarianism. I shall first discuss some of the relevant features of Benthamite utilitarianism, and then show why Mill could not go all the way with it.

For Bentham the aim of both moral and legal rules is to achieve the greatest happiness of the greatest number, each person counting as one. Bentham's utilitarianism, however, contains one other feature which is of great importance. All pleasures and pains are relevant no matter what their nature or what the context may be. Any two lots of pleasures and pains which are of the same 'value' as measured by his 'felicific calculus' are of equal relevance. It is this feature which Mr John Rawls so vividly drew attention to in his well-known article, 'Justice as Fairness': '. . . the individuals receiving these benefits are not conceived as being related in any way: they represent so many different directions in which limited resources may be allocated. The value of assigning resources to one direction rather than another depends solely on the preferences and interest of individuals as individuals. The satisfaction of desire has its value irrespective of the moral relations between persons, say as members of a joint undertaking, and of the claims which, in the name of these interests, they are prepared to make on one another: and it is this value which is to be taken into account by the (ideal) legislator who is conceived as adjusting the rules of the system from the centre so as to maximize the value of the social utility function.'[3] Thus if we are deciding whether the institution of slavery is just, we must treat at the same level both the pleasures of the slave-holder on the one hand, and the miseries of the slaves on the other.[4] And if we are deciding whether or not to prohibit murder, incendiarism and robbery it is as relevant to cite the pleasure enjoyed by the offenders as it is to cite the pain suffered by the victims.[5] All pleasures and pains are to be weighed on the same scale, and none may be given a privileged status over the others.

Among the pleasures and pains to be taken into account are those of malevolence. Bentham defined the pleasures of malevolence as 'the pleasures resulting from the view of any pain supposed to be suffered by the beings who may become the objects of malevolence . . . .'[6] But even these pleasures are in themselves good because every pleasure is as such good, and as good as the same quantity of any other pleasure. This being the case there is no reason why morality and the law should be other-regarding as Mill

3. *Philosophy, Politics and Society*, 2d ser., Peter Laslett and W. G. Runciman, eds., pp. 150–51.
4. *Ibid.*, pp. 152f.
5. *Mill on Bentham*, F. R. Leavis, ed., pp. 48–49.
6. *The Principles of Morals and Legislation*, chap. 5, sec. 11.

understood the term. Consider the case of homosexuality between consenting adults in private. In a society where the majority regard such behaviour with repugnance, it may well be that pleasures of malevolence are aroused by the prospect of homosexuals being punished for their conduct. These pleasures may not be sufficient to outweigh the pain inflicted through the punishment of homosexuals, but they are always relevant and are to be weighed on the same scale as the suffering caused by punishment. It is also possible that under certain circumstances there are pleasures of malevolence which would exceed the pain inflicted by the punishment of 'private immoralities'. We may approach such a situation when the overwhelming majority in a society feel very strongly about the private conduct of a very small group of people, and demand that the latter be fined or imprisoned for a short spell. There would then be a good utilitarian reason for punishing that private conduct.

It is precisely the introduction of this type of reason that Mill tried to rule out with his principle. He realised that individual liberty is insecure so long as reasons like this are regarded as relevant. In the example of the prohibition on the eating of pork which I have already alluded to, and in other similar examples, he pointed out how futile the case for liberty would be if the majority's genuine feelings of horror and repugnance are recognised as having a claim for serious consideration. Mill clearly rejected Benthamite utilitarianism when he said that '. . . there is no parity between the feeling of a person for his own opinion, and the feeling of another who is offended at his holding it; no more than between the desire of a thief to take a purse, and the desire of the right owner to keep it'. He refused to treat the resentment of the religious bigot towards another person's religious observances which he finds abominable, on the same level as the latter's regard for his own form of worship.

I think that we are now in a position to understand Mill's sense of utility 'grounded in the permanent interest of a man as a progressive being'. Liberty is necessary for 'the free development of individuality', and without liberty 'there is wanting one of the principal ingredients of human happiness, and quite the chief ingredient of individual and social progress'. Thus Mill is still appealing to utility or the promotion of human happiness as the standard for appraising the value of liberty. He also argued that because of the diversity of the sources of human pleasures and pains and their different effects on different human beings, men will 'neither obtain their fair share of happiness, nor grow up to the mental, moral and aesthetic stature of which their nature is capable' unless they are allowed freedom to pursue their own modes of life.

It looks as if Mill was claiming that the sum of human happiness would increase where there was liberty. But it becomes clear as the argument proceeds that the goal is not really happiness in any sense that is detachable from 'development' or 'progress', and these are equated with the growth of 'individuality'. This is what 'utility in the largest sense' means. Liberty is not to be valued because it increases the sum total of human happiness, for this implies that the connection between the two is a contingent one, but because it is the necessary condition for the growth of individuality. It allows men to cultivate pleasures of a particular type, namely, 'native pleasures' or pleasures of 'home-growth'. Mill strongly attacked 'the despotism of custom' and men's blind and mechanical conformity to its dictates. Men must be allowed to choose for themselves not because this will lead to an increase in their happiness, but because this is in itself the most important ingredient of happiness. The sort of happiness Mill wanted to promote is logically tied up with liberty as it is involved in the very act of rational and independent choice. Men who choose in conformity with custom not because they independently agree with it, but blindly and without thought or because they are pressured to do so, cannot by definition be happier than those who choose freely and in independence. Happiness is not what Bentham conceived—a goal that is distinct from individual liberty, and as a matter of fact achievable through it. For Mill, happiness is not something that can be got through any means: 'It really is of importance, not only what men do, but also what manner of men they are that do it'. It is not just what men believe or how they feel which is important; the manner in which they come to have certain beliefs and feelings is also important. He also said that, 'If a person possesses any tolerable amount of common sense and experience, his own mode of laying down his existence is the best, not because it is best in itself, but because it is his own mode'. The importance of choosing and acting independently and in a rational manner was further emphasised by the use of expressions like 'an intellectually active people' and 'the dignity of thinking beings'. Rational choice, as Mill's arguments in the chapter on freedom of thought and discussion make clear, implies that one knows the correct grounds for believing something and that one is prepared to listen to conflicting views whenever they arise. It thus implies the existence of freedom for those who may disagree with us.

The appeal to 'utility in the largest sense' is therefore very different from any simple appeal to utility. Though Mill still appealed to human happiness, the concept of human happiness that he uses is so different from that used by Bentham that it would be misleading to say simply that *On Liberty* provides a utilitarian defence of freedom. But if one still insists on calling Mill a utilitarian, then it is important to remember that he was a utilitarian who wanted to limit the type of utilitarian considerations which can be brought in. There are some pleasures and pains which are irrelevant and should not be appealed to as a basis for restricting individual liberty.

III

I shall now draw together the different parts of my analysis of Mill's notion of self-regarding actions. Self-regarding actions are those actions which, if they affect others, do so only indirectly. This means that they affect others only because they are disliked or found to be immoral or repugnant. Mill claimed that the individual's freedom with respect to such actions should not be restricted because he ruled out certain reasons for interfering with liberty as irrelevant. Unless we are prepared to reject appeals to society's feelings of repugnance and dislike and similar feelings towards certain actions, individual liberty can never be secure from the 'tyranny of the majority'. In thus restricting the types of reasons which may be taken into account, Mill was not strictly a utilitarian because the gratification through punishment of those feelings he regarded as irrelevant could be treated as the gratification of the pleasures of malevolence, which on strictly utilitarian grounds are in themselves as good as any other type of pleasure of the same quantity. Mill's reason for allowing liberty in self-regarding actions was not that human happiness would thereby be increased, but that without such liberty there can be no 'individuality'. His defence of freedom is not in terms of utility, but of 'utility in the largest sense', i.e. individuality.

H. L. A. HART

Immorality and Treason†

The Wolfenden Committee on Homosexual Offences and Prostitution recommended by a majority of 12 to 1 that homosexual behaviour between consenting adults in private should no longer be a criminal offence. One of the Committee's principal grounds for this recommendation was expressed in its report in this way: 'There must remain a realm of private morality and immorality which in brief and crude terms is not the law's business'. I shall call this the liberal point of view: for it is a special application of those wider principles of liberal thought which John Stuart Mill formulated in his essay on Liberty. Mill's most famous words, less cautious perhaps than the Wolfenden Committee's, were:

The only purpose for which power can be rightfully exercised

† From *The Listener*, 62 (July 30, 1959), pp. 162–63.

over any member of a civilized community against his will is to prevent harm to others. His own good, either physical or moral, is not a sufficient warrant. He cannot rightfully be compelled to do or forbear . . . because in the opinion of others to do so would be wise or even right.

Repudiation of the Liberal Point of View

The liberal point of view has often been attacked, both before and after Mill. I shall discuss here the repudiation of it made by Sir Patrick Devlin, in his recent lecture, which has now been published. This contains an original and interesting argument designed to show that '*prima facie* society has the right to legislate against immorality as such' and that the Wolfenden Committee were mistaken in thinking that there is an area of private immorality which is not the law's business. Sir Patrick's case is a general one, not confined to sexual immorality, and he does not say whether or not he is opposed to the Wolfenden Committee's recommendation on homosexual behaviour. Instead he gives us a hypothetical principle by which to judge this issue. He says: 'If it is the genuine feeling of our society that homosexuality is a vice so abominable that its mere presence is an offence', society has the right to eradicate it by the use of the criminal law.

* * * The most remarkable feature of Sir Patrick's lecture is his view of the nature of morality—the morality which the criminal law may enforce. Most previous thinkers who have repudiated the liberal point of view have done so because they thought that morality consisted either of divine commands or of rational principles of human conduct discoverable by human reason. Since morality for them had this elevated divine or rational status as the law of God or reason, it seemed obvious that the state should enforce it, and that the function of human law should not be merely to provide men with the opportunity for leading a good life, but actually to see that they lead it. Sir Patrick does not rest his repudiation of the liberal point of view on these religious or rationalist conceptions. Indeed much that he writes reads like an abjuration of the notion that reasoning or thinking has much to do with morality. English popular morality has no doubt its historical connexion with the Christian religion: 'That,' says Sir Patrick, 'is how it got there'. But it does not owe its present status or social significance to religion any more than to reason.

What, then, is it? According to Sir Patrick it is primarily a matter of feeling. 'Every moral judgment', he says, 'is a feeling that no right-minded man could act in any other way without admitting that he was doing wrong'. Who then must feel this way if we are to have what Sir Patrick calls a public morality? He tells us that it is 'the man in the street', 'the man in the jury box', or (to use the phrase so familiar to English lawyers) 'the man on the Clapham omnibus'. For the moral judgments of society so far as the law is concerned are to be ascertained by the standards of the reasonable man, and he is not to be confused with the rational man. Indeed, Sir Patrick says 'he is not expected to reason about anything and his judgment may be largely a matter of feeling'.

Intolerance, Indignation, and Disgust

But what precisely are the relevant feelings, the feelings which may justify use of the criminal law? Here the argument becomes a little complex. Widespread dislike of a practice is not enough. There must, says Sir Patrick, be 'a real feeling of reprobation'. Disgust is not enough either. What is crucial is a combination of intolerance, indignation, and disgust. These three are the forces behind the moral law, without which it is not 'weighty enough to deprive the individual of freedom of choice'. Hence there is, in Sir Patrick's outlook, a crucial difference between the mere adverse moral judgment of society and one which is inspired by feeling raised to the concert pitch of intolerance, indignation, and disgust.

This distinction is novel and also very important. For on it depends the weight to be given to the fact that when morality is enforced individual liberty is necessarily cut down. Though Sir Patrick's abstract formulation of his views on this point is hard to follow, his examples make his position fairly clear. We can see it best in the contrasting things he says about fornication and homosexuality. In regard to fornication, public feeling in most societies is not now of the concert-pitch intensity. We may feel that it is tolerable if confined: only its spread might be gravely injurious. In such cases the question whether individual liberty should be restricted is for Sir Patrick a question of balance between the danger to society in the one scale, and the restriction of the individual in the other. But if, as may be the case with homosexuality, public feeling is up to concert pitch, if it expresses a 'deliberate judgment' that a practice as such is injurious to society, if there is 'a genuine feeling that it is a vice so abominable that its mere presence is an offence', then it is beyond the limits of tolerance, and society may eradicate it. In this case, it seems, no further balancing of the claims of individual liberty is to be done, though as a matter of prudence the legislator should remember that the popular limits of tolerance may shift: the concert pitch feeling may subside. This may produce a dilemma for the law; for the law may then be left without the full moral backing that it needs, yet it cannot be altered without giving the impression that the moral judgment is being weakened.

A Shared Morality

If this is what morality is—a compound of indignation, intoler-ance, and disgust—we may well ask what justification there is for taking it, and turning it as such, into criminal law with all the misery which criminal punishment entails. Here Sir Patrick's answer is very clear and simple. A collection of individuals is not a society; what makes them into a society is among other things a shared or public morality. This is as necessary to its existence as an organized government. So society may use the law to preserve its morality like anything else essential to it. 'The suppression of vice is as much the law's business as the suppression of subversive activities'. The liberal point of view which denies this is guilty of 'an error in jurispru-dence': for it is no more possible to define an area of private morality than an area of private subversive activity. There can be no 'theoret-ical limits' to legislation against immorality just as there are no such limits to the power of the state to legislate against treason and sedi-tion.

Surely all this, ingenious as it is, is misleading. Mill's formulation of the liberal point of view may well be too simple. The grounds for interfering with human liberty are more various than the single cri-terion of 'harm to others' suggests: cruelty to animals or organizing prostitution for gain do not, as Mill himself saw, fall easily under the description of harm to others. Conversely, even where there is harm to others in the most literal sense, there may well be other principles limiting the extent to which harmful activities should be repressed by law. So there are multiple criteria, not a single crite-rion, determining when human liberty may be restricted. Perhaps this is what Sir Patrick means by a curious distinction which he often stresses between theoretical and practical limits. But with all its simplicities the liberal point of view is a better guide than Sir Patrick to clear thought on the proper relation of morality to the criminal law: for it stresses what he obscures—namely, the points at which thought is needed before we turn popular morality into crim-inal law.

Society and Moral Opinion

No doubt we would all agree that a consensus of moral opinion on certain matters is essential if society is to be worth living in. Laws against murder, theft, and much else would be of little use if they were not supported by a widely diffused conviction that what these laws forbid is also immoral. So much is obvious. But it does not follow that everything to which the moral vetoes of accepted morality attach is of equal importance to society; nor is there the slightest reason for thinking of morality as a seamless web: one which will fall to pieces carrying society with it, unless all its emphatic vetoes are enforced by law. Surely even in the face of the moral feeling that is up to concert pitch—the trio of intolerance, indignation, and disgust—we must pause to think. We must ask a question at two different levels which Sir Patrick never clearly enough identifies or separates. First, we must ask whether a practice which offends moral feeling is harmful, independently of its repercussion on the general moral code. Secondly, what about repercussion on the moral code? Is it really true that failure to translate this item of general morality into criminal law will jeopardize the whole fabric of morality and so of society?

We cannot escape thinking about these two different questions merely by repeating to ourselves the vague nostrum: 'This is part of public morality and public morality must be preserved if society is to exist'. Sometimes Sir Patrick seems to admit this, for he says in words which both Mill and the Wolfenden Report might have used, that there must be the maximum respect for individual liberty consistent with the integrity of society. Yet this, as his contrasting examples of fornication and homosexuality show, turns out to mean only that the immorality which the law may punish must be generally felt to be intolerable. This plainly is no adequate substitute for a reasoned estimate of the damage to the fabric of society likely to ensue if it is not suppressed.

Nothing perhaps shows more clearly the inadequacy of Sir Patrick's approach to this problem than his comparison between the suppression of sexual immorality and the suppression of treason or subversive activity. Private subversive activity is, of course, a contradiction in terms because 'subversion' means overthrowing government, which is a public thing. But it is grotesque, even where moral feeling against homosexuality is up to concert pitch, to think of the homosexual behaviour of two adults in private as in any way like treason or sedition either in intention or effect. We can make it *seem* like treason only if we assume that deviation from a general moral code is bound to affect that code, and to lead not merely to its modification but to its destruction. The analogy could begin to be plausible only if it was clear that offending against this item of morality was likely to jeopardize the whole structure. But we have ample evidence for believing that people will not abandon morality, will not think any better of murder, cruelty, and dishonesty, merely because some private sexual practice which they abominate is not punished by the law.

Because this is so the analogy with treason is absurd. Of course 'No man is an island': what one man does in private, if it is known, may affect others in many different ways. Indeed it may be that deviation from general sexual morality by those whose lives, like the lives of many homosexuals, are noble ones and in all other ways exemplary will lead to what Sir Patrick calls the shifting of the limits of tolerance. But if this has any analogy in the sphere of government it is not the overthrow of ordered government, but a peaceful change in its form. So we may listen to the promptings of common sense and of logic, and say that though there could not logically be a sphere of private treason there is a sphere of private morality and immorality.

Sir Patrick's doctrine is also open to a wider, perhaps a deeper, criticism. In his reaction against a rationalist morality and his stress on feeling, he has I think thrown out the baby and kept the bath water; and the bath water may turn out to be very dirty indeed. When Sir Patrick's lecture was first delivered *The Times* greeted it with these words: 'There is a moving and welcome humility in the conception that society should not be asked to give its reason for refusing to tolerate what in its heart it feels intolerable'. This drew from a correspondent in Cambridge the retort: 'I am afraid that we are less humble than we used to be. We once burnt old women because, without giving our reasons, we felt in our hearts that witchcraft was intolerable'.

This retort is a bitter one, yet its bitterness is salutary. We are not, I suppose, likely, in England, to take again to the burning of old women for witchcraft or to punishing people for associating with those of a different race or colour, or to punishing people again for adultery. Yet if these things were viewed with intolerance, indignation, and disgust, as the second of them still is in some countries, it seems that on Sir Patrick's principles no rational criticism could be opposed to the claim that they should be punished by law. We could only pray, in his words, that the limits of tolerance might shift.

Curious Logic

It is impossible to see what curious logic has led Sir Patrick to this result. For him a practice is immoral if the thought of it makes the man of the Clapham omnibus sick. So be it. Still, why should we not summon all the resources of our reason, sympathetic understanding, as well as critical intelligence, and insist that before general moral feeling is turned into criminal law it is submitted to scrutiny of a different kind from Sir Patrick's? Surely, the legislator should ask whether the general morality is based on ignorance, superstition, or misunderstanding; whether there is a false conception that those who practise what it condemns are in other ways dangerous or hostile to society; and whether the misery to many parties, the blackmail and the other evil consequences of criminal punishment, especially for sexual offences, are well understood. It is surely extraordinary that among the things which Sir Patrick says are to be considered before we legislate against immorality these appear nowhere; not even as 'practical considerations', let alone 'theoretical limits'. To any theory which, like this one, asserts that the criminal law may be used on the vague ground that the preservation of morality is essential to society and yet omits to stress the need for critical scrutiny, our reply should be: 'Morality, what crimes may be committed in thy name!'

As Mill saw, and de Tocqueville showed in detail long ago in his critical but sympathetic study of democracy, it is fatally easy to confuse the democratic principle that power should be in the hands of the majority with the utterly different claim that the majority, with power in their hands, need respect no limits. Certainly there is a special risk in a democracy that the majority may dictate how all should live. This is the risk we run, and should gladly run; for it is the price of all that is so good in democratic rule. But loyalty to democratic principles does not require us to maximize this risk: yet this is what we shall do if we mount the man in the street on the top of the Clapham omnibus and tell him that if only he feels sick enough about what other people do in private to demand its suppression by law no theoretical criticism can be made of his demand.

Bibliography

This is intended as a select bibliography for undergraduate students and is therefore limited to those works in English that bear directly on the essay *On Liberty*. Advanced students will find further bibliographical guides in the footnotes to the text and to the critical articles included in this volume, and in *The Mill News Letter* (periodically issued by the University of Toronto Press). Works excerpted or reprinted above are not included here.

I. RELATED WORKS BY JOHN STUART MILL

Considerations on Representative Government (1861).
Principles of Political Economy (1848), vols. 2 and 3 of Mill's *Collected Works*, Robson, ed., (Toronto, 1965).
The Subjection of Women (1869).
A System of Logic (1843), vols. 7 and 8 of Mill's *Collected Works*, Robson, ed. (Toronto, 1974), Book 6.
Utilitarianism (1861), in vol. 10 of Mill's *Collected Works*, Robson, ed. (Toronto, 1969).
Of the many anthologies of Mill's writings, *see:*
John Stuart Mill, *Essays on Politics and Culture*, Himmelfarb, ed. (Garden City, N.Y., 1962).
Prefaces to Liberty: Selected Writings of John Stuart Mill, Wishy, ed. (Boston, 1959).
John Stuart Mill, A Selection of His Works, Robson, ed. (Toronto, 1966).

II. WORKS ON MILL'S LIFE AND THOUGHT

Anschutz, R. P. *The Philosophy of J. S. Mill.* Oxford, 1953.
Bain, Alexander. *John Stuart Mill, A Criticism.* London, 1889.
Berlin, Isaiah. "John Stuart Mill and the Ends of Life," in his *Four Essays on Liberty*, chap. 4. Oxford, 1969.
Britton, Karl. *John Stuart Mill.* London, 1953.
Halévy, Elie. *The Growth of Philosophic Radicalism*, trans. Morris. London, 1928.
Hayek, F. A. *John Stuart Mill and Harriet Taylor: Their Friendship and Subsequent Marriage.* Chicago, 1951.
McCloskey, H. J. *John Stuart Mill: A Critical Study.* London, 1971.
Packe, Michael St. John. *The Life of John Stuart Mill.* New York, 1954.
Robson, John M. *The Improvement of Mankind: The Social and Political Thought of John Stuart Mill.* Toronto, 1968.
Russell, Bertrand. *Portraits from Memory*, pp. 114–34. London, 1956.
Ryan, Alan. *The Philosophy of John Stuart Mill.* London, 1970.
Stephen, Leslie, *The English Utilitarians*, vol. 3. London, 1900.
Street, Charles L. *Individualism and Individuality in the Philosophy of John Stuart Mill.* Milwaukee, 1926.
Woods, Thomas. *Poetry and Philosophy: A Study in the Thought of John Stuart Mill.* London, 1961.

III. WORKS ON *ON LIBERTY*

Aiken, Henry David. *Reason and Conduct*, chap. 14. New York, 1962.
Berlin, Isaiah. "Two Concepts of Liberty," in his *Four Essays on Liberty*, chap. 3. Oxford, 1969.
Bouton, Clark W. "John Stuart Mill: On Liberty and History," *Western Political Quarterly*, 18 (1968), 569–78.
Brown, D. G. "Mill on Liberty and Morality," *Philosophical Review*, 81 (1972), 133–58.
Day, J. P. "On Liberty and the Real Will," *Philosophy*, 45 (1970), 177–92.
Dworkin, Gerald. "Paternalism," *The Monist*, 56 (1972), 64–84.
Dworkin, Ronald. "Lord Devlin and the Enforcement of Morals," *Yale Law Journal*, 75 (1966), 986–1005.
Friedman, Richard B. "A New Exploration of Mill's Essay *On Liberty*," *Political Studies*, 14 (1966), 281–304.

Friedrich, Carl J., ed. *Liberty*. New York, 1962.
Gildin, Hilail. "Mill's *On Liberty*," in *Ancients and Moderns*, Cropsey, ed., chap. 14. New York, 1964.
Hart, H. L. A. *Law, Liberty and Morality*. London, 1963.
———. *The Morality of the Criminal Law*. Jerusalem, 1965.
Himmelfarb, Gertrude. *On Liberty and Liberalism: The Case of John Stuart Mill*. New York, 1974.
Holloway, Harry A. "Mill's Liberty, 1859–1959" [comment on Levi], *Ethics*, 71 (1961), 130–32.
Honderich, Ted. "Mill on Liberty," *Inquiry*, 10 (1967), 292–97.
Lichtman, Richard. "The Surface and Substance of Mill's Defense of Freedom," *Social Research*, 30 (1963), 469–94.
Lindquist, Emory. "John Stuart Mill's Essay on Liberty: A Centennial Review." *University of Wichita Bulletin*, 39 (August, 1959), 3–24.
McCloskey, H. J. "A Critique of the Ideals of Liberty," *Mind*, 74 (1965), 483–508.
———. "Liberty of Expression: Its Grounds and Limits," *Inquiry*, 13 (1970), 219–37. *See also* Monro, D. H.
———. "Mill's Liberalism," *Philosophical Quarterly*, 13 (1963), 143–56. *See also* Ryan, Alan.
———. "Mill's Liberalism—A Rejoinder to Mr. Ryan," *ibid.*, 16 (1966), 64–68.
Magid, Henry M. "Mill and the Problem of Freedom of Thought," *Social Research*, 21 (1954), 43–61.
Megill, Allan D. "J. S. Mill's Religion of Humanity and the Second Justification for the Writing of On Liberty," *Journal of Politics*, 34 (1972), 612–29.
Monro, D. H. "Liberty of Expression: Its Grounds and Limits," *Inquiry*, 13 (1970), 238–53. *See also* McCloskey, H. J.
Radcliff, Peter, ed. *Limits of Liberty*. Belmont, Calif., 1966.
Rees, J. C. *Mill and His Early Critics*. Leicester, England, 1956.
———. "A Phase in the Development of Mill's Ideas on Liberty," *Political Studies*, 6 (1958), 35–44.
———. "A Re-Reading of Mill on Liberty," *ibid.*, 8 (1960), 113–29.
Ryan, Alan. "Mr. McCloskey on Mill's Liberalism," *Philosophical Quarterly*, 14 (1964), 253–60. *See also* McCloskey, H. J.
Scanlan, James P. "J. S. Mill and the Definition of Freedom," *Ethics*, 68 (1958), 194–206.
Spitz, David. "Pure Tolerance: A Critique of Criticisms," *Dissent*, 13 (1966), 510–25. *See also* Wolff, Robert Paul, *et al.*
———. "The Pleasures of Misunderstanding Freedom," *ibid.*, pp. 729–39. *See also* Wolff, Robert Paul, *et al.*
Ten, C. L. "Mill and Liberty" [reply to Cowling and Himmelfarb], *Journal of the History of Ideas*, 30 (1969), 47–68.
Wolff, Robert Paul. *The Poverty of Liberalism*, chap. 1. Boston, 1968.
———, Barrington Moore, Jr., and Herbert Marcuse. *A Critique of Pure Tolerance*. Boston, 1965. *See also* Spitz, David.
Wollheim, Richard. "Crime, Sin, and Mr. Justice Devlin," *Encounter*, 13 (1959), 34–40.
———. "John Stuart Mill and the Limits of State Action," *Social Research*, 40 (1973), 1–30.
———. "Without Doubt or Dogma: The Logic of Liberalism," *The Nation*, 183 (July 28, 1956), 74–76.

Index